GREEN RIVER
SERIAL KILLER

Biography of an Unsuspecting Wife

Pennie Morehead

BrandenBooks
Boston

Library of Congress Cataloging-in-Publication Data

Morehead, Pennie.
  Green River serial killer : biography of an unsuspecting wife / Pennie
Morehead.
      p. cm.
  Includes bibliographical references and index.
  ISBN 978-0-8283-2153-2 (pbk. : alk. paper)
  1. Ridgway, Judith, 1944-
  2. Ridgway, Gary Leon, 1949-
  3. Serial murderers' spouses--Washington (State)--Green River Region
      (King County)--Biography
  4. Serial murders--Washington (State)--Green River Region Region
      (King County)
  5. Serial murderers--Washington (State)--Green River Region Region
      (King County)
  I. Title.

  HV6534.G757M67 2007
  364.152'3092--dc22

                                    2007007260

www.brandenbooks.com
Branden Publishing Company, Inc.
PO Box 812094
Wellesley MA 02482

Contents

Introduction 5

Chapter 1: Buried by Bricks 6

Chapter 2: Beginnings 17

Chapter 3: First Marriage 37

Chapter 4: Finding Her Prince: Gary 58

Chapter 5: The Married Years...............................76

Chapter 6: The Truth Comes Out...........................97

Chapter 7: A Future For Judith 121

Chapter 8: Best Friends of the Ridgways........... 133

Chapter 9: Gary's Comments from Prison 145

Chapter 10: Interview with Gary 148

Chapter 11: Professional Analysis of Gary's Handwriting...... 159

Photos, Cards and Letters.................................... 178

Victims (list of known victims) 237

Bibliography 238

Index..239

Dedication

**To all those who have had their futures stolen
by deceitful lovers**

Acknowledgments

Judith, thank you for your courage and trust in me to tell your story. You made the decision to come out of hiding, gather up your wounded self, and take the first step forward. It has been a thrill for me to watch you become stronger.

Jim and Linda Bailey, your support, encouragement, and committed friendship with Judith perpetuated this project. All the work you did, from tedious errands to liaison coordination with critical personal contacts, was appreciated.

Professors Phil Jack and Marcie Sims, I hope that the folks at Green River Community College in Auburn, Washington, recognize the talent and high-caliber character you two possess. Your mentoring and excitement for this book were incredibly inspiring to me.

Mr. Adolph Caso at Branden Books, thank you for taking a chance on me and giving this book a publishing home.

Finally, to my family, thank you for your support. You teasingly referred to me as "certified intense"—a name I deserved.

Introduction

When I first met Judith Ridgway, she was still clinging to the hope that her husband, the infamous Green River Killer, was innocent. She struck me as being someone who had endured a lot in her life, and I assumed this was the result of her relationship with Gary, her husband. However, I soon discovered that there was more to her story than that, and the true irony was that the man, known to have murdered more victims than any other serial killer in the United States, was the hero in Judith's story.

So, this book is more than a biography. It not only provides a picture of Gary Ridgway through Judith's eyes, but includes interviews, personal documents, and a professional analysis of Gary's handwriting. By taking this approach, I am able to provide multiple lenses through which to view the Green River Serial Killer.

To accomplish this, I begin the multi-prong format with a bird's eye view of Judith, Gary's wife, as she experiences what begins as a typical day. Without warning, she feels the support walls of her life come crashing down when detectives deliver the devastating news that her husband *is* the Green River Killer. By taking this personalized approach, I hope to help the reader understand her feelings and reactions to the terrible news.

Then I provide information about Judith's background so that the reader can learn about Judith Ridgway's difficult entry into the world and her dramatic, painful childhood. Before Gary, Judith was married to a man who had challenged her will to survive. But Judith did survive!

This will help the reader understand how Judith felt when she met the man of her dreams—Mr. Gary Ridgway. Intimate details of the Ridgway courtship and marriage unfold as the reader is led to the day that Judith's world ended—November 30, 2001—when the long search for the Green River Serial Killer ended at her doorstep.

At this point, I have included interviews with Gary's close friends, co-workers, and Judith. Even Gary speaks out from prison about his feelings for his wife and what he hopes will happen in her future.

I've also included a chapter that includes private photos, cards, and letters from Gary to Judith over the years before and after his arrest, which leads to my professional evaluation of Gary's personality using graphology, or handwriting analysis.

Chapter 1
Buried by Bricks

November 30, 2001:

At exactly 3:30 a.m. he got up from his warm bed. The master bedroom was dark and silent on this chilly fall morning. He did not flip on any lights. Didn't need to. He moved about the room with the automated gestures of a workingman who had been doing this ritual for 32 years.

He's going in early for two hours of overtime, his wife sleepily acknowledged, partially awake.

His routine was intimately familiar to her. She smiled to herself without opening her eyes, rolling over onto her other side. She thought that she was one of the lucky ones. She had finally made it to a place in life she had never thought possible before. She was Mrs. Gary Ridgway. She had a good husband—a non-abusive husband—who earned a nice living so she could stay at home and pursue her hobbies.

This morning was no different. Gary was quietly dressing himself: climbing into his work jeans; buttoning his plaid, long-sleeve, flannel shirt down the front of his slim torso; always having his white cotton tee-shirt underneath. He crouched down, using both hands to pull white, cotton crew socks over his feet, one at a time while balancing on the opposite foot, and then finally guided his feet into his sturdy, steel-toe work boots. He laced them up tightly.

She knew he would not shower in the early morning. Why bother? He would surely get dirty at work painting trucks all day. She appreciated the fact that when he got to work, he would put on big, industrial coveralls to keep his own clothing from being ruined.

She stretched her legs and moved them to a spot in the bed that still held Gary's warmth. As she fell back to sleep, she could imagine Gary finding the hot coffee ready downstairs that she had set up the night before. They had a fancy coffee maker now with a timer that could be set at bedtime, and somehow the machine would make the coffee at the precise time she had set it for. She was simply amazed by this advancement in coffee- making technology. Gary's habit was to pour himself a cup of hot coffee to begin sipping after adding a dribble of cold milk from the refrigerator. Then he would pour all but one cup of the coffee into his dented, several-year-old, Thermos bottle, leaving the remaining cup for his wife to drink when she would get up later in the morning.

The next step in the morning ritual would be for Gary to take two peanut butter and jelly sandwiches, his favorite of all sandwiches, out of the freezer. There he would find about a dozen pre-made sandwiches, all peanut butter and jelly, of course, neatly displayed in individual plastic sandwich bags in the freezer that Judith had lovingly constructed. Once in a while, Judith changed up the pattern and made a few ham and cheese with lettuce sandwiches, but she didn't freeze them. That would ruin the lettuce. She would giggle to herself later, knowing that she had surprised Gary with something different. It gave her a warm, ticklish feeling in her stomach to treat her man to something special for his lunch. And why not? He deserved it. He worked so hard to provide a comfortable lifestyle for the two of them.

Each work morning Gary packed his own gray, weathered, plastic lunchbox with two sandwiches, one orange, and a few additions his wife referred to as "munchies."The definition of munchies was potato chips or nuts or something else, but it definitely had to be crunchy and fun. A munchie had to be fun.

Judith often wrote short love notes or smiling faces on scraps of paper and tucked them in the lunchbox. Once a week she placed a twenty-dollar bill in the lunchbox so Gary could fill the tank of his truck with gas. He never had to ask. She always knew when it was time.

On this morning, well before it was time for the sun to rise, Gary quietly jogged back upstairs to the dark bedroom where Judith lay sleeping, bent down, kissed her silently on the cheek, then headed back down the stairs and out the front door toward his truck with lunchbox and Thermos bottle in hand. Judith heard the lock on the front door go "click."A few seconds later, Judith recognized the sound of Gary's red Ford Ranger start in the driveway just below their second story bedroom window.

Gary warmed the small truck for about five minutes, tuned in his favorite country and western music radio station, and started out on his commute from the driveway of his home in Auburn, near Lake Geneva, to Kenworth Trucking in the Seattle suburb, Renton, Washington (positioned at the southern most tip of Lake Washington), where he held the title of Advanced Painter, Grade l. It had taken three decades for him to reach this level of achievement—working in the elite, enviable class of truck painters at Kenworth.

While Gary drove in the darkness toward work, humming along with the country music on the radio, and Judith peacefully slumbered, neither could know that this would be the last day of their morning routine.

Gary would not come home again.

Judith woke up on her own between 8:30 and 9:00 a.m. feeling rested and ready to rise. There was enough filtered, gray sunlight, typical of the Seattle autumn, seeping in the room around the drapes to provide adequate lighting for her morning thanks and visual inventory of her blessed surroundings. While Judith did not view herself as a stereotypically religious person, having no membership in a church, she did possess a reverence for her Almighty God. She had asked for His help on many fearful occasions, and she remembered to give Him thanks for the good things in her life. Judith had reminded Gary countless times, "Remember, honey, the good Lord works in mysterious ways," a mantra she believed in with all her heart.

From her sitting position in the middle of the imitation French Provincial canopy bed dressed with floral cotton sheets, matching cotton bedspread and pillow shams she had picked up at a garage sale, she surveyed their bedroom. The room was large with plenty of open space. The furnishings were cobbled together like a quilt made of many different scraps of cloth that had been lovingly collected over the years. The beige carpet and white walls throughout the home gave a neutral background for this multi-colored quilt to contrast with. Against one wall stood a dark, wooden, 1930's chest of drawers, containing Gary's clothing. On another wall, Judith's newer, white, French Provincial dresser, a matching part of her bed set, stored her clothing and personal items. And, a miniature, antique, crystal chandelier hung from the ceiling of the bay window sitting area; the chandelier's tiny size added daintiness to the overall largeness of the room.

Judith decided to leave the bed. At 5' 1" she felt diminutive in the large master bedroom. She slid her tiny feet into slippers on the floor next to her side of the bed, then reached for her glasses on the nightstand and pushed them on her face. She walked with an obvious teetering motion, back and forth, from left to right, as she headed for the closet. She typically woke with stiffness in her back and hips. The many years of chronic back pain she described to friends and family as "the needles" had affected her ambulation.

The third wall was dominated by a roomy, wide, double closet; clearly one side designated for Gary and the other for her. It held the couple's nicer clothing: dresses, blouses, and shirts and slacks that should to be stored on hangers. Cardboard boxes with clothing that Judith wouldn't hear of parting with were stacked, covering the floor of the closet. *I really am a pack rat. Someday I should go through these boxes and give something away, but, shoot, you never know when you might need these again. It's a shame to get rid of perfectly good clothes!* Judith removed a fuzzy, dark-blue bathrobe from a hanger in the closet and wrapped it around herself.

In the corner furthest from the bed, a door opened into the master bathroom that housed a large garden tub. Judith quietly padded into the room, slippered feet on carpet. She sucked in her breath quickly and crossed her arms against the bosom of her soft, cotton, knee-length robe. *Oh— my garden tub. If people only knew how much fun we have in that tub! But the water! It takes so much to fill it.* She hugged herself even tighter. This was her favorite room in the house.

As Judith passed through the bedroom door and into the hallway, she turned her head over her shoulder and took a wide, sweeping look around the room. This room is so pretty. Plants, jewelry boxes, fancy pillows, collectibles, candles, and photos in frames remained as evidence of the feminine fingerprint Judith had stamped on this room.

Gotta get downstairs. Time for the Regis show! Judith hurried herself along.

Judith moved from the master bedroom to the hallway landing at the top level of the tri-level home. Another bedroom door joined this hallway. She went down a short flight of stairs and entered the main floor. The foyer stemming from the front door, the dining room and kitchen, laundry room, and living room all shared this floor. Another short flight of stairs from the dining room went down to the bottom floor that hosted two small bedrooms, a second bathroom, and a recreation room. The garage could be accessed through a door off the recreation room.

Judith settled in to enjoy the morning on the main floor. She entered the living room and switched on the television, a 27" color television on one shelf of the oak colored entertainment center, the first piece of furniture she had purchased on her own after her first marriage ended. She raised the volume on the television with the remote control so that she could listen to her favorite morning television host, Regis Philbin, while she went in the kitchen and poured the cup of coffee Gary had left for her in the fancy coffee maker. A tall, brick fireplace formed a barrier between the living room and kitchen. But it was open on both sides with screens as doors, and, if the television volume was high enough, she could easily listen to her favorite morning show while shuffling around in the kitchen.

The two Siamese cats of the Ridgway household suddenly appeared in the kitchen. They tunneled between her feet, rubbing and arching their backs against her legs. "Hello my sweet kitties," Judith gently crooned.

"You want your breakfast now, don't you?" Smiling, she bent down and gave the brother and sister adult cats equal petting time, noting the thicker winter fur increasing on their bodies. Winter was coming. The cats pressed the flat tops of their heads harder and harder into her petting hand, each cat trying to wedge in closer to their mistress. But she admitted to herself that she could not love these cats, or any other animal for that matter, as much as she had loved her poodle, Oscar. Would she ever get over the loss? The dog that she and Gary had raised from a pup and had loved like it was their own child had died only four months prior, and the painful grieving had not lessened. She missed him every day. And, as if that were not enough pain for her to endure, Gary's mother had passed away just one month after Oscar in August! Tears were forming in her eyes now, and her nose began to drip. She reached for a tissue and quietly blew her nose, releasing a bit of her aching sadness. *You know, bad things happen in threes. One was my poor Oscar dying. Then my beautiful mother-in-law passed. Dear heavens, what will the third be?* She accepted as stone-cold fact that the third, awful event could hit them at any time. The acceptance gave her gooseflesh.

After the cats were fed, Judith prepared herself a bowl of cereal, the usual shredded wheat with sliced bananas and milk, to have with her coffee. She made a quick mental note to take her vitamins later. She carried her breakfast to the living room and carefully placed the cereal bowl and mug on one end table. She opened the light, cream-colored drapes with a pink, mauve, and blue floral pattern. She looked out the floor-to-ceiling windows at the gray, wet day and thought it might be best to stay inside this day to organize some boxes of clothing she had acquired for future garage sales. Indeed, today would be a perfect day to sort and prepare for their final garage sale of the year before winter came in full.

She settled in comfortably on the dark, burgundy LazyBoy sofa. The couple had inherited Gary's mother's living room furniture when she passed away only three months prior. Judith felt a surreal connection to her mother-in-law whenever she sat on the furniture that both comforted her and coarsely reminded her of the painful loss.

Judith spent about two hours watching television with the cats napping on the floor, hidden among the voluminous, green leaves from a cluster of potted plants. All of the houseplants flourished under the nurturing of Judith's green thumb. Yes, she was fully aware that she probably had too many plants growing in the house now, but she couldn't bring herself to give any away. She accepted little starts from friends and took satisfaction in watching the starts develop into mature, lovely plants. She had asked Gary if it bothered him—the over-crowding of plants in the house—but he showed no signs of irritation, so she continued on, starting more and more plants.

Knowing how cool the temperature was outdoors, Judith gave silent thanks for the home's heat and yet another modern gadget—an automatic thermostat.

When it felt like time to shower and dress for her day's work, Judith returned to her master bathroom upstairs. She quickly showered and slipped into old jeans, a tattered sweatshirt, thick wool socks, and worn, slip-on gardening shoes. While she dried her hair with a hand-held blow dryer, she fashioned a plan in her mind to attack the boxes in the garage and determine what might be deemed garbage. On Saturday or Sunday, she planned; Gary could help her take the garbage items to the dump. The nicer items would be tagged and sorted for her next garage sale. *I'll quit in time to get cleaned up and put on some make-up before Gary gets home.* It was Friday and she was envisioning the weekend with her husband.

Judith went to the main floor, passing the formal dining room where the dark wood, antique dining furniture sat, rarely used. Oddly, it did not bother her that this was the dining room furniture her first husband had insisted they dine at every night, formally, with fine china place settings, polished silver, candlelight, and wine—always wine in elegant, crystal goblets. He had even demanded that Judith wear a formal dress for every dinner. Meals, thankfully, were pleasant with Gary. They ate in the nook just off the kitchen. Judith had set up a small, round, light pine table with two matching chairs in the bay window area. Lace curtains partially covered the bay window. In this small space, the couple chatted lightly with each other over deliberately informal meals. Occasionally, on special evenings, Judith carried snacks into the living room for the couple to enjoy while watching a rented movie.

Judith continued down to the bottom floor, passing through the recreation room and out the door into the garage.

The garage was stuffed full, floor to ceiling, with only a few pathways for walking between stacks of cardboard boxes, plastic storage bins, gardening products, tool boxes, buckets, baskets, furniture, camping gear: a pack-rat's cache that had been multiplying since the Ridgways moved into the home. Judith shook her head and made a clucking sound with her tongue, hands resting on her hips. She wished she could park her car in the garage. When it wasn't being driven, her 1992, mocha-colored Mercury Sable sat in the driveway next to Gary's pick-up. However, she recognized the loftiness of her goal to get the garage cleared out for enough space to park a vehicle. She charged ahead with taking one cardboard box at a time, emptying the contents, and separating into piles what she determined to be either trash, garage sale merchandise, or fabulous treasures that she could wrap up and give as gifts for special occasions and holidays. People didn't need to know how she acquired gift items. That was her secret.

Judith worked in silence, puffing quick breaths, pushing her glasses back up her nose with the back of her hand, bending, lifting; repeating the actions again and again, feeling no hunger for food. Her passion for garage sales was the only fuel she needed for hours.

Judith's proclivity for spotting a bargain and stretching a dollar had brought her to the closest thing that could be called her working career: garage sale steward. She knew the business from shopper to seller. She and Gary had spent the majority of their weekends cruising garage sales and estate sales. They made special note of annual neighborhood garage sales they should remember for the next year. They regularly visited the "swap meet" up on Highway 99 between Seattle and Tacoma for bargains. When they felt like dressing it up a bit, they went to liquidation stores and searched for the ultimate prize in bargain hunting— new merchandise marked down to nearly free. Several years into the marriage, Gary had introduced Judith to a new twist in bargain hunting: "dumpster diving." Her task was to stay in the truck and watch for people approaching the area while Gary inspected dumpsters behind stores, looking for discarded merchandise he could take home and sell or use around the house.

Indeed, Judith had the ability to spot items on sale that she could put to use at home or easily sell at her next garage sale. Sometimes she came home with large quantities of one item like bottles of shampoo. Another time she might bring home dozens of picture frames, some in disrepair, but that was fine because she would get Gary to fix them for her.

Judith examined articles of men's clothing in a box that an acquaintance of the Ridgways had donated for her use in a garage sale. She held up a large pair of men's jeans and gave them a sniff. *Yeeuck! This is disgusting. Everything in this box smells like saltwater!* Well, Wally did work as a fisherman, so it made sense to her that his things would smell of the ocean. Judith decided to categorize the contents of the whole box as trash. While she disliked parting with anything useful, she knew that customers would be repelled by the odors coming off this clothing. The next box she inspected was no better than the first. This time she found clothing that had been obviously worn by a large woman. A neighbor had dropped it off as a contribution to the next garage sale. Each piece of clothing she held up had distinct wear patterns in areas where an obese woman would likely have body parts rubbing, making the fabric thin, and, in some places, the thin fabric actually gave way to holes. Judith's years of experience browsing garage sales taught her that signs of obesity such as this are a turn off to women shoppers. No. No. Garage sale shopping should be fun, and that is what she aimed to offer her customers. This box would also be added to the trash pile.

At approximately 3:00 p.m. Judith's body froze in place as she heard a distinct sound. The sound that had given her a startle was the crunching sound of tires on gravel. A car had come off the main thoroughfare, traveled down the shared, private road, turned, and was coming in the Ridgway driveway. It stopped right in front of the garage where she was sifting through boxes. The engine shut off. She heard the muffled thud of two doors slamming.

She glanced at her wristwatch. It was too soon for Gary to be home from work.

Cars did not typically enter their driveway. Sure, they had Gary's son from his second marriage over to visit sometimes on weekends. The two daughters from her first marriage occasionally came by. But unexpected visitors? No way. Solicitors avoided this area. The houses that shared the private road were all situated on one acre or more. With the houses spaced farther apart than typical neighborhoods, and with an abundance of trees and thick bushes blocking the view from one house to another, it wasn't efficient for solicitors to call on this area.

Judith heard two people walk to the front door and ring the doorbell.

She bit her lower lip.

After a few moments she inhaled deeply, straightened up her back, and decided to go find out who was at her front door. She walked through the smaller garage door and entered the bottom floor of the house. She climbed up the short flight of stairs to the main floor foyer. She opened the heavy wood door and immediately realized she was looking up at the faces of a man and a woman—professional-looking people-who had already opened the screen door and were leaning in toward her. *Who on earth are these people? They look so serious.* Judith felt small looking up at the tall strangers.

The professional-looking people pressed identification toward her face and quickly introduced themselves as Detectives Sue Peters and Matt Haney. Judith frowned and mouthed the word detectives, but no sound came out. *Detectives? Did they really say detectives? I must have heard them wrong.*

Judith swallowed hard against her dry throat. Her eyes zigzagged back and forth between the man and the woman. Solemn faces stared back. Something was wrong. The strangers looked too serious.

Somehow the detectives and Judith had moved into the house and were heading for the living room. The detectives said they had some important questions to ask her and wondered if they could tape record their conversation. She said of course. Thoughts were racing in figure eight patterns like an airplane with no pilot inside her head. She could not understand why these authoritative people were in her house.

Something about the scene felt familiar and frightening to Judith. Her body initiated symptoms that she loathed. At the center of her core she began trembling. The trembling rumbled deep within and then began moving out to her extremities. A wavy sense of lightheadedness began. Judith's heart was beating faster and faster, throat dry as hot sand. *I'm going to have a seizure!* Her last seizure had been in the 1960's when she was only twenty-three years old. To Judith, that had been a lifetime ago, and she believed she was free and clear of seizures. Judith whimpered internally.

The detectives asked Judith about Gary and his relationship with his son. They asked about Gary's family and what kind of people they were. They questioned her about Gary's arrest a couple of weeks ago. Did she know about it? Judith pressed the palm of her right hand to her forehead and explained that Gary had told her about the arrest. He said it was a silly mistake. He was on his way to work, pulled his truck over to push up the tailgate he had left lowered, and waved at a woman as a friendly gesture. She explained how her husband was always smiling and saying hello to people when they were out in public. Police arrested him for solicitation of a prostitute. But he was released the same day, and he and Judith were relieved that it was some kind of a crazy mix up.

Judith fought for control over her body. She was racking her brain to figure out why the detectives were at her house, on this day, asking her so many questions. She tried desperately to hear what the detectives were saying and give them answers, but the buzzing in her ears was blocking out sound. At times she only saw the detectives' faces, mouths opening and closing like fish, as they gestured their questions to her. The floor felt like it was tipping now.

After a few moments, she could hear the detectives again. They pressed on with questions. At times they were aggressive. Then they would back off. They asked Judith about her relationship with Gary. Had he ever been violent toward her? She protested vehemently with fists clenched and explained that her husband was funny and kind and always smiling. She could not understand why they were asking her these questions.

Judith told the detectives about the sad year they had been though with Gary's mother dying of cancer. Gary's father had passed away in 1998 from complications of Alzheimer's, and they had always imagined his mother coming to live with them. It was a terrible shock when they found out she was dying of cancer.

The detectives asked Judith if she knew that her husband had been arrested back in May of 1982 for offering to pay for a sex act with an undercover police officer. Anxiety had Judith in its full grip now. Her fingertips felt numb. Her lips began to tingle. She wondered if she would lose consciousness in front of the detectives. As she answered that she didn't know anything about the arrest, and that she didn't know Gary in 1982, her fingers violently wrestled with the fingers of the opposite hand, pinching and pulling flesh so that she could feel something real.

The female detective aggressively asked Judith questions about Judith and Gary's sex life. Judith felt a brief surge of strength from anger. Judith stammered angrily at the detectives. She defended Gary, describing him as gentle, soft-spoken, always smiling and polite to her. Their sex life was beautiful. The best she had ever had.

Had they ever done anything kinky such as tying each other up or having sex in the outdoors? No, Judith protested. Why would they do that?

As the detectives pushed on with more questions about the Ridgway's sex life, the doorbell rang, and then the telephone began ringing a few seconds later. Judith asked, "Should I answer it?" She motioned toward the telephone in the kitchen. The detectives nodded for her to go ahead.

The incoming caller was Judith's sister-in-law. Judith quickly ended the call by saying, "I'm busy right now, goodbye."

Judith then walked toward the front door, still feeling shaky and disoriented. As Judith opened the front door, Detective Peters quickly inserted her body between Judith and the front door, partially blocking Judith from the view of the news reporter who was ringing the doorbell. Apparently, word had gotten out about Gary's arrest and the first reporter had arrived at the Ridgway home in Auburn. But Judith was still in the dark about why a reporter would be at her home. The detectives had not yet told Judith that Gary was under arrest and that the biggest story in two decades was about to break in Washington.

A cameraman taped a few moments of Judith's pale face staring out, expressionless, just before the door was slammed shut by Detective Peters. The reporter failed to get any comment from Judith.

Ms. Peters guided Judith back to where they were before to resume questioning. But by now the telephone was ringing continuously. Judith pulled away, "I should answer that. It might be my mother calling."

Detective Haney suggested they unplug the phone. They had something very, very important to tell Judith.

After the phone was disabled, the detectives told Judith that her husband, Gary Ridgway, had been arrested earlier that day because of some new evidence that linked him to the victims of the Green River Killer. In fact, they were certain now that he was the Green River Killer.

Judith felt her heart slide downward in her chest. She felt weaker. She broke down. Her composure dissolved away like sugar granules in warm water. The idea of her husband actually being the Green River Killer was completely overwhelming. Inside her head, she cried out for Gary. *Gary, where have they taken you? I need you to hold me!*

Haney and Peters explained that Gary had been a suspect for a long time—several years. Specimens of DNA collected from several victims of the Green River Killer matched Gary's DNA. Three cases had already been confirmed as a match.

Judith shook her head side to side, openly crying. No, she didn't know that Gary was a suspect. No, she didn't know he was seeing prostitutes. No, she didn't know anything. Her head motion finally stopped after several minutes, and she fell into still silence. She was unable to move or think.

As the detectives continued on, offering more details about how the task force had been following Gary and monitoring his activities, Judith felt like a giant wall was collapsing down on her, squeezing the air out of her lungs.

Judith heard a voice echoing toward her from the far end of a long tunnel. It was Sue Peters. "Judith, let's get a bag packed for you now. We are going to take you to a hotel and check you in under a different name. The reporters will not know you're there. You are going to stay there for a few days while we search your home."

Judith compliantly followed Ms. Peters' instructions as the support walls of her life cracked, tumbled, and buried her.

Chapter 2
Beginnings

Judith Lorraine Mawson (Ridgway) was born on August 15, 1944. Her eighteen-year-old mother, Helen Downing, quietly delivered her at only seven months into the pregnancy, alone, at the St. Helens Hospital in Chehalis, Washington.

During the years flanking Judith's birth, it seemed the world had gone mad. In 1939 the U.K. and France had declared war on Germany, pressing the start button for World War II. Canada followed suit in September of the same year. 1941 brought a shocking and deadly attack on the U.S. Pacific Fleet when the Japanese attacked Pearl Harbor, Hawaii, December 7th. The United States officially declared war on the Empire of Japan December 8, 1941. Just two months prior to Judith's birth, United States soldiers waded onto the beaches of Normandy, France, under devastating enemy fire. And, like the soldiers in Normandy, Judith's father was far away from home, a nineteen-year-old soldier himself, battling for America in World War II. American soldiers and their anguished families had no means of predicting that World War II would end in 1945 after the U.S. bomber, Enola Gay, would drop atomic bombs on Hiroshima and Nagasaki, Japan. And they, in their wildest dreams, hadn't foreseen that the United States would be back at war just five years later in Korea.

Helen did not know the location of Judith's father when she gave birth to their baby. In fact, as she lay in the hospital bed with no smiling, well-wishing visitors, no flowers, and no gifts, she did not know if Wesley Mawson was living or dead and whether he would ever come home and meet his new daughter. Her chest ached with worry for her new baby and for the life of her lover. Of course she would write him a letter… tell him the good news…it would take weeks to reach him.

What the new, young mother acutely knew as fact was that she had just become the mother of a premature baby girl, that she was not married, and that she had only one living soul to help her survive and to care for the new baby: "Uncle Si."

Uncle Silas was a man who had executed multiple roles in his life. Had he volunteered for the challenging roles in a benevolent spirit? Or, had he accepted the roles with resentment when they were rudely thrust upon him? The answer is not known. But Uncle Silas, a carpenter and widower with no children of his own, took custody of Judith's mother, Helen, when she was sent to him at approximately three years of age. Helen's biological mother had become erotically active by the age of thirteen and was drinking alcohol excessively. She married six times and gave birth to several children. She abandoned Helen to pursue men, and later, committed suicide after four failed attempts. The identity of Helen's father was unknown, and her maternal grandparents had been killed in a car accident. Uncle Silas was the brother of Helen's grandfather who had died in the car accident.

Great Uncle Silas became both mother and father to Helen while he worked in his trade as a carpenter. Young Helen and aging Uncle Si lived together near the tiny town of Vader, Washington, in a small, modest home that he had built with his own hands on five and one-half acres of fertile land—land that he had made claim to when he came to the area as one of the early settlers. The simple, square home had no indoor plumbing and no running water, but it was a cozy home and the occupants were mighty thankful to have it.

Vader, Washington, at the time of this writing, has a population of approximately 600; however, the town is considered to be a semi-ghost town. Incorporated in 1906, the town covers a total area of approximately one square mile and is located twenty miles southwest of Chehalis, Washington, along the Interstate-5 corridor that runs north and south in western Washington, on state route 506.

Vader experienced its paramount energy in the early days with a steady, dramatic, decline until present day. The community rose up from nothing in the early 1800's when settlers arrived from the east. A post office, general store, hotel, and a one-room school gave the town a fresh, new face— a face that would later be blemished by brothels and saloons.

Helen and Uncle Si worked together as a competent team during the years that Helen grew through childhood, adolescence, and then as a young mother. Si's modest income from his sporadic carpenter jobs and his skills as a handyman supported the basic financial and maintenance needs around the home. A well on the property supplied all of their water. They fed themselves with locally butchered meat and plentiful vegetables that they nurtured each year in their expansive garden. Potatoes served as a major staple for the household as they were easy to grow, easy to dig up in the rich, dark, loamy soil, and they did not require much for preservation—simply a dark, cool, area for storage. It seemed they ate potatoes as a part of every meal. They even ate raw potato wedges for snacks. Fruit trees on the property yielded abundant crops each summer.

Helen treasured the once-a-year pleasure of tasting fresh, sun-ripened fruit. Most of the fruit was preserved to last the remainder of the year. It was endless, backbreaking labor for the duo, but somehow they made it work. They had all the basics for survival: water, food, shelter. But most importantly, they had each other.

When Helen was sixteen years old, Uncle Si sent her to work as a riveter at a Boeing airplane factory in nearby Chehalis. It was wartime and the United States needed more airplane riveters just as much as Uncle Si needed more cash. Helen went to work at her first paying job without question, and quietly slipped out of school, never to return.

At seventeen, Helen discovered who her biological father was and that he was living in California—a universe away from Helen's small world in Vader. Uncle Si encouraged Helen to go meet her father. So, Helen left Uncle Si and the mini-farm in western Washington and courageously went to live with her newly found father who was, in fact, a total stranger to her. During her one-year stay in California, she worked at a purse factory and began a relationship her father. Then, at the end of the year, Helen felt a powerful yearning to go home to Uncle Si. Uncle Si welcomed her back, and the duo picked up where they had left off: working in the yard, tending the garden, hauling water up to the house, chopping wood, and preparing and preserving food.

At eighteen, when Helen realized she was pregnant after getting involved with Wesley Mawson, a handsome, restless, and charismatic young man she had met while hanging out at the local train station (one of the few sources of entertainment in the tiny town). Neither Uncle Si nor Helen had any experience with pregnancies or babies to reference. However, they did not panic. They simply continued moving forward, calmly accepting that they would just *figure it out*, like everything else they had faced in life. In the meantime, Wesley had already been drafted into service for World War II.

Helen's pregnancy developed normally while she performed her usual chores with Uncle Si. With no woman available to offer advice and experience about pregnancies and birthing, Helen observed, with fascination and a child-like delight, her belly growing tight and round, and she felt movement from strong kicks by the baby. Once, she exclaimed to Uncle Si, "You know, it's just like when a calf kicks inside the mother cow...my gosh, it feels like there's a baby cow inside of me!"

Labor began unexpectedly and early at seven months when Helen slipped and fell over a large rock while crossing a creek near their home. The jolt to her swollen abdomen initiated labor, and the very worried Helen and Uncle Si walked quietly together down their long driveway and then down the first dirt road to neighbors who owned a car. The neighbors drove Helen to the St. Helens Hospital (named for Mt. St. Helens, an active volcano that would violently erupt in 1980) in Chehalis and dropped her off. Uncle Si walked back home to wait for news from the hospital.

Premature baby Judith was born and placed into an incubator. She was tiny but thriving. After sixteen days, Helen and her baby were discharged from the hospital. A staff person at the hospital kindly offered Helen and the baby a ride home. But they were gruffly dropped off at the mouth of Uncle Si's driveway as the driver did not want to attempt to maneuver the car up the perfidious terrain. Helen, weakened from inactivity for sixteen days, thanked the driver for the ride home and then slowly carried her tiny bundle up the long, nappy driveway and introduced the sleeping baby Judith to Uncle Si.

The duo became a trio.

Shortly after Helen returned home from the hospital, a woman from the Red Cross paid a visit to the new mother, offering chatty, warm, advice and a layette, a starter kit for a new baby including diapers, blankets, and some clothing. Someone at the hospital had noticed that Helen did not have any supplies for her newborn. Uncle Si had polished up the wooden cradle that he had constructed years ago for Helen to sleep in when she first came to live with him. Carefully, Helen gently placed her baby Judith in the same cradle. A second baby girl began life in Uncle Si's hand-crafted cradle.

Uncle Si and Helen silently stared down at the new miracle, watching her sleep, each fast-forwarding in their mind's eye to the infant's life ahead, wondering what kind of person she would become. Would she look like her mother or her father? Would Uncle Si live long enough to see her graduate from school? Marry? Neither Uncle Si nor Helen had a whisper of a premonition that little Judith would grow up and marry a notorious, dangerous, serial killer.

Just one day short of Judith's first birthday, the Japanese surrendered to allies on August 14, 1945, ending World War II. Wesley Mawson came home shortly thereafter with his U.S. Army combat engineers battalion, based in Fort Lewis, Washington. He met his one-year-old daughter, instantly recognizing his eyes and nose on her little face. He asked her mother to marry him.

Having been raised a Mormon Wesley Mawson married Helen in a Latter-day Saints Ward in Seattle, Washington, about one hundred miles north of Vader. He and his new family began a life together, staying with Uncle Si. Wesley quickly found work in the booming logging industry very close to home. But Wesley, feeling restless and hungry for more excitement, grew weary of the mundane logging job in the first year of employment. Like so many other returning soldiers, he may have been having difficulty transitioning into normal life after fighting in the war. One day in 1946, Wesley abruptly packed up his family and moved to Salt Lake City, Utah, leaving Uncle Si behind. Judith was a two-year-old toddler. The young family lived with Wesley's parents, and Wesley went to work in a cement block yard. Helen began to observe the Mormon ways of life.

Again, Wesley did not bond with the colorless work routine, so he moved his family back to Vader, Washington. Again, they lived with Uncle Si. Wesley worked off and on at different jobs and began a new pattern of behavior that afforded less and less time with his wife and daughter. It seemed to Helen that her husband was always away, searching for something. Helen confided in Uncle Si that she felt like she had an exciting lover to meet occasionally for dates but not a husband. Uncle Si was not pleased with what he saw in Wesley's behavior. Wesley had developed a reputation as being a highly excitable Tomcat, always on the prowl for mates. No, Uncle Si's women deserved better.

In 1949 Helen's father moved from California to Kennydale, Washington, and he invited Helen and little Judith to live with him. Helen agreed. She thought it was time to leave Vader, try something new. By now Helen's husband had severed all contact with her.

Helen's father, according to gossip, was doing well financially. Maybe he could help Helen with Judith's upbringing and offer her opportunities that were not available in Vader. Uncle Si, she reasoned, was getting on in age and perhaps it was time to bless him with some well-deserved quiet in the home.

Judith's first memories of her life originate in her grandfather's home, a new rambler, in Kennydale, a suburb of Seattle. Even at Judith's young age, she understood the significance of living in the first home on the block with a television set. She sat, motionless, enthralled, watching her favorite shows in black and white: Wanda Wanda and Howdy Doody.

Five-year-old Judith entered kindergarten and her mother got a job, again with Boeing, at the Renton plant where she hand-painted numbers on airplanes.

Life was good for Judith in grandfather's house. They enjoyed modern appliances and indoor plumbing. Grandfather's new wife prepared hearty meals of store-bought food. Frequently they shared meals with interesting guests seated all around the table. The adults showered affection upon the only child in the group, little Judith, in an attempt to fill in for her absent father. The adults indulged little Judith by laughing at her antics and listening intently whenever she interrupted the adults.

Grandfather owned a beautiful, shiny, black car. Judith and her mother enjoyed a fantastic new sense of freedom and great fortune as they traveled about the busy Seattle area by car, always driven safely by grandfather.

In 1950 Helen had saved enough money from her earnings to make a down payment and purchase a small home in Renton, very near the Boeing plant at which she worked. She could walk to work and save bus fare. Home ownership for a single, young woman in the 1950's was unusual. However, Helen was determined to forge ahead and do whatever necessary to secure a sense of stability for herself and Judith. Helen and Judith left grandfather in Kennydale and moved into their new home. For a brief time, mother and daughter lived alone together, without any men. Helen worked a full schedule at Boeing, managed all of the household chores, cared for Judith, and tended a small garden in the back yard. Naturally, she grew potatoes like she had at Uncle Si's place. Evening entertainment for the two was curling up together on the sofa, in pajamas, watching television and munching on bite-size pieces of raw potato.

With no other people in the house, Judith began to receive undiluted attention from her mother. "No" was not a word that Judith recognized. Helen dropped what she was doing to play with Judith, giving in to her demands. Judith had no rules to abide by in the home. She could freely jump on the furniture, spill food on the floor, and get into her mother's things with no consequences. In a generation when "spare the rod, spoil the child" was advocated as good parenting wisdom, Helen chose to throw out the rod.

In June of 1950 President Harry Truman authorized General Douglas MacArthur to send U.S. military support to South Korea. The Korean War had begun. Wesley Mawson re-enlisted as soon as he heard the news. He was going to be a soldier again.

On September 2nd of the same year, Sgt. Wesley Mawson stepped on a land mine near Seoul, Korea. His body was decimated, leaving scant remains to send home to his parents in Utah. Judith would not know until she was a sixty-one-year-old woman, while doing a genealogy search on the internet, that her grandfather, Wesley's father, desperate to end the sickening grief he had felt after losing his son, walked out to the barn behind his house in Utah and fatally shot himself in the head on the two-year anniversary of Wesley's death.

Judith became a six-year-old fatherless child and Helen a 24-year-old widow. Immediately, without contemplation, Uncle Si decided it was time to sell his home and land in Vader and, shortly thereafter, he moved in with Helen and Judith in the little home in Renton.

Judith seemed upset when she was told that her father had been killed in the war, but having only interacted with him for about six months out of her six years of life, she did not have any memories of her father that she could cling to. Helen gave Judith a wallet size, black and white, head and shoulders photo of Wesley—the only tangible evidence to Judith that she had ever had a father. She only knew that she had suffered some kind of loss and that her mother seemed to be sad. The mutual loss worked to reinforce the bond between mother and daughter.

When Uncle Si moved in, Helen transferred Judith out of her small bedroom and into Helen's bedroom to allow Uncle Si his own room. Judith and Helen had to walk through Uncle Si's bedroom, however, to access the tiny bathroom. Quarters were close but they moved around each other with respect for one another's privacy.

The trio was together again.

In 1952, when Judith was eight years old, a group of boys from the neighborhood coaxed her into the little playhouse that had lived up to its name thus far—a cute little house that Judith played in. The playhouse was only steps from the house in her back yard. Having successfully isolated Judith from view of her mother and Uncle Si, the bigger, older boys shoved Judith down on the floor and quickly stripped her clothing off from the waist down. They slapped her across the face repeatedly and threatened her with serious injury if she cried out. The boys pressed her firmly down, arms above her head, yanking her legs apart, as they each attempted penis insertion. Penetration was not possible, and this disappointment enraged the boys who slapped and punched Judith even more violently. Having their goal of gang rape foiled, the boys ran off, leaving a beaten, shocked, eight-year-old lying on the floor of her beloved playhouse, naked on her bottom half.

When Helen discovered what had happened, she rushed Judith to a doctor who examined her and confirmed that her hymen was still intact. Good news, Helen thought. Meanwhile, Uncle Si smashed the playhouse with a heavy sledgehammer, swing after angry swing, until it was a pile of disarrayed pieces of lumber. Judith's physical wounds healed quickly. The actual memory of the attack was sent away to a distant corner of her brain where it would be repressed.

Judith was not disturbed by the memory of the assault from the neighborhood boys, however, she was disturbed about her lovely little playhouse being destroyed. One day she marched out to the back yard to discover that her playhouse was gone. Demolished. Her mother and Uncle Si gave no explanation. Judith wondered for the next fifty-four years why her playhouse had inexplicably fallen down.

And so, with one vicious attack to Judith's body and soul, a course that would take her through a series of tragic happenings was set.

Uncle Si, now in his eighties, spent most of his time sitting at the kitchen table in their house. The table and chairs were 1950's diner-style with chrome framework and red vinyl seat covers. A toaster—the kind that opened up in the middle for placement of bread—resided in the center of the table. Uncle Si prepared himself toast at the table throughout the day. Dressed in either denim overalls or jeans with suspenders and a cotton shirt, the toothless Uncle Si sat for hours at the kitchen table chewing tobacco and spitting into a coffee can on the floor near his feet. He was bald with a white goatee beard that hung long and thin from his chin. Wire frame glasses anchored over the top of his large ears and balanced on his strong, pointed nose. Unfortunately, Uncle Si's declining health prevented him from doing household chores or helping in the garden, but Helen and Judith weren't concerned. Uncle Si was never a burden. His energy and humor sparked laughter and warmth in the home.

Judith would always remember her mother carrying in potatoes from the garden in the back yard. The garden had one, large, signature, yellow sunflower each year that rose up so high, Judith had to look up toward the sky to get a good look at it. Judith stomped up the back porch and through the screen door that opened into the kitchen, carrying in produce with her mother from the garden for dinner. Countless times she watched her mother's hands holding potatoes and deftly peeling potatoes with a small paring knife. Sometimes Helen declared, "This potato is just too small to waste my time on," and she would discard it. Potatoes, it seemed to Judith, brought a sense of normality and continuity to her life and to the household.

On a few thrilling occasions, Judith got permission to run the two-block distance from their house over to Katie's Corner, a small grocery store, where she would purchase a few pieces of penny candy. Then, she slowly walked home, sucking on something delicious, while happily flicking her skirt in a circular direction around herself with her hands.

Judith felt excited and downright giddy while running down the sidewalk to the end of their street to meet "Clyde" the mailman. She skipped along next to Clyde and prattled at him while he delivered mail to the houses on the block until they reached Judith's house where they would say goodbye until the next time. Clyde was a nice mailman and one of the characters Judith held dear in her tiny world.

One summer afternoon, Judith was pleasantly surprised when a traveling band of sales people came to the door of their house offering to take pictures of Judith while she sat atop one of their rental ponies in the front yard. They had cowboy hats and related costume garb available for an additional small fee. Helen said yes, of course, always wanting to make life better for her daughter, so Judith donned the cowboy gear and joyfully posed on a pony for a photo.

Uncle Si looked after Judith while Helen went out on occasional dates. Helen had finally accepted her title of "widow" and believed enough time had gone by for proper grieving. She dated casually but always kept her guard up. It would not be easy for any man to penetrate the invisible safety barrier she had constructed around her precious family trio.

One date, however, in 1953, brought a man named George Pillatos right through the front door of their lives. Helen had been set up for a blind date with George by a female co-worker at Boeing. George was the co-worker's brother-in-law. After a few more dates, it seemed like they had always known George and he slowly became part of their new normal life. Judith liked George very much.

George and Helen dated exclusively over the next two years and George became a welcome, extra hand and sounding board for Helen as she faced a twofold difficulty: One, Judith growing into a bigger girl who was becoming more forceful, physically, in getting what she wanted. And two, Uncle Si's heart condition. Could Helen continue to manage both issues?

George assisted Helen in moving Uncle Si into a nursing home facility so that he could receive daily medical care and the additional help he now required for bathing and dressing. Fortunately, the proceeds from the sale of his home and land were available to cover the costs for Uncle Si. His heart was failing, and it broke Helen's heart to see it happening. Uncle Si had been her mother and her father and her everything for her entire life. She closed her eyes tightly and cried whenever she imagined life without Uncle Si. She leaned heavily on George during this time and, with his reassurance, felt convinced moving Uncle Si out was the right thing to do. The couple regularly took Judith to the rest home to visit Uncle Si.

George tried to lighten the mood for his new women by taking them on car trips for fun. They regularly visited "the cow," otherwise known as Herfy's Hamburgers in Renton for 19-cent hamburgers. The restaurant had a very large cow statue mascot in the parking lot. It was a fabulous treat for Judith when they got to go to "the cow" for hamburgers.

Occasionally, George drove Helen and Judith to the middle of the state, near Kennewick, Washington, to visit his family. It was on one of these trips that George inadvertently injured Judith. It was August 1954. Judith was ten years old. George was swinging her around in a garage with a cement floor in a playful, familiar exercise they had developed over the past months. On George's cue, Judith would jump up and wrap her legs around George's waist. He would then hold her hands while she tossed her head backward, away from his chest, and flipped her legs along after her head, through her arms, making a circle back to the ground, over and over again, squealing out laughter the whole time. "Let's do it again George. I want to do it again!" Judith begged. On this occasion something went wrong, George lost his grip on her hands, and Judith smashed her head down on the concrete floor with a horrible clunk sound. Judith immediately felt a large bump on the back of her head. Then she had nausea and vomiting.

Short, robust, Judith, with yellow-blonde hair, trusting eyes, and a wide smile, held no anger toward George. She simply viewed it as a bad accident, just like her mother said it was. And she fervently continued to wish he would be her father.

Two months after the accident, a brain seizure disturbance began. Suddenly, the good times ended. Seizure episodes in Judith terrified Helen for years and left Judith with too many gaps in memory, pieces of her childhood forever lost.

Helen took her little girl to see a very special doctor, a *neurologist,* in Seattle. The two traveled by bus, as Helen had never cared to learn how to drive a car. Judith was put through a series of neurological tests that included gluing wires all over her head. It was all strange and frightening to Judith. She knew that something was terribly wrong with her, and she had never seen the strained, pale look on her mother's face that she was seeing now. The neurologist diagnosed "petit mal seizure disorder" and prescribed Dilantin. Helen and Judith walked to a Bartell's Pharmacy and sat at the soda fountain, sipping on delicious tasting ice cream sodas in tall, frosty glasses while the prescription was filled. A bus ride home finished the day.

The seizures diminished in frequency for a while. The medication was apparently working.

In 1955, at age eleven, Judith's wish came true. A Justice of the Peace married George and her mother, and then George moved in with his new wife and stepdaughter. The newlyweds took Judith along on their honeymoon to Kennewick where they visited with George's family again.

Judith could see how happy her mother was, and this knowledge, in turn, made her feel very happy. Finally, Judith had a real, complete family. She began calling George "Daddy."

A new trio was formed.

George took his responsibilities of stepfather to heart. He immediately implemented new, strict rules in the household, including asking Judith to finish eating the food on her plate and not to interrupt adults while they were talking. It was no longer acceptable for Judith to jump on the furniture like a rambunctious puppy. A sense of structure and order came into place with regular bed times. More rules. And— punishment for Judith when she broke the rules? George spanked Judith in the hallway of the house when she disobeyed the rules, and he sternly, with an authoritative voice, delivered lengthy lectures to Judith on why she must not break the rules. This change of rules planted some seeds of conflict in Judith. On one hand, she had wished for a father with all her being—and got one. On the other hand, this new father unleashed awful rules upon her—something she instantly loathed and rebelled against. Why couldn't she just have a daddy and keep living the way she was before with her mother? Why did everything have to change? None of it made sense. It was a great relief to Helen to be able to share the responsibilities of raising a child with another able adult. With her new husband in the home, she possessed more hope for the future and felt optimistic that things would somehow work out for the best.

In 1956, twelve-year-old Judith began menses. With the onset of her periods, the Dilantin, unfortunately, no longer controlled the seizures. Seizures fired up again, with, curiously, an increase in seizure activity around Judith's periods. Sometimes her periods would last for three whole weeks with heavy flow the entire duration. With seizures manifesting while Judith was in school, her classmates witnessed behavior they had never seen before—dizziness, Judith falling down to the floor, wetting herself, making strange noises, acting goofy and disoriented afterward. The children did the only thing they knew to do—they teased Judith mercilessly. She was deemed a freak. In addition to the health difficulties in school, Judith was only reading at a fourth grade level when she was in the seventh grade, inviting further mocking from her peers when she was asked to read aloud in the classroom. Judith began lashing out in anger at her classmates when they teased her. Teachers took note and made reports to the school counselor and principal.

The next year, at age thirteen, Judith watched her world and the new trio explode painfully, like a firecracker in her soft hand. Judith became a big sister. Her mother and George had their first child together—a baby girl named "Georgette." While it was, at first, wonderfully exciting having a cute little baby to study with fascination, Judith quickly began to realize that this *baby* was ruining her life. She was losing her mother to the small, needy, bawling, creature. Her mother was completely wrapped up in the baby's needs. Helen had quit her job at Boeing to focus on caring for her new daughter. George earned a decent living for the family at Bethlehem Steel in Seattle. It had been thirteen long years since Helen had given birth to Judith, and she needed to re-orient herself to caring for a newborn. Naturally, George and Helen were on top of the world with joy in producing a child together. But Judith felt as though she were pushed to the outside, looking in on this newly-formed trio.

A trio that no longer included herself.

George and Helen sold the small home in Renton and moved. Judith had to leave behind her neighborhood with all its familiar happenings; had to leave behind the lovely garden with the tall sunflower; had to leave Clyde the mailman. The family moved into a single-wide trailer home, situated in a mobile home park in Federal Way, directly across from the Lewis and Clark Theater, very near Highway 99—the strip of highway that would later be famous for being the highway that Gary Ridgway cruised in search of sex acts with prostitutes and candidates to murder.

Then Uncle Si died. He passed peacefully in his rest home in 1957.

As Judith and her mother adjusted to Uncle Si being gone forever, Judith realized the big sister thing really wasn't working out for her. Not only did her mother love the baby more than her, Judith wasn't permitted to babysit or even *hold* the baby because she could go into a seizure at any moment and drop the baby. Everyone knew it was dangerous for Judith to be around the baby. The damn seizures were ruining her life. Sometimes, in fits of sheer frustration, Judith poked baby Georgette or pinched her to make her cry. One time she roughly shook the baby. Judith was in big trouble with her parents.

Judith's childhood entered a long tunnel of darkness. She was kicked out of school in the eighth grade as, in addition to her seizure disorder, her anger and aggression had increased to an unacceptable level. Teachers complained that "Judy" would do almost anything or create any kind of a disturbance to gain attention, especially where boys were concerned. She destroyed property, broke rules, and slammed her desk to the floor when challenged. She often acted ridiculously silly. Ultimately she was suspended from school for exhibiting indecent behavior in school.

The young, blonde, teenager with a body that was beginning to blossom into the full flower of womanhood, posed in front of a much nicer trailer home, probably the fanciest one in the park, while the man took pictures of her. She wore a bathing suit for him and posed for the camera. He told her that she was very pretty. He wanted to take some photographs of her so that he could have them to look at.

His yard was lovely with neatly landscaped flowerbeds, colorful flowers, a big tree stump. She felt beautiful, posing for the nice man in the pretty flowers.

But then mother found out and got so angry with her! She shouldn't have gone down to the man's trailer. Mother told her to never, never go there again. Why did she have to ruin something so nice?

Helen made an appointment for Judith to see a *hypnotherapist* in downtown Seattle. George and Helen walked Judith into the large, brick building. They waited in the waiting room while Judith was with the hypnotherapist. Judith sat face to face with the therapist, defiant, arms crossed in front of her chest. Nobody was going to hypnotize her! The doctor went back to the waiting room and shook his head. It hadn't worked. George and Helen asked themselves what they could try next.

A subsequent visit to the hypnotherapist was more successful. While in a moderately deep hypnotic state, the therapist asked Judith to describe a perfect life. Judith, relaxed, compliant, verbally outlined her vision. She fancied herself out parked in a car with a boyfriend, in lover's lane, and his arms would be around her, and he'd be kissing her gently, placing a ring on her finger and asking her to marry him.

One night Judith woke her sleeping parents and said she had something to tell them. Could it wait until morning? No, she had told them. She went on to describe to her parents' stunned faces that George's nephew had repeatedly molested her. She offered matter of fact details of how he had done it. Many times, Judith asserted, when the families got together, the nephew had insisted that she put her hand inside his open trousers and manipulate his penis with her hand. At other times, he had demanded that she take her pants down. Then he lay on top of her, rubbing his erect penis against her pubic area. She said all of this bothered her, and she knew it was wrong. She wanted to tell them about it. George, highly skeptical, asked Judith, "If you really saw a penis, what did it look like?" Judith replied that she couldn't really explain it but she could draw a picture. After being given pencil and paper, Judith sketched a remarkably life-like image of the male genitalia. George and Helen instructed Judith to go back to bed. No follow up took place after the nighttime confession. It was not spoken about again. Later, Judith wondered if she had simply dreamed the whole thing.

Two years later, at age fifteen, Judith became a big sister again. This time Helen delivered a son, Wesley, named after Judith's deceased father. By now the family had moved into a house in White Center, near Seattle, so that George could have a shorter commute to his work at Bethlehem Steele in Seattle. Judith retained no memory of the event, however, her mother later explained to her that once she was allowed to hold Wesley when he was a tiny baby. Unfortunately, Judith dropped him like a slippery bowling ball onto the floor when a seizure started. Years later Wesley accused Judith, tongue-in-cheek, of causing his own "grand mal seizure disorder." In fact, his lifetime of seizures began at the age of ten after a passing car in front of their house had struck and nearly killed him.

Shortly after Wesley was born, with Judith's temper tantrums escalating and deemed to be utterly dangerous to those around her, Judith's parents admitted her to the Ryther Child Care Center in Seattle, November 23rd, where she would live and have round the clock care and monitoring. A clear message had been sent to Judith that she was now too dangerous to be around her own family.

Her parents had heard of the Ryther facility and decided they had no choice but to give it a try to see if something changed in Judith. The public school system would not take her back. She was becoming impossible to manage at home with her frequent seizure activity and horrible outbursts. And it was more and more difficult to keep her in the home, safe, with so many boys noticing her maturing, curvy, body and all. Judith thoroughly enjoyed mowing the lawn in her bathing suit, but Helen and George told her she could no longer do that in the front yard. It wasn't right for a young lady to display herself in that way to the neighbors. Judith had been caught smoking cigarettes behind an abandoned building with boys. She was beginning to engage in sexual activities with young men—something respectable girls absolutely should not do. Judith was undeniably running wild. The Ryther Child Care Center, her parents were advised, had a reputation as being a home with firm, but loving discipline, and nothing but the best intentions for wayward youths. Helen and George were hopeful that this would be the winning ticket for Judith.

Founded in 1883, The Ryther Home was created by "Mother Ryther" (a.k.a. Olive Spore Ryther) who had a vision for a warm, safe home in Seattle where prostitutes, orphans, runaways, pregnant girls, and the like could live and be free from the dangers on the city streets. But the home was more than mere shelter. Mother Ryther insisted that everyone be responsible for household chores; she taught new mothers the skills needed to care for babies, and her ultimate goal was for every guest to reach a point of self- sufficiency. She encouraged everyone in the home to learn skills that would increase chances of finding employment.

In 1934, at the age of eighty-five, Mother Ryther died, having mentored over 3,100 children in her house. However, successors to Mother Ryther continued her work and the facility was open in 1960 when Judith's parents checked her in. At the time of this writing, the Ryther Child Center remains open in north Seattle, funded by public and private donations, and serving adolescents with chemical dependency, mental disorders, and criminal histories. Prostitution, pregnancy, physical and sexual abuse, and general neglect cases are also admitted.

Judith lived at the Ryther Child Center for approximately twelve months. Most of Judith's memory of the habitation is blurred by numerous seizure episodes. Judith did not know how long she would have to stay there. Even though she felt estranged from her family, she did miss them and longed to go home. It hurt her deeply to be sent away, but Mother and George had reassured her it was for her own good that they were doing this. Judith believed her parents thought they were doing the right thing. And they were faithful in visiting Judith on the weekends. Helen and George brought the little siblings, all dressed up. The family posed for photos on the sidewalk in front of the Ryther facility, trying to look like an ordinary family.

Judith recalls sharing a room with approximately five other girls, dormitory style. A separate boys' dorm was on the other side of the home. She was required to attend high school classes. A heavy-set, black woman, named Chaney, worked as the cook for the facility. Judith instantly bonded with the woman, proclaiming she was the nicest woman in the whole world. Judith slipped away whenever possible to share a few moments of conversation and hugs with Chaney. Even on Judith's darkest days, Cook Chaney could lift her up with kind words and loving smiles.

Judith ran away from the Ryther home on several occasions, only to be rounded up and brought back. She never stopped plotting to escape and go home. During one runaway episode, Judith attempted to hitchhike her way home, even though she wasn't sure which direction home was. All she knew was that she was going home. A man picked her up at the roadside, and the next thing Judith remembered was trying to escape from his vehicle like a bunny rabbit from the open mouth of a wolf. Between the time of being picked up and crawling frantically out of a back window of the car in her escape, Judith's memory had vanished. Judith was found and taken back to the Ryther facility. Later, she wondered if she had had a seizure in the car with the strange man. What had he done to terrify her so?

After twelve months of receiving counseling and attending classes at the Ryther Center, sixteen-year-old Judith gratefully went home to live with her family November 15th of 1960. But, by the next year, at age seventeen, her life was tumbling ferociously toward the edge of a cliff. She was about to receive yet another little sister, Lori, and a new home— Western State Hospital, a mental facility, where she would live, with no chance of escape, (it was assumed) for the next year.

Meanwhile, Judith's parents and three young siblings moved to a larger home in Lake City, near Seattle. Living space was getting tight.

Western State Hospital, in Tacoma, Washington, a *funny farm*, a *nut house*, a *lunatic asylum*, was a hospital in the 1960's where the very mentally disturbed were checked in and did not have the option of leaving. Established in 1871, it was first called an "insane asylum" and was located on the site of Fort Steilacoom. Most mental patients were deemed a danger to society and were locked up, having little chance of ever leaving the facility. Many served life sentences there. Radical treatments such as ice water immersion, frontal lobotomies, and electric shock therapy had been practiced on patients at the insane asylum for years. However, the 1960's brought in a new wave of treatment for the mentally ill—antipsychotic drugs, which tipped the treatment scale heavily toward drug therapy. The 1975 movie "One Flew Over the Cuckoo's Nest," starring Jack Nicholson, later dramatized the life of patients in mental institutions such as this. For the first time, the public got a peek into the mysterious, daily, at times horrifying, happenings within the walls of a mental hospital. Today, with new treatments available, Western State Hospital continues to treat the mentally ill and evaluates the alleged criminally insane.

How is it that young Judith became a patient in such a facility? She was "voluntarily committed" at seventeen years of age, and was coaxed into signing a voluntary commitment form.

Judith does not remember much about May 19, 1961, just three days before her sister Lori was born, when she was left at Western State Hospital. She cannot remember the majority of her stay at the hospital. One day, mother simply told her, "Okay, Judith, it's time to go to the hospital now." Very pregnant mother and George swiftly loaded up Judith and the young ones into the car. The next thing Judith knew, having no idea how many miles they had driven—they could have traveled into another state, according to Judith's perception—she was looking out the car window at an intimidating, large, brick building. It was the biggest building she had ever seen. She was told that she would be living in this hospital, just for a while, so that doctors could experiment with strong medications to help get rid of her seizures. To Judith, it sort of felt familiar, like just another visit to a doctor, an exercise she and her mother had been performing most of her life. They never stopped hunting for a "cure" to her ailment. If mother told her that this place would help, then it was just the next stop in a never-ending series of medical appointments. Judith did not protest or cry or ask questions. At the hospital, she silently followed medical personnel, away from her mother, stepfather, and young siblings. She was introduced to her small, dormitory-style room, with a narrow rectangle shape. Judith felt like she was stepping into a skinny shoebox. A single bed was situated parallel to the right wall of the room, with a small cabinet on the left side for her clothing. Everything looked stark. *I don't see anything here that looks like home.* Judith knew in a moment that this place was nothing like the Ryther Child Center. No, no. Authority was thick in the air. A much bigger authority than the Ryther Child Center had. And the place was gigantic! Judith worried about getting lost in the endless hallways. She looked up and down, left and right, with her eyes; she was certain there were other eyes in all the walls and ceilings looking back at her. *Man. There's no way I can run away from here.*

Judith retained only a few, crystallized memories of her eighteen-month stay. She retained a powerful memory of being viscerally afraid of the nurses. Early into her stay, she had formed the impression that the nurses were mean spirited toward her, even—astonishing as it was to Judith—accusing her of faking the seizures. Judith worked to avoid interaction with the nursing staff whenever possible. She had been firmly coached by the nurses to ring a special bell that was situated near her bed whenever she felt a seizure coming on so they could come in the room and observe Judith during seizure activity. But Judith wasn't inclined to ring the bell: she dreaded the wrath of the nurses after a seizure. It was easier to just "go out" alone.

Judith got a great surprise in the hospital. She noticed and then recognized a young female patient as a classmate she had attended school with for a brief time back home. *Oh, so there are other girls like me having problems. Maybe we can be friends!* But the surprise quickly turned ugly. Judith noticed that the girl had only hostile energy toward her. One day, while working in the laundry room, a duty that the girls were expected to perform routinely, the ex-classmate switched some of the clean, folded laundry around, relocating the piles to incorrect bins. When the staff discovered the switch, Judith was squarely blamed for purposely placing clothing in the wrong patient bins, just to cause trouble. Judith was outraged. She angrily cast her protests of innocence up against faces of stone. She was told she must be punished for her disrespectful prank, and Judith was placed in "solitary," a tiny room, approximately four feet by six feet, with only one little window, about he size of Judith's face, that she could look out if she rose up as tall as possible on tip-toes. Solitary confinement went on for four agonizing days. Judith screamed hysterically at the guards through the door. It wasn't fair! The other girl did it! Judith asked herself over and over, *Why would anybody do this to me? What did I do to deserve this? Why would anybody do this to me...why would anybody do...why would anybody...why would...why...*until she slipped into another seizure and then—nothing.

Many years later, Judith would connect her extreme claustrophobia to being locked up in solitary.

Some days in the mental hospital were pleasant for Judith. Every other weekend, her parents and little siblings made the drive over to visit her. At each visit they gave Judith five dollars so that she could make purchases in the hospital store if she needed something. As soon as the family left, Judith hustled over to the hospital store and spent all the money on Payday candy bars. She thought they were especially wonderful candy bars: Salty globs of peanuts and something chewy, pure heaven to Judith's tastebuds.

When the family came for visits, Judith was allowed to stroll the grounds outside with them. Western State Hospital, with its original core brick building and multiple add-on buildings stood, side by side, like a row of tall people holding hands on acres of neatly trimmed grounds. In 1868, Fort Steilacoom officially closed and the site and building were given to the Washington Territory (Washington State had not yet been established). In 1871 Washington Territory used the facility for housing "lunatics." In 1948 Washington State remodeled the building, making it a state-run insane asylum. Over subsequent years the building was expanded to become the present complex of multiple buildings and parking areas. Just adjacent to the hospital on the east end, original Fort Steilacoom officers' quarters remain. The doors are open to tourists. Old cannons sit, rusting, along Cottage Row.

Judith and her family, on visiting weekends, sat on picnic tables scattered across the green lawns. It was as if the quiet calm and order of the park-like grounds on the outside of the facility offered balance to the illness and disharmony on the inside of the facility.

One day, Judith was going through the movements of a typical day as a patient at Western State Hospital when she suddenly froze, staring blankly down at her hands for a long while as a realization set in. *Today is my eighteenth birthday. I guess I'm not like other teenagers. I've never been to a dance...I've never driven a car...I didn't even get to graduate from high school.* While Judith denies memory of it, her Western State Hospital medical record documented escapes or "unauthorized leaves".

"July 8, 1961. Return from unauthorized leave. Returned from unauthorized leave by a state car this p.m. Having been apprehended in Vancouver, Washington, and detained in a Vancouver hospital since 7-6-61. Ran away from hospital auditorium, a high school girls gym class, because she was unhappy with staff criticism of her behavior (i.e., flirting with boys), claims hitchhiked for several miles then met a friend who took her to Greyhound Bus and bought ticket to Vancouver. Friend, Jack, claims he gave her five dollars (to buy eats) so she bought a new purse. In Vancouver, met a taxi driver who directed her to a State Patrol officer and he, in turn, to Vancouver General Hospital. She was there two days and today picked up and returned to WSH by hospital staff...abrasions on her legs and ankles..."

During hospitalization at Western State Hospital, nursing staff alleged that Judith was faking her seizures. Doctors decided to perform some tests.

"July 18, 1961. 5 days ago Dr. Barber and I decided to discontinue patient's Phenobarbitol and Dilantin. Since that time she has had 6 or 7 grand mal seizures according to the nurse. She described 1 this morning as a generalized seizure lasting 3 minutes, manifested by a shaking movement of her arms and legs, turning of the head to the right, dilation of the pupils, which failed to react to light and confusion of a few minutes afterwards, followed by 10-20 minutes of sleep. There was no tongue biting or voiding at this time. This sounds like a pretty good description of a grand mal seizure and I think that we can state definitely that the patient has a seizure disorder as well as a strong tendency to feign seizures. Accordingly, at Dr. Parrott's request, I have suggested that her Dilantin be resumed at the rate of Grs. 1 ½ t.i.d. I would expect a good control of her grand mal seiures on this medication..."

Judith escaped yet again. "October 25, 1961 unauthorized leave. October 26, 1961, returned from unauthorized leave." She was clearly not happy in the mental hospital.

Another chart entry described Judith as "quite aggressive, active, and at times, mischievous in behavior. Must be told every day in order to get routine duties done...is constantly seeking attention by these spells and other attention getting devices...recommend close supervision..."

As the months ticked by, chart notes indicated signs of improvement in Judith. Finally, a chart note read, "November 24, 1961, it is felt that the program of group therapy and school activities is of help to patient. The length of time patient will need to profit from this to the degree which would make for essential changes is seen as several years. It appears unreasonable to have patient hospitalized for this length of time seeing the fact that the help needed could be provided by any out patient clinic and/or epileptic clinic..."

Then, miraculously, one day in December of 1962, at the age of eighteen, Judith was released from Western State Hospital, back into the care of her family. Doctors had her seizures under fairly good control now with two effective drugs: Dilantin and Phenobarbitol. Helen was instructed to make sure that her daughter take her medications four times daily without fail. Judith would hear her mother say hundreds of times for the next several years, "Judith, did you take your medicine? Remember, 8:00 am, 12:00 noon, 4:00 pm, and 8:00 pm; 2 capsules and 1 pill." This reminder reverberated in Judith's head for six more years.

To say that Judith's feelings about going home were complex would be a gross understatement. She had lived in a mental hospital, witnessed the behavior and treatment of some of the most deranged individuals, endured the abuse (she was sure of it) of hospital staff, and lived like a prisoner, with bland food (except for the Payday candy bars) and none of the freedoms she had known before. She hadn't been allowed to have her only material possessions, a few record albums, with her. Oh how she had missed listening to Elvis Presley and Ricky Nelson and Pat Boone. One would think she might be euphoric or even downright giddy moving home, back to her family and things. But as Judith slowly and quietly acquainted herself with the newer home her family had moved into while she was in the hospital and cautiously observed her two little sisters and one little brother who had grown taller and much more clever over the last year, she wasn't sure she fit in anymore. It looked like this healthy, growing family was moving forward, without any need for her presence. Judith felt like she was standing outside, utterly alone, looking in through a window to her home, realizing she was invisible to her family.

Maybe I do belong in a mental hospital.

Chapter 3
First Marriage

After enduring over a year at Western State Hospital, Judith re-joined her family in the Lake City home, north of Seattle. She felt relieved to be out of the mental hospital and thankful to be with her mother again.

While she was away, Judith's height and figure had transformed into a remarkably similar rendering of her mother. Judith especially noticed similarities when she stood beside her mother, both looking at the same mirror. She felt a new, intimate connection to her mother when Helen suggested they share clothes—because they were the same size.

Over several weeks, Judith, judiciously medicated, settled into a fairly predictable routine of helping her mother with the younger children: giving baths, changing diapers, serving meals, washing dishes, and sweeping the porch. However, she was still not allowed to tend the children without any other adults present. Judith's seizures were finally under some control, but they never knew when another could hit.

Judith was paid a small weekly allowance for her assistance with the children, cleaning the house, and doing yard work. Sometimes, wearing her mother's clothing, Judith walked to the local WigWam store and purchased her own cigarettes for fifty cents a pack. Her mother and stepfather had caught onto the fact that she was sneaking some of their cigarettes to smoke, and her stepfather had firmly explained, "Now that you're an adult, Judith, you should buy your *own* cigarettes."

Something changed for Judith with that admonition. She felt a new acceptance by her parents as an equal, and she began spending hours with her parents at the kitchen table playing cards, drinking coffee, and smoking together. It seemed like smoking had allowed her special admittance into the exclusive club known as "adulthood." It was something that she could do that her younger siblings could not. This made her feel mature. Privileged.

One day Judith tried on the role of *confident woman,* just like she had been trying on her mother's dresses, and bravely walked to the nearest church to inquire about activities that she could participate in. Having missed almost as many years of school as she had attended, Judith felt a need to re-connect socially with people her own age. Yes, she was told, the church had a youth group and she was welcome to come back whenever she wanted to. Judith felt nervous and wondered what on earth the young people would think of her, but her need to interact with young people was stronger than her fears, so she pressed forward.

Judith's exposure to religion had been nothing but confusing to her as she grew up. Her mother had married her father, a Mormon. Helen had explained to Judith that when she was younger, Judith had been blessed in the Mormon Ward also. That made her a Mormon. After Helen's husband died, she received visitors at her door from Jehovah's Witnesses and had been converted. Then her second husband, George, joined the Jehovah's Witness religion after they were married. However, the Mormon visitors still regularly came to their home. Judith observed the visits by both groups and listened in on the conversations in the living room while she towel-dried dishes in the kitchen and shushed the children, having more questions than answers when the visitors had left. Most visits, it seemed to Judith, were intrusive to the household and a nuisance to her busy mother, who was too polite to protest. She and her mother, it seemed, always had more important things to do and they did not appreciate the interruptions. Besides, the Jehovah Witness people did not celebrate Christmas! That seemed outrageous to Judith who had experienced several traditional Christmas holidays and had really enjoyed herself. Judith decided that she was not Mormon and not Jehovah Witness. She wanted to be something else. But what?

Her mother had told her previously, "Judith, honey, when you turn eighteen, you can believe in whatever you want." Judith, therefore, felt no guilt about attending the local Presbyterian Church so that she could meet young people and find something to do with her free time.

In 1963, at the age of nineteen, Judith was baptized in the nearby Presbyterian Church. She became active in the youth group, attending various functions each week. She either walked alone to church or had her stepfather drive her when he was headed in the same direction.

The people at church were very nice to Judith. Everything around her seemed unbelievably pleasant in comparison to the year she had spent in a mental hospital. To say it was a difference like night and day was not enough. It was more like the difference between death and life. She began to feel peace and a gentle, quiet, happiness for the first time in her life. Her anger was breaking up and dissolving. Judith felt like she belonged somewhere. And she was making new friends.

One new friend, Bob, owned a shiny, red, convertible car, a stunningly beautiful car, in Judith's opinion. Bob kindly offered Judith rides to and from church. In a short time, Judith and Bob became casual friends. Judith had secretly hoped for more, but she knew Bob would never want to date her like boyfriend and girlfriend because he made it clear how much he disliked cigarette smoke. He would definitely want to date a non-cigarette smoking girlfriend. It never occurred to Judith to give up cigarettes.

On several weekends, Judith also cheerfully accompanied her family on weekend visits to George's father's home in Cumberland, Washington, about a one-hour drive from Seattle near the Cascade Mountain foothills. Grandpa picked fresh nettles in the surrounding forest of evergreen trees for salad, and he killed a chicken for dinner each time they visited.

Judith marveled over how delicious her Grandpa's food tasted. Her appetite had definitely awakened since leaving the mental hospital. These visits were pleasant for Judith—pleasant enough for her to ignore the times when her step-grandfather caressed her buttocks over her slacks whenever people weren't looking. And pleasant enough to ignore step-grandfather when he took his flaccid penis out of his trousers and shook it toward Judith, while chuckling to himself as if someone had just whispered a funny joke in his ear. Most times when Judith ran out back to use the outhouse, as the farmhouse did not have indoor plumbing, she was acutely aware that step-grandfather was peeking in at her through cracks of the wooden outhouse. She urgently relieved herself so she could sprint back to the big house without looking back.

One evening at church, in 1964, twenty-year-old Judith was chatting with Bob in the kitchen after a youth group dinner. She was wiping dishes and storing them away in cupboards when she heard the church organ. The music delivered a powerful beauty. Judith felt gooseflesh all over her skin and stopped wiping the plate she was holding to intently listen. After several minutes of listening she asked Bob, "Do you know who is playing that music?"

"Yeah, that's my friend Lee."

"Boy, oh boy, he sure can play beautiful music on that organ!"

"Would you like to meet Lee?" Bob asked.

"Sure," Judith shot back, eyes sparkling and mouth in an open smile.

Judith did not know that she was about to meet the man who would become her first husband, and the first of two husbands who would carefully use her to frame their lives so as to appear normal to society as they secretly led darker lives.

After the music stopped, Bob introduced Lee to his friend Judith. They chatted for a while, and then one person in the group suggested they all go roller-skating. Judith felt a moment of panic and went silent. She had never been roller-skating, and, even though she was an adult who smoked, she still had to get permission from her mother to go anywhere. After several moments, Judith self-consciously explained to the group that she needed to call home and ask for permission first. She waited for her friends' incredulous looks and maybe some whispering among them, but they only shrugged their shoulders and agreed. Judith phoned her mother, asked if she could go skating, and her mother repeated a mantra that had been cemented into Judith's brain, "Judie, remember to tell them that you have epilepsy, and that you have to take your medication at eight, noon, four, and eight."

Judith looked squarely at Lee and stated, "I can go skating, but I have epilepsy and I have to take my medication."

"So, does that mean you can't skate?" Lee asked sarcastically, dark eyebrows lifting up.

"I don't know. I've never tried skating before."

"Well, let's go give it a try then."

At the skating rink, Judith and Lee paired up and held hands as they slipped and rolled, nearly falling down, holding each other up, laughing, attempting to slowly make one revolution around the floor while everyone else whizzed past.

Judith stole several glances at Lee while they flopped around the skating floor. She absorbed details about him like the corner of a paper towel just touching the edge of a puddle of water. At about five foot, six inches, Lee appeared tall to Judith. He had dark hair, cut short and neat. He wore glasses that gave his clean-shaven face an academic look. His build was slender and lean. He dressed in nice clothing. Overall: he was a smartly dressed, intelligent, older man. And there was a bonus feature: Lee was a smoker.

Judith and Lee skated until their physical exertion brought on an urgent thirst. The skating rink featured a refreshment bar at one end so the two tired skaters, with muscles that would surely be sore the next day, sat down together and each downed a soda pop. Some real conversation began. Judith learned that Lee was twenty-two, and that he had a good job at Bethlehem Steel (just like her step-father!). Lee had served two years in the Army. He owned a home and a car, and he lived alone. Besides, he played the organ and piano, and musical talent was something Judith had always admired.

But the most impressive thing that Judith observed about Lee wasn't something that he had said, it was something that he did—he *looked* at her as if she were a normal person. Judith had never felt that before. Not from her parents or friends or teachers or doctors. When she had attended school, children teased her mercilessly. In the mental hospital, she had felt like a freakish monster. Judith was already falling in love with Lee. She couldn't believe her luck.

Judith and Lee began dating exclusively. There wasn't anything about Lee that Judith could find fault in. He was patient with her; he spoke politely, laughed at her stories, and he kissed her hand. Judith felt a powerful synergy with Lee when he told her that his father was also killed in the Korean War, and that his mother had re-married, giving him a stepfather and half-siblings—just like Judith. Their backgrounds were remarkably similar, except for the fact that Lee didn't have epilepsy.

In November of 1964 their friend, Bob, who was in the Marines, suggested that he and his girlfriend attend a Marine Corp Ball with Judith and Lee. It was the most elegant event Judith had ever imagined. Feeling like she had stepped into the pages of Cinderella, Judith wore her mother's best dress, had her hair carefully piled up high and classy-like, wore costume jewelry that her mother had loaned her, and sheathed her legs in real nylon stockings. The stylish pumps on her feet clicked on the dance floor as Lee, in a dark suit, white shirt, and dark tie, whirled and twirled her around for hours.

The dance was quickly passed in a warm blur, blissfully, seizure-free for Judith. She did not want the night to end. Afterward, Lee and Judith said goodbye to Bob and his date, and Lee, who also did not want the night to end, took Judith to a small bar in downtown Seattle called "The Black and Tan." Judith had a drink with Lee (alcohol was a definite violation of the doctors' orders) and stared, dumbstruck and a bit drunk, at a heavy-set black woman who was blasting out songs from her lungs, accompanied by a live band. Judith felt like she had literally stepped through a door, from one world into another.

How life had changed! *One year I'm living in a mental hospital, and the next year I'm out on the town with a handsome date, wearing fancy clothes, listening to live music!* It was wondrous and magical. Judith felt electrically charged. Her parents had always been classic homebodies, typically preferring to play cards around the kitchen table with friends. Knowing that she was out participating in something that her parents never had—something edgy like drinking alcohol in a nightclub—gave Judith a sense that she had somehow surpassed their sophistication level. It was a heady rush.

Three months later, Judith boldly left her home, parents, and young, half-siblings to move into Lee's house on 917 N. 72nd St. in Seattle. Wedged tightly in between the adjacent houses, it appeared disproportionately tall with its extremely narrow width, and it did not resemble any other houses on the block. The odd looking house eventually became a symbol of Judith's odd marriage to Lee.

Judith packed up her belongings, clothing and record albums, easily in just a few cardboard boxes. Feeling rushed and very excited about starting her new future, she did not take time to gauge how upset and concerned her parents might be. She was an adult, as her stepfather had told her many times, old enough to smoke, and everyone knew there was no stopping her from going. At the time, her parents decided it was pointless to try.

Around Christmas time, Lee proposed to Judith, giving her a traditional wedding ring set. Judith gleefully said yes and began to imagine herself as a married woman, keeping her husband's home clean and tidy and tending to their beautiful children. It would be grand. The perfect life she had described to a hypnotherapist years ago was about to begin.

In January of the next year, 1965, Lee went alone to visit twenty-year-old Judith's parents and ask for permission to marry their daughter. Lee asked George first—man-to-man, but George abruptly waved him off and instructed Lee to ask Judith's mother. After all, George was only the stepfather, and a biological mother had more weight in this decision, George explained. Helen then listened to Lee's request quietly. As Lee was delivering his carefully planned, polite words, she wondered, "Isn't it interesting that this guy wants to marry Judith the same year she's going to have access to her trust fund? I bet he just wants her money!" Helen had set up the trust fund for Judith when Wesley had had died, and had deposited the social security checks faithfully into the account, using only a small portion of the funds when necessary to pay doctor bills for Judith. She had hoped the $10,000 that had accumulated over the years would help her daughter make a good start in the world. Still, at the end of the conversation, Helen kept her doubts to herself and acquiesced, believing she had no choice in the matter. Judith was a grown woman and could marry whomever she wanted. She just prayed that Lee wouldn't take the money.

The following week, both George and Helen broke their silence and tried to change Judith's mind about marrying Lee. They expressed their concerns about Lee having access to Judith's money, explaining that the money was to have been her nest egg and safety cushion. It was the only thing she had to hang on to from her real father. George and Helen felt they never had any right to spend it. It had been their solemn responsibility to protect it and save it for Judith to use one day. They cautioned her about how difficult the world was to survive in. Had their daughter thought about all this? But Judith would not be turned back. She had a man who loved her and a fortune in the bank waiting for her to turn twenty-one later that year, and nothing could stop her. Finally, her life was going to be on her terms. Simply, she had had enough of other people making all of her decisions.

Judith and Lee were married on January 16th, 1965, in the Trinity Episcopal Church in Seattle. Lee had chosen the church, not because he was a member of it, but because it had the old-fashioned, beautiful, *formal* look that he wanted for his wedding. And in that church, on what was designated as the bride's side, not one person from Judith's family was present. The emptiness was a silent but bold statement to everyone in the church, including Judith, that Judith's plainspoken people thought the marriage was wrong—so wrong they would not witness it. Nor had they helped in planning the wedding. Judith had made all of the arrangements with oversight from Lee. She had purchased a simple, short, white dress for herself from a Lerner's store for twenty dollars that she had earned by babysitting for a girlfriend. Judith was not yet able to tap the funds in her trust account, so everything for the wedding was done on a shoestring budget.

Lee's mother was friendly and bustling about with a welcoming attitude toward Judith at the wedding. However, it wouldn't be long before Judith would know that her new mother-in-law looked down on her, judging her to be an uneducated high school drop out, plagued with a *disease* for goodness sake, spawned from a lower class, and unquestionably not good enough for her son. Why, if they produced grandchildren, heaven forbid, they would probably be deformed like Judith! But one needed to keep up appearances, so Judith's mother-in-law conducted herself with grace when in the view of others. Ultimately it hurt Judith deeply that her mother-in-law did not embrace her as family.

Lee's stepfather behaved with decent social manners, but with cool distance and snarling remarks made under his breath that would remain his style for all the years that Judith would know him. Curiously, Judith could not detect any love between her new husband and his stepfather.

The newlyweds honeymooned in Lee's house that looked rather like a clothespin. Being a self-titled connoisseur of Victorian era homes, Lee had done his best to decorate his first home with heavy tapestry drapes, framed art work he had picked up from estate sales and antique stores, a crystal chandelier, tall candle holders, lacey tablecloth— anything that looked old and formal.

And so was the style in which the new couple lived all aspects of their life per Lee's mandate: old-fashioned and formal.

Even their car stood out as being unusual. Judith still hadn't learned to drive and was, in fact, not permitted to obtain a driver's license because of her epilepsy, but the car Lee drove her around Seattle in was a 1947 Chrysler limousine. At first Judith felt ridiculous riding in it with only herself and her husband to the grocery store in an enormously long limousine car. As they sat for traffic lights, Judith self-consciously glanced out her passenger window to see if people were gawking at her. But fairly quickly Judith began having fun in the car and playing along with the *character* Lee acted out more and more. "Madam or My Lady," Lee would greet his wife with as he extended his arm to her, "allow me to drive you to the store." Lee habitually kissed her on the cheek formally and at some point developed a habit of carrying around a cane with which he could point and gesture while in character.

All of this was fun fantasy to Judith. She giggled at Lee's antics. *What a funny husband I have. Everything is so fun!*

Judith and her charming husband settled into what she had imagined married life would be like. She saw her husband off to work in the morning with a lunch she had made herself; then worked about the house doing chores that were not unlike the kind of chores she had done for years at her family's home: laundry, dishes, sweeping, vacuuming, dusting, and making beds. Then, with the day charging forward, it would be time to cook dinner and carefully time it for when Lee returned home from work. Judith experimented with different dishes, trying to zero in on what her husband enjoyed the most. Provoking some praise from her husband was the best reward for her efforts. Straight away into the marriage, Lee advised Judith that he liked to eat at least two plates of dinner and he did not appreciate being left unsatisfied. He preferred some kind of meat, potatoes (Judith knew plenty about potatoes), vegetables, and wine.

After dinner, with classical music albums spinning on the turntable of his stereo, Lee lectured Judith, like a professor to a young pupil at his feet, about the kind of life he had always dreamed of and the expectations he had of how his wife should dress and talk and behave. On and on he would pontificate, repeating his important points, using dramatic body gestures for punctuation marks. Judith listened carefully.

Lee began a long process of overseeing the necessary makeover of his new wife. As Judith did not drive a car and had no connections or activities outside of their home, it was easy for her to direct 100% focus on complying with Lee's new rules. He was so smart. So worldly. Everything he said to her seemed to make sense— like he had a complex plan developed that was going to benefit them both ultimately—but she hadn't been given all the details yet.

She simply trusted. And she worked hard at her lessons.

Some of the activities related to the makeover were enjoyable. Lee took Judith out shopping at high-end clothing stores in downtown Seattle where he resolutely selected items, like a wealthy benefactor with his newly-acquired foster charge. Judith tried on dresses and turned in circles in front of him, watching his facial expressions closely, waiting for his cane to rise up and point at the dresses he liked best. When he was satisfied that the proper dresses had been chosen—dresses that made his wife look like a classy lady— he instructed the sales clerk to package up the selections and give him a sum to pay.

Judith felt special. Taken care of. She had never dressed so fine in all her life. But she sensed the clothes might be impractical. How many housewives, she puzzled, wore fancy, long, dresses while cleaning a house? She thought it best to keep the question to herself.

Lee instructed Judith on how to perform wifely duties in the bedroom as well. Having lost her virginity as a teen while she was "rippin' and runnin'" (an expression her daughters would later use to describe their wild times), which was the reason she was sent to live at the Ryther Child Center in the first place, she was not shocked about what took place in the marriage bed. Judith was compliant, finding sex to be neither a good thing nor bad thing—just a thing that she did with her husband. Feeling awkwardly uncertain about what exactly she should touch on her husband's body, or what she should do with her own body, she followed his lead. She put no emotional investment into the act. It was similar to her other household chores. Other wives must be doing the same thing, she reasoned, so it was just part of being a wife. And, she frequently reminded herself, quietly, deliciously, when she was alone, *this is what must be done to make a baby.* So many times throughout her life she had painfully overheard adults whispering, "You know, Judith can never have children… because they won't be normal…"

Nonsense, Judith thought. *I will have a baby. And it will be all mine to take care of.*

A baby was born shortly thereafter, but it wasn't Judith's baby.

One day in March 1965, Judith phoned her mother, Helen, to ask how things were going at home. Helen said, "Well, my pains are about five minutes apart, and your father isn't home, so I think I need a ride to the hospital."

Lee drove Judith in the limousine to her family's home where they picked up laboring, tired Helen, and took her to a hospital. A neighbor agreed to watch the younger children. Judith and Lee remained at the hospital until the baby was born. George wasn't able to leave his shift at work. A couple of days later, the couple picked up Helen and Judith's new baby sister. In the limousine, Judith held her mother's fifth child and declared, "Mother, I want you to name this baby Charlene."

Helen sighed, "Fine, Judith. I will name her Charlene."

"And mother."

"Yes, Judith."

"I want to have my own baby."

"Well, go ahead, honey. You are married now."

Exactly nine months later, December 16, 1965, Judith gave birth to her first baby. It was a girl. Judith named her Marie.

And she was normal.

Judith adjusted to motherhood quickly and relatively easily. The functions of caring for a newborn baby didn't seem too complicated. After all, she had watched her mother care for several little siblings over the years. Lee appeared happy to be a father. When he was home, he tenderly held baby Marie, sometimes rocking both the baby and himself to sleep. Sometimes he played the piano while Judith rocked the baby to sleep.

A few months later, Lee became active in the union for Bethlehem Steel workers, so he was attending meetings in the evening, after work. He became more fatigued and, over the subsequent months, showed diminishing interest in his wife and baby.

Earlier in the year, part way through Judith's pregnancy, in the hottest part of the summer, Lee decided they needed a larger home—with the baby coming and all. So, they sold the strange-looking house and bought a larger, early 1900's home, for $12,000. 4407 Sunnyside Avenue was the address of their new place in the quaint Seattle community known as Wallingford.

Judith went to the bank and asked to withdraw $5,000 from her trust fund. She wanted to contribute to the home purchase. The bank lady was very nice in accommodating Judith's request.

Their "new" house had a covered front porch that spanned the front width of the house where they stacked up boxes from the move. Judith worked every day at unpacking, cleaning, and preparing a room for the baby. She acquired a used bassinette from a neighbor and some cloth diapers. Judith went back to the nice lady at the bank and withdrew enough money from her trust fund to buy a new washer, dryer, refrigerator, and stove for the kitchen to replace the old wood-burning stove. With a baby coming, it was time to modernize. The well-stocked Sears store had everything she needed.

Judith and Lee talked about what to do with the remaining money in her trust fund. They decided it would be great to buy a new car. So they spent $1,500 on a big, yellow Mercury at a car dealership that Lee's grandfather and grandmother operated in White Center. Of course, Judith still couldn't drive as she was still taking seizure medication. But she enjoyed watching Lee enjoy driving it. With more of the trust fund money Lee took Judith shopping and selected more clothing fit for a "lady." He told her she needed to dress up more. He liked her best in long dresses. For her twenty-first birthday, Lee took his "madam" to the Alaska Arctic Furs store and bought a mink stole and a blue fox fur jacket with, naturally, her inheritance money.

She labored with her housework during the daytime, often wearing her "Earthquake Dress," (earlier that year, a shakiness quite different from the typical seizure symptoms went through Judith's body and caused her utter, speechless, terror. At 7:30 a.m. on April 29, 1965, an earthquake with a 6.5 magnitude rocked the Seattle-Tacoma Region, one of the strongest earthquakes on record for the area since 1850. Judith sat, trembling, wailing, with her husband's arms around her as they watched news reports on their television. The earthquake had killed three people. Judith sobbed, "This was probably the most frightening day of my life." She explained to Lee as he held her, "It was more frightening than a seizure because I had to stay awake and *feel* the whole thing. At least when I have seizures, I don't remember what happened." After several hours, having sufficiently calmed his wife, Lee declared they should go out and buy Judith a fancy new dress to celebrate surviving the great earthquake of 1965! They went to Bon Marche in downtown Seattle, laughing and carrying on as if nothing had just occurred, and bought a dress that would forever be called the "Earthquake Dress." It was floor length, dark black print, with puffy sleeves, tight waist, and full skirt.), Judith entertained herself by listening to her record albums on Lee's stereo. She still enjoyed her Elvis Presley and Ricky Nelson albums, but she was nurturing a new love for country and western music that she was tuning in on the local radio station. The country music had a different beat to it and real life stories in the songs that warmed her heart. She felt like the songs described real people, unlike stupid classical music that didn't even have words! But, it was critical that she switch everything back to the classical station on the stereo before Lee got home from work. He would not allow anything but classical music to play in his home and Judith knew she must never get caught listening to anything but classical. Lee said that classy people only listen to classical music. That was the first rule she learned to never break.

The second was dusting the house thoroughly and regularly. One Sunday afternoon, Lee was roaming around the house, inspecting Judith's cleaning proficiency. He found thick, accumulated dust on a high shelf that Judith couldn't reach. Standing at five foot, one inch, many things were out of reach for Judith in the big, old house. So Lee wrote the date in the dust, using his finger as a writing instrument, and then waited to see how long it would take Judith to dust the dated shelf. After several days, and the date still in the dust, Lee sternly scolded Judith for failing to dust the high shelf and told her that he had written the date on it, had watched it for days, and was extremely disappointed to see that she continued to neglect it. Judith was humiliated and silent. A heavy blanket of shame fell over her. She had already failed as a wife. Since she badly wanted to please Lee, Judith employed chairs and stepladders to help her reach everything in the house that he might inspect. From that time on, she carried a new, spooky sense that she was always being watched.

Union meetings. Then more and more union meetings.

Lee called Judith when he was not going to come home after work for dinner. She always told him to be sure and pick up a hamburger before the meeting so he wouldn't be too hungry, and he promised that he would. He advised her to not wait up for him. She told him what a hard worker she thought he was.

It would be years before she discovered what he was really doing after work when he was supposed to be at union meetings.

As Lee worked more hours and Judith became more involved with raising her first daughter, Lee's physical appearance took on a visible change. He began wearing his hair longer, in a casual shaggy style. He grew a full beard. He seemed to identify with the "hippy" look that was in full swing at the time in Seattle. Months later, he would be wearing button down shirts opened half way, exposing a chest adorned with necklaces, and sporting bell-bottom trousers—a dramatic departure from the conservative, narrow black slacks, white shirts, and thin dark ties. But even though Lee's attire was changing, he continued to insist that Judith dress like a lady from the past.

And the doctors continued to insist that Judith take her seizure medication.

Occasionally on weekdays, when Judith had finished all of her housework, she would put little Marie in a stroller and walk down the wide sidewalk with the neatly trimmed grassy strips that bordered the large homes on her block, to a bus stop on 45th Street. From there, she and the baby traveled by bus to the University District where she slowly pushed the stroller past store front windows and cafes and coffee shops, quietly staring with fascination at what other people were doing and how they were dressed. At first she was surprised to see so many men with long hair. They were so unlike her stepfather. She saw people her parents had disapprovingly referred to as "hippies." She saw women in cotton peasant dresses with sandals on their feet selling handcrafted jewelry from outdoor tables.

On one trip to the University of Washington campus Judith was frightened when she saw bonfires burning and people her own age holding up signs and yelling out angry words. Judith was completely unaware that the opposition to the Vietnam War among university students had begun in the spring of 1965, manifesting into demonstrations, hostile debates, and even violence on college campuses across the country. She had no idea that a war was taking place in Vietnam, as Lee shielded her from news. He regularly read the Seattle newspaper but did not comment on what he read with Judith. Being a poor reader, Judith had never felt inclined to look at the paper herself.

One Sunday Judith and Lee took baby Marie to be baptized as a Christian in a fancy church. Lee had given Judith a little mink hat to wear on top of her blonde head for the special occasion. He also chose an expensive, gray dress for her to wear that would complement the hat perfectly. The godparents, friends of Lee's family, attended the baptism with their teenage son who seemed to admire Lee. Her husband had a special way with people, Judith thought, as she observed her husband chatting warmly with the son of the godparents after the ceremony.

That December Judith had her one and only Christmas holiday with Lee and baby Marie because the next year Lee decided they should become Jewish. Another big change. No more Christmas holidays.

Having been raised in a strict Catholic home, Lee explained to Judith he had always felt dissatisfaction with his upbringing. Something had been missing. He had spent many evenings at a friend's house down the street where their Jewish faith was practiced. Lee was often invited to share the family's Friday night Sabbath dinners with elegant place settings on a formal dining room table. Even the children drank wine from crystal wine glasses. Lee was fascinated with the formality and the traditions that seemed to hold the family together like an unbreakable glue. Being a stepchild, he had always felt different than the siblings his mother and stepfather gave life to. He was sure his stepfather did not love him.

Now that Lee had a family of his own, it was finally time to implement the lifestyle he had always fantasized about. They would become Jewish and have elegant meals just like his boyhood friend's family had. In 1966 Lee, Judith, and Marie began attending a Synagogue in Seattle where Judith did not understand a word of what was being said. The customs, symbolisms, and language were as foreign to Judith as the planet Mars. She was miserable. But she dared not challenge Lee.

So the new Jewish family learned about the Jewish holidays and Jewish foods. Judith worked extra hard at absorbing what she needed to know, mostly in the area of setting the table and preparing kosher foods. She could only nod and pretend to understand the Hebrew preaching of the Rabbi at Synagogue. She sorely missed the Christmas holiday each year. She missed the tree with colorful lights. She missed the presents wrapped in shiny paper and ribbons. She never got to play Santa Claus with her daughter.

In 1967 Judith became pregnant again. In July of 1968 she gave birth to her second daughter, Rachel. The twenty-four year old mother had waist-length, thick, wavy blonde hair and dressed in long formal dresses. She saw her husband less and less. He was working over-time shifts at the steel mill as well as keeping up with the very important union meetings. But Judith didn't consider herself lonely. She had her two babies to keep her company and chores that never were finished.

When Rachel reached toddler age, the next-door neighbors announced that their children could no longer play with Judith and Lee's children because they did not associate with Jewish people. Judith was deeply saddened but did not protest.

There was another delivery in 1968—a miracle. Judith's seizures inexplicably, completely stopped that year. She quit all her medication and still had no seizures.

Could she finally drive a car? No. Judith was told she would have to be ten years seizure-free before she could apply for a driver's license. Another ten years? No problem. If she could drive a car all by herself, go wherever she wanted, whenever she chose to, then she could easily be patient for another ten years.

Judith took up sewing on a machine that she and Lee had purchased on one of their shopping outings. In the evenings, after the girls were put to bed, and Lee was away at union meetings, Judith began designing custom clothing on an old sewing machine. She had had a few lessons years before from her mother on a treadle sewing machine which had a foot pedal that required continuous pumping in order to turn a belt that made a needle move up and down, creating stitches in fabric. With her newer sewing machine, Judith crafted matching outfits for her daughters, long dresses for herself, pillows and curtains for the house, and later—at Lee's request, she would design and sew outrageous costumes for the couple.

Judith's head snapped up from her sewing project. Had someone just walked into the room? She had been concentrating so intensely, the shuffling noise startled her. Oh, it was Lee. Why was he looking so troubled? Had something happened to his mother? Judith's heartbeat quickened.

Lee cleared his throat. "Judith, I have something I need to tell you."

"Uh-okay."

"You know how I told you I was going to union meetings?"

"Uh-yes."

"Well, that's not where I was really spending my time. You see, Judith, My Lady, I am what they call bisexual. I have been going on dates with men."

Judith felt complete bewilderment. She had trouble forming words. After several moments, she asked, "What is 'bisexual'?" She had never heard the term before.

"It means that I enjoy having sex with both men and women."

"Oh." Judith, thinking that her husband had unfortunately contracted some contagious bug that created the bisexual symptoms just as a viral infection might induce coughing and fever, asked hopefully, "Is there anything that will cure you?"

"No, My Lady, there is not."

"Then, what do we do?" Judith implored. Lee always knew what to do.

"We don't do anything. I will meet other men and go on dates with them, and we will still be married—just like before. But it is absolutely necessary that you never, never tell anybody about this condition that I have. That's just between the two of us. And, Judith, we must never speak of this to any of the people at the synagogue. If they found out, we would be in big trouble. Do you understand Judith, My Love?"

Lee and Judith added two Siamese kittens to the family. Judith discovered a deep well of passion that she apparently possessed for animals. She and the girls delightfully cared for the kittens as a part of their normal, daily, activities.

The view for any person looking in at this family was that of a middle income, white, Jewish, husband-breadwinner, wife-homemaker, normal, happy family.

But the scene was deceiving.

Judith learned that the son of her daughters' godparents was one man her husband had been going on dates with. As Lee had instructed earlier, Judith kept the information strictly to herself. When the godparents and their handsome son came to visit, Judith put a lovely meal on the table, and then it was laughter, story telling, exclamations of how very lovely the house looked, and photo taking to remember these good times for all.

As Marie approached school age, Lee landed a new job at the University of Washington in the audiovisual department—a big switch from his job at Bethlehem Steel. His position at Bethlehem Steel involved heavy, dirty, physical labor. The new position would be a desk job. Lee's good fortune brought him a pay increase as well as an increased opportunity to meet interesting, exciting people. The campus was flush with liberal thinking faculty as well as students of all makes and models.

Judith continued sleeping with Lee, knowing that he was engaging in sexual activities with other men and possibly women, still unable to share her secret with anyone—not even her mother. Lee occasionally asked for sex with Judith. She complied. But, even though Judith stoically wore the daily mask of being a "typical, dutiful, smiling, wife and mother", a tiny bud of resentment was beginning to grow within her. She had left her parents to be free and to control her own life. Was this the freedom she had sought?

Lee decided they should start having people join them for formal dinners. He liked the idea of having many people gathered around a large table, covered with a lacey, white tablecloth, with tall candles giving off soft light, reflecting off the crystal wine goblets and silverware. The guests would laugh and compliment Lee on how beautiful his home looked and how great the food tasted.

So they started practicing with family members: Lee's mother and stepfather, Lee's grandparents, occasionally Judith's mother and stepfather and siblings. Judith prepared full-course meals. Lee took note of what was working and what wasn't, according to his fantasy.

As they perfected the formal dinner routine, they shifted to having work associates and students from the university. That's when Lee received confirmation that he was on the right track. The meals grew longer in duration. Wine was consumed in larger quantities. At some point, marijuana was introduced before and after the meals. Laughter shook guests until they complained their sides were aching.

As Lee embraced his new role of formal dinner host, his wife and children began to lose color in Lee's eyes.

One day, he came home from work and told Judith he had just made a down payment on a gorgeous Victorian mansion. They were going to move to 6205 Latona Avenue Northeast so that he could be closer to his job at the university. And, he excitedly gushed, they would decorate the mansion with all antique furnishings and have the best parties in town.

When Judith first saw their new house, a three-story, elegant, Victorian home on a large corner lot, she gasped. It was exactly what her husband had been sketching on paper with pencil in his free hours. The porches, the dormers, the detailed craftsmanship, had all been described to her by Lee as the kind of house they should own.

Nice young men (from the university, Judith guessed) helped them move into the new home. Judith stood on the grassy lawn and snapped a photo of about a dozen men who were heaving Lee's heavy piano up the steep front steps and into the house.

Lee, Judith, Marie, and Rachel settled in to their spacious home, feeling lost at times as their voices echoed throughout the mostly empty extra rooms.

Over the next couple of years, every chore Judith performed in the home threw some frustration back in her face. The laundry piled up higher and higher. The meals became more elaborate and time-consuming to prepare for the increasing number of guests Lee was bringing home on a regular basis. It seemed like Lee had become a hotshot entertainer since he started working at the university, so there were more dishes to wash after dinner.

Also, the girls were beginning to act out, defying Judith's clipped instructions. They weren't little babies anymore who could be put down for naps or contained in a playpen with a rattle to play with. On some days, Judith locked her daughters in their bedroom for a "time out" as she sensed her anger toward them was not healthy, and she needed space between herself and the children so that she would not strike them. She recognized that she did not have time to chase them around with the great many chores she had to complete each day. Lee wanted the house sparkling at all times. What would the guests think, coming in to a messy house?

When Judith felt her anxiety rise to its highest level, she overcame an almost hysterical panic and complained to her husband that she couldn't keep up with everything and that the girls were being naughty and throwing tantrums while he was at work. She desperately needed his help and understanding.

Lee did not show any outward empathy to his wife, but he silently contemplated what Judith had reported to him. He later admitted that perhaps his wife could use some help around the house. Things could run a bit smoother. He crafted a plan and laid out the details to his wife. What they would do is utilize the extra bedrooms in the huge house by having boarders move in. Lee would collect monthly rent from each boarder, and each boarder would have some responsibility assigned that would contribute to the household efficiency. Lee said he couldn't believe the cleverness of his plan. Why hadn't he thought of it before? He could bring in more money without doing any more work. They had an enormous house with multiple levels, including quarters that were once used by servants. Lee said it was thrilling to take them back in time to use the house as once before.

Before long, Judith had her own chauffeur, a young male boarder assigned to be her driver. Whenever she needed to go to the grocery store or wanted to take her daughters to Greenlake Park to play, she notified the boarder, gathered up the girls, and off they went.

With more people in the house, the girls were constantly entertained. Judith's inner tension relaxed.

Another young male boarder was put in charge of cooking and cleaning. Judith suddenly had free time on her hands. She joined a women's sewing guild, and made friends with other women. She left the house to go bowling. Lee started telling people that Judith was the "Madam" of the house and that she was to be treated like no less than a queen at all times. Judith was delighted, at first, to be referred to as a queen, but eventually realized it was just part of Lee's playacting and not a statement of how he really felt about her.

It was helpful and pleasant for Judith to have people around, but an evolution had already begun for the household that would change all of their lives.

With boarders occupying every room in the house, it occurred to Lee one day that he didn't need to go out so often in the evenings. The boarders were interesting, and they brought home stimulating guests. He had brought a perpetual party to his home! Lee gave the go-ahead for drinking alcohol and smoking marijuana openly in his house. It was, after all, the early 1970's—a time when everyone was trying to understand serious social and political debates that were agitating the country and to find a way to have peace and love and harmony. Why not start at home? Judith asked if smoking and drinking in front of the girls might be harmful, but Lee shushed her. He curtly said the girls were too young to know what was going on. Judith sadly determined that Lee seemed more interested in planning parties than interacting with his own daughters.

As the parties grew larger in size and frenzy, the presence of Judith and the girls got smaller and smaller. If Lee's daughters attempted to get his attention, he showed immediate irritation and snapped at them. "Judith, I'm not going to tell you again! Get these girls out from under my feet!" he would order, as if she were a hired nanny, not a queen.

When an associate at the university introduced Lee to the Society for Creative Anachronism, a local club whose primary focus was reenacting medieval times, he quickly ushered members of the society into his home so that he could learn more about it. He could not get enough details fast enough. It seemed that Lee had discovered something even better than Judaism.

Over the next decade, Lee immersed himself, Judith, and their daughters, into a grand fantasy that would ultimately become his new reality: Medieval times.

Outside of normal work hours, Lee wore medieval costumes that Judith sewed. Tights, velvet tunics, gold rope belts, and hats with feathers, were as normal to Lee as Levi jeans and flannel shirts were to other fathers. Weekends and vacations were spent at Society for Creative Anachronism camp outs and festivals. Judith and the girls wore full medieval costumes as well.

At the festivals, club members strolled the grounds, in costume, holding silver wine goblets, addressing one another as "My Lord" or "My

Lady." Men bowed and women curtsied. Men and women locked arms and danced on the grass.

Everyone had titles and roles to play. Lee refused to take part in the mock battles using wood swords and shields; however, he quickly rose through the ranks to become a "chancellor." Judith watched Lee salivate with anticipation when opportunities to exert his authority came up. He especially enjoyed officiating mock weddings at festivals.

The great problem for Judith was that it appeared her husband did not know when to turn off fantasy and get back to reality. He wanted to *live* in the medieval times. He wanted to *be* a chancellor. And he always wanted to get drunk, laugh, and end up in a tent (or one of the bedrooms in their home) with an attractive young man. He was, after all, "bisexual."

One day when Marie was kindergarten age, Judith went out for bowling with friends, and was five minutes late getting back to meet Marie as she was walking home from school. When Judith arrived at the meeting place, a horrifying scene met her. Marie had been hit by a car and lay bleeding, unconscious in the street. People were gathered around the young victim, murmuring, "Oh my God, is she dead?"

Judith could not tell if her daughter was alive or dead. She could see that her five-year-old's head was dented on one side. An ambulance raced them to a hospital in Seattle where Marie underwent emergency surgery to remove chunks of skull bones that were pressing into her brain. Judith and Lee paced the halls of the hospital. Lee called in his Rabbi.

Marie survived but endured a protracted recovery. She needed extensive follow up medical care and suffered from learning disabilities as a result of the brain injury. Lee grew more impatient with Marie, finding her needs to be a distraction from his social life. From that point on, in Judith's opinion, Lee favored his younger daughter, Rachel, barely tolerating anything Marie said or did.

In 1975, after ten years of marriage, with Lee's parties stretching their boundaries into unrestrained indulgence, including sex orgies, Judith knew she had had enough. At any time, on any day, she could open a door to a bedroom and find a couple or a group of individuals engaging in sex. On one occasion, one of the girls opened a bedroom door and screeched, "Mommy! Daddy is naked with a man!" Judith reached the point of feeling nauseous in her own home. The sound of Lee's raucous laughter at their parties made her sick. Witnessing Lee degrade Marie made her sick. The thought of having to live like this forever made her physically sick. She decided she needed to leave him. He didn't want her anymore. Why would he care if she left? He had plenty of people to keep him company. Besides, he actually preferred men for company.

On a warm summer day, Judith walked out of the house and sat down in the front yard next to Lee. She bluntly told him that she was leaving him—that it was time for a divorce. Lee screamed at her, "Are you out of your damn *mind*? You can't leave! What are you thinking? You have no work skills. You have no insurance. You didn't even finish high school. What kind of a job could you get? You are so stupid Judith! If you leave, I swear, you'll never see your daughters again."

Judith knew that Lee was right. She hadn't finished high school. She had no money. Where would she live and who would take care of her? And what would happen to the girls?

Judith agreed to stay.

Lee suggested they have separate bedrooms.

Judith stayed for another nine years.

During the final nine years of the marriage, Judith exercised more freedom in terms of going out with friends to movies, shopping, eating in restaurants, and going bowling, but if she talked about dating a man, Lee angrily roared at her.

During the final nine years of marriage, Marie and Rachel became teenagers. Having no tolerance for Marie, Lee treated her terribly by yelling at her, calling her names, and even slapping, shoving, and, at the worst times, kicking and punching her while she was down on the kitchen floor. Ultimately, Marie took herself out of the house to live in the streets of Seattle with other runaways. Judith lost contact with her oldest daughter for several years.

In 1984 Judith finally decided that she could leave Lee. She had been working in a daycare at a local synagogue, earning $4 per hour, and had been driving a car (at age 34, having been 10 years seizure free, Judith finally learned to drive). Having the ability to earn money *and* drive gave Judith the confidence she needed: two of the reasons Lee gave for her being unable to leave were no longer valid.

In the end, Lee let her go peacefully. The fight was over. He loaded her personal possessions and some of the shared furnishings in a truck. He carried the items into an apartment that Judith planned to share with a female friend. Lee gave Judith $5,000 for her share of the equity in the big house that they sold for $50,000. She did not question the amount. Lee and Judith agreed to have their younger daughter live with Lee while Judith got on her feet.

Lee assured Judith that if she ever needed his help he would be there for his "Madam".

Only a few months later, Judith had to call Lee for help. Her room-mate came home drunk one night and grabbed Judith, began kissing her on the lips, murmuring that she wanted to love Judith. Judith wanted to get away as quickly as possible.

Lee came back and helped Judith move out of the apartment into a house where she rented a single room.

Each night, as Judith lay crying in her bed in the small rented room, her desperate prayer was to live a normal life and just be a normal person.

Chapter 4
Finding Her Prince: Gary

The dream re-played, night after night. And each night, after waking to realiz she had had the dream again, she was stricken with horror.

The house is silent and dark. I feel myself rise from the bed and haltingly walk the hallway, arms reaching out from my sides, skimming the walls with my fingertips. When I get to the living room, I stop. Where is he? I see blocky, dark objects that are furniture. Where is he? I so desperately want to see him, and yet I am afraid! I stand completely still, hearing my breaths inside my head. Wait! My eyes detect a quick movement across the room. Suddenly, like a monster, popping out at me in a horror house, Gary jumps up from behind the sofa, and my body is paralyzed with fear. I see him only from the waist up. His body is one dark shadow, like the furniture, but his head—it's illuminated like a dark green light bulb! His glowing green face stares at me, expressionless. "Gary, darling. You got out of jail?" I ask as I step toward him. "Please, hold me." I call out to him—but he is silent. Then the green light bulb face goes dark. He vanishes. Oh! My head jerks to the left. He reappears, crouched by the chair, ready to bolt. His head lights up again in the horrible green color. My heart feels like a cannonball bouncing inside my chest. My limbs tremble. "Go away," I angrily yell! "Get out of the house!" He darts across the room and hides behind the television. "Why won't you come out and talk to me? I've been waiting and waiting! I just want you to love me like before. Please Gary," I plead. My chest jerks with sobs and hot tears run down my face.

The nightmare terrified Judith for weeks after Gary was arrested in 2001. It tormented her mind. She felt like she was standing on the border between sanity and insanity, not knowing which side she would land on. Had Gary been inside the house to see her in the night? Or was it really just a dream? The dreams were so vivid and realistic. She experienced several minutes of debilitating confusion each time she woke from the dream. Part of her secretly hoped that Gary had somehow escaped jail and was checking on her—that he missed her as much as she missed him. Another part of her felt ice-cold terror when she allowed the words she had been hearing on the television news flow through her mind: Green River *Killer*.

As Judith lay in her bed, smearing tears across her cheeks with the palms of her small hands, the silent morning making its way in, head throbbing from too much wine the night before, she remembered her life with Gary. How utterly happy they had been! Why did it have to end? It was all so unfair. Her husband had been taken away from her in a moment, and she was left with nothing of her previous life. Could she summon the energy to get out of the bed one more time? What, she wondered, was the point?

It was February of 1985. Judith was forty years old, and finally free from the stranglehold of her dysfunctional, nineteen-year first marriage. She was learning how to function as a single woman and was living in a tiny, low-rent apartment on Highway 99, south of Seattle. She had found a decent roommate with whom to share expenses.

A tavern called "White Shutters" was located near her apartment, on the opposite side of Highway 99. Local Country and Western bands played in the tavern on weekends for dancing patrons. For Judith, there was sweet justice in having the freedom to choose to listen to country music. Her first husband hadn't allowed her to listen to it. "Country music was for low class people," he had told her. To make his point, one day he took all of Judith's country music albums, without any regard for her feelings, tossed them one by one into the air like Frisbees, and blew them to bits with his shotgun. Judith had watched her beloved albums—the only personal possessions she had brought to the marriage—splatter into tiny pieces and fall to the ground as she choked back sobs.

But now she was free to listen to country music. She heard about an organization called "Parents Without Partners" that regularly sponsored country music socials for single men and women at the White Shutters Tavern. Judith and a woman she knew from the daycare center where she was working attended one such function on February 21st. Judith was wholly drawn to the country music. She wasn't thinking about finding a man; it was too soon after her divorce.

Judith and her acquaintance sat at a small table, nursing beers, and tapping their feet along with the western beat. Two men at a nearby table initiated eye contact. Soon they walked over and began talking to them. After exchanging proper introductions, the men asked the women if they would care to dance. The women looked at each other for a moment and then stood up to dance.

Judith paired up with the smaller of the two men—the one who had introduced himself as "Gary Ridgway." Gary told Judith he had been out celebrating his birthday, which had been on February 18, over the past few days. She wished him a happy birthday and asked about his age. He had, after all, opened up the subject. When he politely informed Judith that he was thirty-six years old, she immediately pulled back the reins on herself and did some quick calculating in her head: she was forty, and he was thirty-six, so she was four years older than him—five years older for part of the year when she had had birthday in August! She decided that Gary was probably too young to be interested in her. He was cute, but too young.

Dressed in slim jeans, cowboy boots, and a long-sleeve, western-style shirt, Gary appeared refreshingly wholesome and *straight* to Judith in comparison to the many gay men she had been surrounded by in her first marriage. In fact, Judith noted, everyone in the tavern that night looked straight. She felt comfortable in the environment.

The evening passed quickly as the two couples danced to all the popular country tunes. At closing time, the men casually suggested they all go out for some breakfast. Gary's associate offered to drive the four in his van which was parked outside. After a night of dancing with two men who seemed harmless and likable, the women agreed to breakfast. Judith's friend climbed up in the front passenger seat, and Judith and Gary were seated at the rear of the van.

Each time the van made sharp turns, Gary and Judith intentionally leaned into each other, sometimes completely falling over into the other's lap. They radiated the excitement of body chemistry. They giggled like children. Judith began to re-think her earlier judgment that Gary was too young for her. She enjoyed the feeling of his lean body pressed up to her side. Once, when the van stopped for a traffic light, Gary looked down at Judith's face and flashed her a wide, boyish grin. Then, without warning, he popped a quick kiss on her lips. Judith gasped in surprise. Then they both giggled again. The game of flirtation was on—full throttle.

At about 2:30 a.m., the group ate breakfast in a local 24-hour diner on the Kent East Hill. When they finished, the women declared they really should be getting home. "Oh no," the guys argued.

"Why can't we keep the evening going?" Gary asked, shrugging his slender shoulders. "How about we have coffee at one of our houses? We're having fun, right?" He flashed his boyish smile. Again, the women looked at each other, and agreed through eye communication that it would be fine to continue with the men. Gary's acquaintance said they could all go to his house as they were already in his neighborhood.

A few moments after entering the house, Judith's friend and Gary's friend slipped off to a bedroom, leaving them standing awkwardly with one another in the front room. Gary suggested they take a seat on the sofa. Within an hour, the two were cuddling comfortably with Gary's arm draped around her shoulders, Judith's hands resting on his legs. They talked for several hours.

The longer Judith looked at Gary's face, the more she liked him. Long, thick bangs swept across his forehead to one side, giving him a boyish look. When he smiled, she could see that one of his "eye" teeth was rotated, pushing out the upper lip on one side. Her heart actually beat faster each time he smiled. She carefully studied his demeanor. It seemed to be offering clues that the young-looking Gary was energetic, fun loving— possibly mischievous— yet he always maintained a strict code of gentlemanly manners.

Judith learned that Gary had been married and divorced twice. In his second marriage, he had fathered a son: Matthew. Gary spoke warmly about his son and he told Judith how he kept up with regular weekend visits and sometimes went on special trips with him.

Gary had been working for sixteen years at Kenworth Trucking in Seattle. He also owned a home in the SeaTac area. A remarkably stable guy, Judith concluded. She was impressed that he had worked at one job for so many years. She praised him in her head at she stared at him. *You must be a very good worker!*

It occurred to Judith that it had been hours since they had consumed alcohol, yet she felt completely, warmly drunk. *How very odd*, she thought. The only desire she felt was to sit close to Gary. His soft, male voice held a matter-of-fact calmness that was soothing to her ears. There was very little rise and fall in his intonation. Gary's voice was the opposite from her ex-husband's. Lee had yelled, threatened, screeched, and criticized Judith until she covered her ears with her hands and tried to block out the sound.

Judith had a premonition that everything was going to be all right as long as she knew Gary.

The couple remained on the sofa for the rest of the night. They kissed. Gentle, shy pecks at first. Then they forged into long, open-mouthed kisses. With each kiss, Gary stopped and asked Judith how she was feeling. "Judith, can I kiss you that way? Are you comfortable?"

"Uh-huh, this is just fine."

"Is there anything I can get for you? Water?" Another charming smile.

"Nope. I'm fine." Judith grinned as she stared up at his face.

When morning brought light into the house, the men drove the women back the White Shutters on Highway 99 where their cars were parked.

During the drive back, Judith wondered if she would see Gary again, or if the night had been merely a Cinderella-like fantasy. Judith was willing to accept her one night of fun, and walk away, believing that Gary would prefer a younger woman.

In the White Shutters parking lot, as Judith said good-bye to the group, Gary casually said, "Well, I should probably get your phone number." He opened up a brown, 4"x8" address book and clicked a pen into ready position.

Judith smiled as she recited her phone number and address. She watched Gary slowly and deliberately print, "Judith, 148 Egewood A Pl 62, 246-95 08." She noticed that he misspelled "Edgewood" and that he got the "Pl" out of order with the apartment number, but it really didn't matter. He got her phone number down correctly. Gary said he might call her sometime. She hoped that he would call, but doubted it. Again, she thought about their age difference.

After driving to her apartment, she collapsed into bed, exhausted. But she couldn't stop thinking about the remarkably polite man she had just met. She remembered every detail of his face and could see it, as though it were right in front of her, as she finally fell into heavy sleep. As she fell into deeper sleep, dreams about her childhood began.

Judith's childhood had been a blur of seizures, medications, and doctor appointments. Her mother had laboriously protected her from the cruel world outside their home. For many reasons, Judith had never developed an interest in current events in her community—let alone national civics. She did not know the difference between a "democrat" and a "republican." She had never voted. And, when she was living under her first husband's oppressive control, she was completely shielded from news. "It is the man's job to read the news," he had told her.

As a single woman, free to make choices, Judith still had no concern with catching up on the news. Therefore, she was completely unaware that a serial killer in her community was being vigorously hunted—a killer who had been dubbed "The Green River Killer" because he had dumped the first five young women he killed into or along the banks of the Green River in 1982. She was oblivious to the fact that young women with connections to street life along Highway 99, near the Seattle-Tacoma Airport, were disappearing by the dozens. That year, 1985, was the fourth year that female bodies were showing up in clusters or solo in both heavily populated and remote areas of western Washington. Bodies had been found in and around Kent, Des Moines, Auburn, Enumclaw, Maple Valley, and Sumner.

In fact, a special task force had been created by the King County Police Department the previous year to focus entirely on locating and arresting the Green River Killer. Judith did not know about the task force either.

By 1985, the Washington public found it incredulous that the killer had not yet been apprehended. Victims' advocate groups were starting to speak out. What would it take to catch the killer? Did the police have a plan? If Judith had read the newspapers, she would have known that the public was putting intense pressure on elected officials and police departments to *do something*.

Judith was not aware of another chilling fact: Only two days after she met her prince—February 23rd—Gary Ridgway was sitting in the presence of Green River Killer Task Force detectives. He was being questioned about his connection to prostitutes who worked the Highway 99 strip. During the questioning, Gary admitted to choking a young woman named Rebecca Garde Guay in 1982 while on a "date." He said that she had bitten him and he was angry about it. Ms. Guay had run off after he choked her. The detectives asked Gary if he knew any of the Green River Killer's victims. He said no. They showed him photos of victims. He admitted that he may have "dated" some of them over the years.

The detectives told Gary he could go home.

By the end of the week, Gary called Judith for a date. She was both surprised and thrilled to get his phone call. They made plans for Gary to pick up Judith at her apartment and go out to dinner that night.

Judith hung up the phone and excitedly babbled to her roommate. "That nice, polite guy I told you about called back! We're going out to dinner!" Judith dashed into her bedroom to select an outfit and begin work on her hair and makeup.

She was in the bathroom putting the finishing touches on her shoulder-length, blonde hair and thinking about how nice it felt to wear slacks and a blouse (Lee had never allowed her to wear pants) when she heard a knock on the apartment door.

Judith opened the door and was first struck by what she smelled. She smelled a man.

Gary stood, smiling, framed by the doorway, with the second story balcony rail running behind him, and said, "Hi. Are you ready?"

It took Judith a few seconds to answer. She looked him over. It seemed like more than a week had passed since she last saw him. His hair had recently been cut short, he was fresh-shaven, except for his neatly trimmed mustache, and he was again dressed in western garb. The only thing missing was a cowboy hat, Judith thought.

But it was the *smell* she was analyzing. Gary smelled like masculine soap, deodorant, and aftershave that she would later know as "Old Spice." Then it hit her: Lee had always worn women's perfume when they went out. Over the years, it had become normal to Judith. A flashback raced through her head of Lee dabbing perfume behind his ears and on his neck, and him dressing in her underwear and pantyhose, prancing through the house, laughing wildly.

In amazing contrast, here stood a man—a man who smelled so differently—waiting to take her out on a date.

"Well, are you ready to go?" Gary asked again, still smiling.

"Uh, yes!" Judith replied as she grabbed her purse.

They walked down the outdoor stairway to the ground level where Judith saw Gary's brown, full-size pick up parked.

Gary opened the passenger door and helped Judith get in. He slammed the door shut and went around to the driver's side. When he got in and started the truck, he was still smiling. Judith appreciated that warm smile. It put her at ease.

"Was it hard to find my apartment?" Judith asked.

"No, not at all. I know this area like the back of my hand." Gary went on to name several of the nearby streets and cross-streets.

"Gosh, you really know this area," Judith replied, impressed. "I'm still struggling to find my way around, haven't lived here that long."

"Well, where would you like to eat?" Gary asked with a brilliant smile before starting the truck.

Judith thought for a moment and answered, "How about you decide, since you know the area better and all."

They ate a casual dinner at a local diner that he selected. Judith thoroughly enjoyed herself in Gary's company. His plainspoken conversation style matched hers perfectly. She had always felt embarrassed about her limited education because she hadn't finished high school. But Gary did not come across as condescending at all.

After that night, Gary phoned Judith weekly for dates. They began a routine of Judith driving herself to the McDonald's on Highway 99 where Gary would meet her in the parking lot at about 2:00 in the afternoon. He was working the second shift, or "swing shift," which ran from 3:40 p.m. to midnight. It was convenient for Gary and Judith to meet on his way to work at McDonald's and eat a light meal before he started his shift. Judith sat up straight and smiled every time she saw his truck turn off the highway and roll in to the lot, never a minute late.

Judith was living on her own for the first time in forty years, and she knew that her four-dollar per hour daycare pay barely covered basic expenses. Therefore, she had cut her food budget down to next to nothing. When she met Gary at McDonald's, he always insisted on paying, so she boldly ordered the chicken sandwich meal—a meal that had previously been out of reach.

Gary and Judith slowly ate their food at a corner booth inside McDonald's, holding hands under the table when they thought nobody was looking. Judith imagined they must have looked like a couple of teenagers, staring at one another with silly grins the whole time they were chewing food.

Judith always felt disappointed when Gary announced, "Well, I'd better get going to work now, can't be late," and another McDonald's date ended.

After about a month of weekly dates, meeting at the same place, at the same time, Gary had a suggestion: "Hey Judith, I have an idea. How about we get together this weekend? I wanna show you my place."

The following weekend, he took her to see his house at 21859 32nd Place South, in the Sea-Tac area. When they pulled into the driveway, Judith saw a small rambler. It looked new, modern, and suburban compared to the Victorian Age homes she had lived in with her first husband. She liked the simple, basic shape. As she stepped out of Gary's truck, she heard the sounds of vehicles speeding by on a freeway that must have been close. She tried to orient herself, knowing they hadn't driven too far off of Highway 99.

Gary escorted Judith through the front door.

"Well, what do you think of my house?" Gary quietly asked as they stepped through the front door directly into the living room.

"It's nice. Modern!" Judith scanned the living room and then her gaze fixed on the floor where they stood.

"I know. The carpet is gone," Gary offered before she could ask.

"Why is the carpet all ripped out?" Judith could see from where she stood that the living room and hallway carpet had been yanked out.

"Yeah. Well, I wasn't planning on replacing it, but I had some kids peeing on the floor. Smelled horrible. Couldn't get the smell out. So I ripped most of it out." Gary went on to explain that he had taken in boarders for extra money. A couple with small children rented a bedroom for a while and they had irresponsibly allowed their children to urinate on his carpet.

"That's just awful!" Judith exclaimed. She remembered what it was like to have boarders in her home with Lee. What a hassle it could be.

"I know, but what can you do. Hey—I know! Maybe you can help me pick out new carpet one of these days?" Gary asked as he tilted his head to one side.

"I would love to." Judith leaned in against his side.

Gary took Judith through the house, pointing out a small bedroom that was set up for his son who came for weekend stays. Judith noted the twin-size bed and toys strewn about the room. That room still had carpet.

At their next McDonald's date, Gary suggested that Judith meet him at his house instead of McDonald's. It might be nice to spend some private time together before he went to work.

For the next date, Judith drove herself to Gary's house. With a huge grin on his face, he pointed to his bed, a mattress set with loose sheets and blankets on the carpetless floor, and asked her if she'd like to get in it with him. "You know, Judith, it's probably about time we make love, dating for a while and all." Judith felt her sexual desire escalate with his. She began undressing. Gary stopped her. "Wait. We have to go wash up first. Gotta make sure we're clean. You know." Gary led Judith to the bathroom where they washed their genitals with soap and water.

Pre-sex washing became a ritual for the couple for the rest of their years together. Gary was always concerned about cleanliness during sex, but he never wanted to use a condom.

Birth control wasn't a concern for Judith. Earlier, she had overhead her mother declare that it wasn't possible for women over forty to get pregnant.

Judith discovered Gary's lovemaking style matched his personality: gentle and polite. Again, she noted differences between Gary and Lee. Lee had always been so "freaky" in bed. She had always felt off-center around him. But Gary was considerate of her needs during lovemaking. That was a brand new experience.

"Hey Judith," Gary teased at a subsequent date before work at his house. "How would you like to have a key to my house?"

Judith sucked in her breath. "You want me to have a key?"

"I don't know. Maybe. Here you go." Gary tossed a copy of his house key to her. " Now, you can be here when I get off work. Spend the night if you want."

"Thank you." Judith felt Gary's trust envelop her like a soft blanket.

She began using Gary's house key to let herself in well before it was time for him to get off work. Humming, she quietly puttered around the messy bachelor's house, first straightening up the kitchen, then picking up dirty clothes off the floor and making his bed. When she made his bed, she flopped her body down, face first, onto the mattress, pulling Gary's scent into her nose. She could not get enough of his smell. Sometimes she rolled over and hugged his pillow to her chest, marveling at how much she was in love.

She checked the clock on the wall often. Approaching midnight, almost time for Gary to get home from his shift, she changed into a nightgown, slid in between the sheets of his bed, pulled the covers up to her neck, and excitedly watched the clock again. Gary walked in the front door at exactly the same time every night.

His greeting was always the same: "Hi there, what's new?" Typically covered in paint over spray, except for a clean area around his nose and mouth where a mask had been, he started stripping off his clothes as he headed down the hall to shower. When he finally slid in to bed next to Judith, he always whispered, "Did you wash?" After she nodded yes, he initiated sex.

Judith would not know until years later that Gary worried about sexually-transmitted diseases. He had contracted numerous STD's in the past and used genital washing as "prevention." Judith honestly believed that only homosexuals gave and received STD's, an impression she had formed after living with homosexuals and overhearing their pensive conversations about AIDS. So, feeling both protected and clean, Gary and Judith proceeded happily with their sex life.

Once, when Judith was studying Gary's lean, naked body after sex, she gently asked him how he had acquired the horrible looking scar on his arm.

"Oh, this?" Gary casually pointed to the long, marbled, strip of scar tissue on the underside of his left arm. "One time I was working on a car and it caught on fire. It was, you know, pretty bad."

Judith got a mental picture of Gary's arm on fire and him swatting at the flames, yelping in pain. "I'm so sorry, Gary. I bet you don't want to really talk about it." She had noticed that he typically wore long-sleeved shirts.

"Yeah, I really don't like to talk about it," Gary replied, head bent down.

During all their years together, they never mentioned the scar again. But Gary hadn't told her the truth. Two years before they met, sometime in 1983, Gary was attacking one of his victims, Marie Malvar, in the very house he and Judith were making love in. During the desperate struggle to escape Gary's strangling hands, the victim badly scratched his left arm with her fingernails. After finally killing her and dumping her body near the Mt. View Cemetery in Auburn, he went back home and poured battery acid over the scratches, creating a deep burn that would form a scar that would disguise the deep scratches.

In May, Gary asked Judith to move in with him. The timing was perfect for Judith as her roommate was preparing to marry and would soon be leaving their apartment. It would be impossible for Judith to cover the full rent.

"Gary, I have to warn you, I have a lot of furniture."

"That's fine, I have a truck." Gary and his "can-do" attitude helped Judith move her furniture from the apartment to his house, and then he collected some additional furniture she had in storage from her first marriage.

As Gary had promised, he let Judith select new "wall-to-wall" carpet from a local carpet store. If Judith had known that they were replacing carpet that Gary had actually torn up and rolled around a body—the body of a woman that he had murdered in his home—and dumped the wrapped body in nearby woods, she would have changed her name and moved out of state, forever terrified that Gary might find her. But, instead, she enjoyed a warm, fluttery feeling in her stomach as the happy couple laid the new carpet and crammed her furniture into Gary's small house.

The warm, new-family feeling continued as Gary took Judith to meet his parents and two brothers who all lived nearby. Gary's tall father, Tom, sat quietly in his recliner chair, seemingly content to let his wife, Mary, tell Judith the family history. As Judith watched Mary's long earrings jiggle around as she charismatically welcomed her visitors, Judith took special note of Gary's smartly dressed mother who worked as a sales clerk at a JC Penney department store. She looked like a classy, smart lady. Judith quickly got the impression that Gary highly respected her opinions. In fact, when Mary Ridgway said something, everybody got quiet and listened attentively. Judith immediately became determined to win Mary's approval. Judith had never had any kind of relationship with Lee's mother because it was obvious she had hated Judith—Judith not graduating from school and all. When Judith heard Mary say, "Yeah, I don't see anything wrong with the woman being older than the man. Do you know, Judith, that I'm five years older than Tom?" she couldn't believe her luck! Gary's mother was older than Gary's father. Judith had initially dismissed Gary as a potential boyfriend because of her concerns about being nearly five years older than Gary. Somehow that just didn't seem right. But Mary's words resonated with Judith. They were the same. Five years older than their men. The beginning of a loving, trusting bond started in Judith's heart with Mary.

Gary also took Judith on a ferryboat ride across Puget Sound to Bremerton to meet his grandmother. Judith instantly fell in love with his grandmother, a sweet, gentle, old woman. Finally, Judith became the "new girlfriend" included in Gary's weekend visits with his ten-year-old son.

In turn, Judith introduced Gary to her parents and her youngest daughter and two of her four grandchildren. Rachel was attending an alternative high school where her two out-of-wedlock babies could be cared for while she attended classes. Marie, Judith's oldest daughter, had also given birth to two babies who were ironically in Lee's custody. Marie had gone back out to street life—the same streets where drugs were bought and sold, prostitutes conducted business, and some prostitutes were extinguished by the Green River Killer.

The first trip Gary and Judith took alone was a camping trip in the Okanogan area of northeast Washington. They made love in the back of his truck under the canopy shell. Afterwards, as they looked up at night sky peppered with stars, Judith slowly and cautiously began revealing details about her strange first marriage. She feared that Gary would reject her when she told him that Lee had been bisexual. But he just shrugged his shoulders and said, "Well, that was before. No big deal now."

Judith felt their relationship was cemented in place after that acceptance. However, they did make a pact to never mention Lee's bisexuality to Gary's parents. Gary told Judith that his parents were sort of "old fashioned."

Judith and Gary settled into a comfortable existence with one another in his house. He continued painting trucks at Kenworth and she worked at Kindercare, another daycare, on Highway 99. They made plans for every weekend and the anticipation of weekend activities carried them through the workweek. Because weekends included visitations with Gary's son, activities were modeled to accommodate a child, which worked out perfectly for Judith because she frequently cared for her grandchildren. It became common for Judith and Gary to take Matthew to a park or zoo, while toting a couple of Judith's toddler grandchildren. Judith flourished in the family environment. She began to feel normal in the eyes of the public, no longer attracting odd stares like she did when she wore medieval garb.

Judith felt especially happy when Gary took all of them, sometimes including her daughters when they came for a weekend visit, to the Kenworth Trucking Open Houses. Several times each year, Kenworth sponsored weekend Open Houses as a public relations function for employees and vendors. Judith and Gary typically dressed in matching jeans, Kenworth tee shirts, and Kenworth hats. Gary walked the grounds of Kenworth with Judith, proudly pointing out trucks that he had painted. It wasn't difficult for Judith to see the company loyalty that he felt when he spoke about Kenworth and the gorgeous trucks they put out on the road. She sensed that Gary felt like he had contributed to Kenworth's success by painting their trucks so skillfully, which made him feel like a success. They climbed up inside giant semi-trucks that were on display. They lunched on free hot-dogs and sodas that were chilled in barrels of ice. Gary happily waved and called out hellos to the many people he seemed to know at Kenworth. Judith surmised that he must be a popular and respected employee.

Other weekends found the new blended family touring Grand Coulee Dam in Central Washington, and the Petrified Forest along the Columbia River. They took ferryboat rides across the Puget Sound from Seattle. They picnicked on the lawns at Pt. Defiance Zoo in Tacoma. They shouted and clapped at monster truck competitions where the loud roar of the engines drowned out their voices.

Judith continued to observe the affection Gary had for his son. At times she felt intense jealousy as she witnessed Gary playing with Matthew, like the two were alone in a bubble, and she didn't exist to them. She worked her way into the bubble by becoming childlike and running and playing with Matthew. At times she felt like a sibling competing with Matthew for Gary's attention. She saw Gary faithfully paying his $275/month child support payment. She viewed Gary's commitment to his son as a deduction in time and resources for her.

Sometimes Judith felt like going off and having an activity, away from Gary and his beloved son. She attended her ex-roommate's wedding alone where she joyfully caught the bride's artificial flower bouquet. *I wonder if I'm going to marry Gary*, she thought. She decided to save the bouquet, just in case.

Five months after she moved in with him, Gary announced he was taking Judith and Matthew all the way to Disneyland in Southern California. Judith had never been to Disneyland and had never traveled such a long distance. Well, she had accompanied Lee once to San Francisco to visit gay bars. But that was different. That was a trip for Lee. She was ecstatic. Disneyland! What could be more fun? They drove south through Washington and Oregon, stopping along the way at tourist sites to pose for photos. They slept and ate in the camper that was fastened to the back of Gary's pick-up truck. The camper did not have a toilet, so they laughingly urinated in a large coffee can—their "toilet." They continued south through California.

Gary stunned Judith when he stopped the truck in front of "Ridgway's Restaurant and Lounge" in Modesto, California. Gary's cousin owned and operated the restaurant. Judith's wide, blue eyes scanned the inside of the restaurant while they dined on hamburgers. She felt star-struck—her man being connected to these successful people. It was thrilling to see the Ridgway name on the restaurant sign, napkins, and menus. These Ridgway people are very successful, she thought. Before leaving the restaurant, they bought hats featuring the Ridgway logo.

When they finally reached Disneyland, Judith cut loose with Matthew. They sprinted from one ride to the next, jumped up and down with excitement, and hounded Gary for snacks and souvenirs.

After returning home from Disneyland, Gary calmly lied to Judith and kept the dark side of his life out of her view, yet he continued to build a trusting relationship with her. He helped Judith pick out a smaller, more fuel efficient car and helped her pay for it. Having worked on cars for most of his life, Gary was adept at inspecting motors of used vehicles and spotting fair prices at dealerships. Judith completely deferred to his judgment when it came to cars.

Then Gary offered a steady shoulder for Judith to cry on when she wrecked her newly acquired car on Interstate 5. A semi-truck veered over and bumped her car, spinning her out of control on the busy freeway. The driver's side of the car was smashed, and Judith's little blue Plymouth Champ was ruined. The disappointment struck deep within her. She had viewed the small, sporty car as a symbol of her escape from Lee. She no longer had to be chauffeured about in an antique limousine. She, for a short while, could hop into her little car and zip around without supervision or accountability to anyone. However, she had Gary to comfort her and other parts of her life got better.

The couple's first Christmas was everything she had long wished for: tree, presents, lights, decorations, a good man, and family stopping by the house. After being forced by her first husband to give up traditional Christmas for the Jewish ways—a religion she had felt absolutely no connection to—the first Christmas with Gary and all the children and grandchildren was redeeming and memorable. Judith's tiny grandchildren pointed to Gary and said, "Grandpa." Gary smiled at them. Rachel and Marie privately murmured to Judith, "It's great to see you so happy, mom. Things are finally good for you." Judith could not stop smiling as she surveyed the peaceful, family Christmas scene in her new, cozy home with Gary.

The blended family way of life continued for three years, 1985-1988.

In 1987, a terrific jolt nearly derailed Gary and Judith's strengthening relationship.

On April 8th, as Judith went about her typical duties at the daycare, she heard deep male voices coming from the front entrance above the drone of children's voices. It caused her to stop what she was doing and stare. Three tall, distinguished looking men, all in nice suits, seemed to be looking for someone, perhaps asking for directions. Then they pointed directly at Judith. She became alarmed. Had they come to tell her bad news? Had something happened to one of her parents? As she set a toddler on the floor that she had been holding on her hip, the three tall men walked toward her.

"Are you Judith?" one man asked her.

"Yes" she barely whispered.

"We need you to come with us for a while." A man who looked like he might have played professional football at one time took her elbow and steered her toward the exit.

Judith felt her co-workers staring at her back as she was went out the front door. One of the men instructed her to have a seat in the back seat of their car.

Oh my God, am I being kidnapped? Judith wondered. She thought about trying to escape and then abandoned the thought. The guys were huge.

They drove slowly for a few minutes while the men explained to Judith that they were detectives; they wanted to ask her some questions. The driver parked the car behind a storage facility, out of view from the main thoroughfare. They began asking questions about Gary. Later, Judith could not recall the specific questions they had asked or how long she had been in the car. Like a patient waking up after being under general anesthesia for a surgical procedure, she only knew that the tone of the questioning had been dark and frightening. Her brain felt fuzzy. Her throat was dry.

The detectives' further stunned Judith. "We're going to have your boyfriend in custody for a few days for questioning in relation to the Green River Killer case. Judith, you need to make immediate arrangements to leave your house for 2-3 days. We need to search the house." After asking several more questions, they drove Judith directly home. She quietly sobbed the whole way.

The phone was ringing as she stepped in through the front door, still crying. It was Gary's mother calling. Mrs. Ridgway heard Judith's panic over the phone and offered a steady stream of reassuring promises: "Judith, you must not worry. This is some kind of horrible mistake. Tom and I are livid! What are these people thinking anyway? Gary did not do anything wrong! Now, now—you're going to be fine, honey. No need to cry. Just pack up a few things. Tom and I are on our way over to pick you up. You can stay with us while this disgusting thing gets cleared up. Mark my words, Gary will be back home in no time."

Judith took comfort and hope in what she heard from Gary's parents while she stayed with them. The parents and Gary's brothers were united in their outrage at the police for picking up the wrong guy, Gary. Judith began to see too that the whole thing was some kind of nightmarish case of mistaken identity.

During the next couple of days, the Green River Task Force detectives questioned Gary. His home, vehicles, and personal locker at Kenworth were searched. Many pieces of evidence were seized and logged. Gary compliantly yanked hairs from his pubic area, chest, and head.

He also gave a specimen that would ultimately end his life as a free man: one cotton gauze, soaked with his saliva.

When it was over, Gary was set free. He went home to Judith.

Judith had dozens of questions for him about why, and what for, and what did they do to him at the police station? She had been so frightened. She couldn't stop hugging and kissing him. She was just so happy to have him back. He answered all of her questions with his signature, calm voice. "Judith, sometimes the police make mistakes. They pick up the wrong guy. They probably picked up forty other guys like me. But, hey—they sent me home, right? Obviously I'm innocent if they let me go home."

Judith felt tremendous relief. She felt joy like never before. Gary was back. Everyone around her was saying it was just some crazy mistake. The only bit of outrage that Gary showed was when he talked about how the detectives had put a big, ugly dent in the hood of his truck. That had him really steamed. He took meticulous care with his vehicles with engine maintenance and washing, and it didn't seem right to him that the police could dent his truck and get away with it. He was angrier about what they had done to his truck than what they had done to him. He asked Judith if she would help him fill out the claim form he had been given to seek compensation from the police for repairing the damage. Judith said she would. But she shoved the forms into a catchall drawer, along with recent newspaper clippings about the Green River Killer that Gary had gathered, and somehow never got back to filling it out. She would find the form and clippings again fourteen years later.

Gary and Judith worked for days to put their home back in order after the search. Their clothing and possessions had been pulled out, rummaged through, and then stacked in piles in the center of rooms. When the clean up was finished, they did not speak of the arrest again. It was as if it had never happened. Judith sensed they were moving forward, as a couple, oddly stronger and more connected his family.

Their routine settled back into place. Matthew came for weekend visits just as before, and they all went on weekend adventures including camping, picnicking, cruising for garage sales, and hanging out at festivals and county fairs. Judith became proficient in packing the camper throughout the workweek so that when Gary got home on Friday afternoons, they were ready to head out of town.

One day in early 1988, after living with Gary for three years, Judith said, "Gary, you know you're not going to get rid of me."

He said, "Okay."

She said, "I think we should get married."

"Okay."

Judith later described her wedding as the most wonderful day of her life: June 12th, 1988, the day she married Gary Ridgway.

They decided to have the wedding ceremony in the next-door neighbor's front yard for a couple of reasons: Jerry and Linda's yard had nicer looking landscaping, and the yard was also slightly shielded from the constant freeway noise.

They mailed out invitations that read on the front cover, "To love and to cherish, from this day forward…" to their relatives, friends, and all of the employees that Gary knew at Kenworth. The reception would be "potluck" style in the same yard as the wedding, and attendees were asked to bring one side dish.

Judith found a raspberry-colored lace dress, calf length, with a wide satin ribbon that tied low across her hips for twenty dollars in a thrift store. It was the most beautiful dress Judith had ever seen. They bought a navy blue suit for Gary with a nice, white shirt and dark tie at a garage sale for twenty-five dollars. Buying clothes for Gary was always a pleasant experience for Judith. Lee had been so picky about clothing and had always insisted on buying expensive suits made of high quality fabric. Gary didn't complain about any clothes she picked out for him.

The ceremony took place at 2:00 pm under pleasant, 72-degree sunshine. Judith, about to become Gary's bride, could barely contain her euphoria as she stood next to her father. Her parents had been a no-show at her first wedding, so it meant the world to Judith that her parents were there, smiling along with her. She felt love coming at her from all angles.

Judith tightly clutched the plastic bouquet of flowers that she had caught and saved from her roommate's wedding. She inhaled deeply and squared her shoulders. *Well, it's really happening—I'm marrying Gary. I only knew Lee for three months before I married him. This time I lived with Gary for three whole years. This time I was smart.*

The theme from Romeo & Juliet, the bridal chorus that Judith had chosen, played softly. Judith looked around at the small group of people who attended the wedding. She saw Linda, the neighbor's wife, standing next to her as "maid of honor" and the one and only co-worker from Kenworth who came, Jim Bailey, standing next to Gary as his "best man" just as he had stood as Gary's best friend at Kenworth for years. Years later Jim would admit that he had felt embarrassment that sunny wedding day as he looked around and realized he was the only person who came from Kenworth. He had felt badly for Gary. He had heard the jokes and whispering about Gary around the plant subsequent to Gary's arrest and locker search in 1987. Many thought that Gary might have been the Green River Killer. He was weird enough, they had said. They called him "wrongway Ridgway" behind his back.

Judith looked out at less than thirty relatives and friends sitting in the rows of mismatched lawn and deck chairs they had assembled on the grass. Many seats were unfilled, but that did not diminish the love Judith felt at her beautiful wedding.

Ellis P. Forsman officiated the wedding and delivered the words: "Dearly beloved, we are gathered together here in the sight of God, and in the presence of these witnesses to join together this man and this woman in holy matrimony. Marriage is an honorable estate and instituted of God. In the beginning, after God created man, he said 'It is not good that man should be alone. I will make a help meet for him.' Therefore shall a man leave his father and his mother, and shall cleave unto his wife: and they two shall be one flesh...Gary Leon Ridgway, will you have this woman to be your wife, and will you pledge your troth to her, in all love and honour, in all duty and service, in all faith and tenderness, to live with her, and cherish her, according to the ordinance of God, in the holy bond of marriage?..." Gary said that he would.

After the ceremony, the reception kicked off with upbeat music that Gary and Judith had carefully selected from their favorite artists: Barry Manilow, Barbra Streisand, Kenny Rogers, Dolly Parton, and Charlie Rich. They dined on potato salad, macaroni salad, scalloped potatoes, chicken cassarole, fruit and meat trays. Gary and Judith laughed heartily with everyone. Gary comfortably shared jokes and quips with his brothers.

Judith then sat in a lawn chair and slowly opened their wedding gifts as Mary Ridgway jotted down the names of the gift givers. Judith opened up packages that contained candles, candleholders, kitchen towels, a crotched tablecloth, steak knives, dessert dishes, and a mini duster. Judith gasped as she opened cards containing checks in the amounts of fifteen dollars, twenty dollars, and even one for thirty dollars. Gary stood behind Judith, looking down and smiling all the while.

They posed for a family photo in front of a fence draped with white garland, Gary and Judith in the center, flanked by both sets of parents.

Finally, it was in to the house to cut the wedding cake, a chocolate marble with pink and blue roses on white frosting that Judith had picked out at Safeway. The crowd cheered as Judith and Gary fed each other pieces of cake. They finished with a champagne toast.

Six days later the new Mr. and Mrs. Ridgway set out on their honeymoon.

Chapter 5
The Married Years

If an architect sat down and drafted a plan, a "blueprint," showing how a traditional, successful marriage should be constructed, phase by phase, to achieve the point of completion when contractors stand back to admire their work and onlookers whisper "that is beautiful," and then one held the blueprint up next to Judith and Gary's fourteen-year marriage for comparison, it would appear that the couple followed the recommended steps in building their own beautiful marriage.

One such "phase," communicating events of past and dreams for the future, started for the newly married Ridgways during their honeymoon along the Oregon coast. It was the kick-off to their married years, lasting nine days, June 18-26, 1988. Judith, still glowing with happiness in her new role as "Mrs. Gary Ridgway," was breathlessly excited about the trip to Oregon. Fearing that one day, in her "old age," she might forget details about her honeymoon with her dream husband, Judith vowed she would carefully document the trip. Her diary listed daily activities and adventures:

Sat 18th Leisure Time Resort, Plants Paradise, swimming and potluck

Sun 19th Father's Day, more swimming, sunburn

Mon 20th Oregon coast, Old Mill Marina Resort

Tues 21st Swimming, walking, Tillamook Cheese Factory (cheddar smoke, cheddar pecan), Blue Heron French Cheese Company (wine and cheese tasting), Debbie D's Sausage & Jerky Factory, Am. Adventure, Lincoln City Resort

Wed 22nd Swimming, ping-pong, movie, Lincoln City, walked the ocean beach, Kite flying, Depoe Bay, gift shops, Dairy Queen, NacoWest, South Jetty Resort

Thurs 23rd Sea Lion Caves, Forest Glen RV Park, Salem, Oregon, walked

Fri 24th Waterslides, drove to I-5 north, LTR plants paradise, Swimming

Sat 25th Swimming, walking, swinging, potluck

Sun 26th Swimming, came home, Kentucky Fried Chicken

Traveling in Gary's truck/camper to the south along Oregon's famous Highway 101, Judith had the better view over her right shoulder and out the passenger side window. While Gary focused his attention on maneuvering the heavily loaded truck through narrow lanes that climbed up steep hills and turned sharply along the jagged coastline, Judith stared down at the place where Oregon's lush, evergreen forest meets the uneven, rocky ledge that drops down to the ocean beach to form a dramatic, picturesque image.

I wonder why the ocean looks like a different color on different days? Judith mused as her body bounced with the truck over bumps. She had noticed that on some days the ocean looked like sweet root beer, rusty-brown with cream foam, spilling onto the tan-colored, sandy beach. Other days, the water looked steel-gray, colder, *ominous*, making her shiver. She saw sea lions resting on rocks, deer crossing the highway, rivers dumping into the Pacific, and white seagulls gliding on wind currents. She saw cargo ships and small fishing boats. She saw a world she had never seen before through the eyes of a woman finally at peace. She still could not believe that she had married a man so perfect for her. As she reflected on the many bad years with her first husband, it occurred to her that Lee had been like the jagged, dangerous, rocky cliff she was staring at and Gary was like the waves gently rolling onto the smooth beach. When people got near Lee, they were wounded by his sharp edges. Gary, on the other hand, did everything in gentle, steady beats, just like the ocean tide rolling in and out, so rhythmic and unchanging. She wanted to savor every moment of time she had with her gentle, polite husband on this trip, and she felt thankful they were able to have the trip without any children or grandchildren tagging along. Finally, it was just the two of them.

The Ridgways stopped frequently each day to take pictures at scenic viewpoints and tour various commercial attractions. They lingered at flea markets and roadside souvenir stands looking for pieces to add to Judith's collections of Garfield, Mickey Mouse, and Donald Duck knick-knacks.

"You know, Gary," Judith shared as they browsed vendor tables, "I didn't have very many toys when I was a little girl. Uncle Si and mom never had much. And when mother and I lived alone, it was hard for her to make ends meet." She was excited by the fact that Gary seemed to understand and support her desire to have "toys" as an adult. As they shopped, they smiled and waved at other tourists, sometimes calling out warm greetings. "Beautiful day, huh?"

The Oregon coastline was speckled with campgrounds, state parks, and recreational vehicle parks from Astoria, the beginning of the drive, to Brookings Harbor, which marked the end of the drive, or the "bottom" of the state, so it was easy to find a place to park the truck for overnight camping after each day's drive. Gary's parents had registered him as an "associate member" on their Leisure Time Resort membership, so he tried to plan each leg of the drive in order to utilize the Leisure Time Resorts, his favorite places to camp. He explained to Judith as they drove into the first one, "These Leisure Time Resorts are really a perfect place to stay. You see, they give you a nice place to park your R.V. with hook-ups. There's a swimming pool, clubhouse, activities, and, you know, nice people to talk to. We should always stay at Leisure Time if we can."

And, just as Gary had described, Judith found them to be accommodating and fun. They plugged the camper in to electricity and water and washed their clothes in the well-maintained laundry facilities. After their chores were finished, they began playing. Judith and Gary went swimming together in the outdoor pool, but after a few minutes Judith wiggled up and sat very still on the concrete edge of the pool, completely absorbed in watching her husband swim laps. Her eyes focused on his tan, lean body undulating under the aqua-blue water, holding his breath for long periods of time, swimming from one end of the pool to the other. It was as if Gary couldn't stop swimming and Judith couldn't stop watching him. She was drawn to his intense concentration. Later she would exclaim to relatives, "Oh, you just won't believe how good Gary can swim. He swims just like a fish!"

During their pleasant trip, they chuckled over jokes and chatted comfortably with each other as they pedaled along on bicycles. Judith practiced saying sweetly, "Honey, I love you."

Gary called back over his shoulder, "Love you too," but *only* when Judith said it first. And the pattern held for all of their married years.

Once during the honeymoon, Gary playfully referred to Judith as "Judie." "No, no, *no!*" Judith shrieked. "Gary, don't ever call me 'Judie' again. I can't stand that name!"

"Why?" Gary went still.

"Because, it reminds me of all those years that my mother told me what to do—like I was a little kid or something." She mocked her mother, 'Juuudeee, take your medication now. Juuudeee, remember to tell them that you have epilepsy.' "I don't want to be called 'Judie.' I want to be called 'Judith' because that sounds like I'm a grown up and I make my own decisions." A firm stomp of her foot on the ground punctuated her statement.

"Okay *Judith*." Gary never called her Judie again.

As they relaxed in a Leisure Time hot tub each evening, sipping on their favorite drinks, dark beer for Gary and wine for Judith, they finished filling in the story of their childhoods to each other. Naturally, stories had been started over the past three years of living together, but somehow—now that they were officially man and wife—there needed to be a finish to the story for them so that they could move on to dreaming about the future. Gary told Judith that his childhood had been rather happy. He believed that he had had a traditional family life with good values taught to him. He had a good mother, Mary, who made tasty food and cleaned the house. His father, Tom, had provided a decent income by working as a bus driver in the King County area. Gary told stories about adventures he had had with his two brothers. He was the middle child, with one older brother, Greg, and one younger brother, Ed. However, Gary confided in Judith, "You know, we have another brother, but we don't ever talk about him. I guess my dad had him with another woman."

"You have another *brother*? Judith asked, completely taken by surprise. "How old is he? What does he look like?"

"We never—you know—we're not supposed to talk about it, so don't say anything around my family, okay?" Gary turned his hands over, palms facing up.

"Okay." Judith ended her questioning about the mystery brother.

Gary went on, telling about his love of cars and fixing up old cars with his brothers. How fun it was to poke around in junkyards, looking for car parts.

Another thing he said surprised Judith: His little brother, Ed, had suffered with seizures when he was a child, and since then, he'd been a little "off" in his ways. Gary and his family had to give Ed some special help now and then, as he had difficulty sticking with jobs and commitments. "He's cool and everything but he—you know," Gary shrugged his shoulders, "we just have to help him out sometimes. My mom gets mad at him when he doesn't work." Judith felt an immediate, empathetic connection to Ed. *Lord. I know what it's like to have seizures and have your family think you're different. Poor guy.*

Gary and Judith exchanged tales about how extremely difficult it was for them in school. They had both especially struggled with reading and writing. In fact, Gary had been two years late in graduating from Tyee High School, finally graduating at age twenty. Judith never did graduate high school. "Oh, talk about graduation," Gary popped up, "I got drafted by the Navy when I was twenty. That really sucked." He went on about how he had started working at Kenworth Trucking in April, 1969, before his graduation, and was looking forward to a career at Kenworth, but then in August he had gotten a notice from the United States Navy saying that he had been drafted into military service.

"What did you do?" Judith asked.

"I didn't want to go. I mean, I really did *not* want to go. I tried to think of some way out of it. But the day came, and there was this guy at the front door to pick me up, and I just got so scared, I shot out the back door and hid in the back yard."

"Oh, *Gary*. You were hiding from the military people?" Judith felt frightened for Gary just imagining that day. Her father had been killed in the Korean War. Wars were bad.

"Yep. I wasn't gonna go."

"Then what happened?"

"They came and got me and put me in the car, and that was it—I was off to the Navy." He described some of the places he had gone, what it was like on a Navy ship, what his uniform had looked like, and promised he could show her photos that he had saved. "Oh yeah, and another thing—I have a kid over there."

"What? You have another child?" Judith's mouth hung open with surprise.

"Yep. A 'love child.' You know, soldiers—they go into town—everybody does it—and we would, you know, visit prostitutes. It was really common. Lots of guys did that." Gary flashed his wonderful smile.

"Oh. I see. Well, uh, do you know where your child is now?"

"No. I never stayed in touch. Lots of guys have kids over there in Vietnam." It was another truth Gary asked Judith not to mention in front of his family.

Gary talked about marrying his first wife, Claudia Kraig, at the Fort Lawton Chapel in San Diego when he was twenty-one. He didn't offer much explanation, but said, "It didn't work out. We got a divorce when I was twenty-three. She cheated on me and stuff." He told Judith about marrying his second wife, Marcia Winslow, the next year when he was twenty-four years old. This was the mother of his son, Matthew, who Judith had come to know through Gary's weekend visits with him. Gary did not have anything positive to say about his second wife. He described her as being fat and annoying, and "then she had a surgery and lost a bunch of weight, and after that—she just went out runnin' around on me."

"I met her one time!" Judith exclaimed. "I saw her playing in a country band at the Eagles Club. It was a Seattle Singles thing. She was really nice to me—I remember that. Then, you know when I went with you to pick up Matthew, and I saw her? I recognized her from that band." Judith remembered Marcia as being warm and friendly toward her when she accompanied Gary to pick up Matthew for a weekend visit.

"Yeah, well. She wasn't that nice." He talked about some of the heated arguments they had leading up to the divorce in 1980 when he was thirty-one years old.

"But now we found each other, Gary." Judith reached over and took Gary's hand. "I think God wanted us to be together." She looked up at his face adoringly while they held hands.

Judith took a turn telling about how painful her childhood had been with all of the seizure episodes and taking medication and, ultimately, going to live at a mental hospital and missing high school. Gary listened in silence. Then she talked about her marriage to Lee and outlined the tragic timeline of events including finding out her husband was gay, finding her oldest daughter lying bleeding in the road after having just been struck by a car, and witnessing countless verbal and physical attacks on her oldest daughter by her husband. She talked about all of the medieval activities they had been involved in and how weird it was, looking back. Gary interrupted her at that point, reminding her not to talk about any of that "gay stuff" in front of his parents, as they wouldn't be able to handle it. Judith nodded.

Then the new Ridgway couple shifted their minds to the future.

As they chatted about things they were looking forward to and what they hoped for in the future, it was easy to see the comfortable alignment taking place with their mutual goals. They both wanted to be homeowners, giving good maintenance to their home and yard. Judith especially wanted to be involved in gardening and landscaping. They embraced the idea of living in a home for a while, making some improvements, and then selling to take the profit and upgrade to a nicer home—"The American Dream."

The same thing with automobiles and recreational vehicles. Soon a master plan developed. They would work very hard, save most of their money, and upgrade homes and vehicles until they reached the ultimate goal: Gary would retire from Kenworth at age fifty-five and they would sell everything, buy a large motor home, and travel the country (staying at Leisure Time Resorts of course), meeting new friends, buying and selling goods at vendor stands, and having endless adventure.

Over the next fourteen years, their commitment to the master plan would remain rock-solid.

As Judith and Gary moved through the communication and goal setting phase of their honeymoon, they were delighted to enter the next phase of building a relationship: discovering how sexually compatible they were. They had been living together for three years prior to marriage so, of course, they had been sexually active with each other. But, Gary's small house had often been crowded with children visiting, grandchildren visiting, and stints of people living with them. Judith's second daughter, Rachel, and her boyfriend and their two children had moved in, sleeping in the family room, for the year leading up to the wedding. With different work schedules and people always in the house, private times for Gary and Judith to explore sex were scarce. The honeymoon provided an extended period of "alone time" for them to be free with their sexual whims.

Letting nature take its course on the honeymoon, they found themselves making love in the morning when they woke. Then they had breakfast with coffee, sitting in lawn chairs on the cement pad next to the camper. After a mid-day activity of bicycling or swimming or hiking, they went back into the camper to "nap." After cuddling and resting for a while, clothes started coming off. They made afternoon love. Then it was dinnertime in the Leisure Time clubhouse. After dinner they headed to the hot tub and, if they were really lucky and got it to themselves, they would make love in there. Otherwise, they headed back to the camper for evening lovemaking.

Judith felt like she was "floating" during sex. Being desired by a man—a man who did not want to have sex with other men—was a rush that she had never known before. Gary represented complete masculinity to her. Seeing him get excited and aroused by her femininity only got her even more aroused. She noticed that he made love to her with the same kind of focus he applied to swimming. Intense. And he wanted *her.* Nobody else. *She* was his wife. *I hope, by some chance, I get pregnant with Gary's baby. I want to have his baby* she fantasized as he made steady love to her, even though she knew she was past forty and probably too old to get pregnant.

But Gary terribly upset her during one lovemaking session. He casually pointed to her vagina and bluntly referred to it as her "cunt." As Judith's eyes flew open wide, she clutched her fists to her naked chest and pushed words out through clenched teeth, "What, did you say?"

"I said, you know, down there, your cunt."

Judith was sobbing by now. "Don't you ever use that horrible word again, Gary, I mean it! That is a *horrible* word."

"Why? It's just your cunt." Gary shrugged, looking truly perplexed.

"Gary, listen to me! My first husband used to scream and yell at me and use that horrible word. It hurt me so—huh—bad! He even called Marie that word when he punched and hit and kicked her. Don't ever use that word again. I *mean it!*" Judith stabbed the air with one index finger.

"Okay—fine." Gary casually answered, not registering anywhere near the emotional level Judith was at. He never uttered the word in Judith's presence again.

When the honeymoon trip was over, the couple returned to Gary's small house, feeling intimately close and ready to live the rest of their lives as husband and wife. And, perhaps their love was contagious because Judith's second daughter—the one who had been living with them—decided to marry her boyfriend and father of her two children. They moved into an apartment shortly after their wedding. Gary and Judith reclaimed their space, moving things back into the family room and cleaning up.

As the Ridgways cruised through their first year of marriage, December of 1988 brought the happiest Christmas holiday Judith had ever known. Feeling secure, safe, and healthy, with all of the desperation she had previously carried gone, she heavily decorated the house with lights, garland, knick-knacks, tablecloths, wall hangings—anything that looked like Christmas to her. She didn't care that some people made remarks about the over-the-top decorations. She was having the time of her life. Again, all of the children and grandchildren stopped by to visit Judith and Gary. There was a wrapped present for everyone.

And Judith experienced her first Christmas as a daughter-in-law to Tom and Mary Ridgway. Judith and Gary spent most of Christmas day at his parents' house, as they would for all their married years, where Mary authoritatively bustled around the kitchen, wearing a holiday apron over her nice blouse, tending to the last minute preparations before the family would sit down and eat Christmas dinner together. While Gary watched television with his father and brothers in the living room, Judith assisted Mary: fastidiously studying everything she did, aspiring to be as lovely and efficient in the kitchen as her new mother-in-law one day.

After dinner, when the mood was more casual, the Ridgway clan reclined in the small living room with their over-stuffed bellies. Judith found herself seated next to Tina, Gary's younger brother's wife. Judith was drawn to Tina. There was something about her pale, vulnerable face surrounded by short wisps of sandy blonde hair that said she had been hurt deeply in the past, and that was something Judith could relate to. The two laughed at the same jokes. They elbowed each other in unison the way twins often do. A sisterhood began that holiday that would endure for the rest of Judith's life.

December of 1988 also brought a special television show to an audience of fifty million viewers, but Judith and Gary had somehow missed it. It was called "Manhunt Live—A Chance to End the Nightmare." Hosted by Patrick Duffy, the two-hour television program aired in both the United States and Canada and brought viewers up to date on the sinister actions of the Green River Killer. The body of Cindy Anne Smith had recently been found in June of 1987 near Green River Community College in Auburn, Washington. In May of 1988, one month before Judith and Gary's wedding, construction workers in Federal Way, Washington, discovered the body of Debra Lorraine Estes. Patrick Duffy pleaded with viewers to call in any tips they might have that would help the police find the killer. It was time to stop the killing he said. The show was even offering a $100,000 reward. At the time of the show's airing, it was estimated that the Green River Killer had murdered approximately forty women, maybe more. But the killer was amazingly still free and probably living innocuously among some of the people who were frightened out of their minds watching the television special.

After the broadcast, only one man was arrested as a result of a tip phoned in. The suspect was a college student at Gonzaga University in Spokane, Washington, approximately three hundred miles from where the Green River Killer bodies had been found. However, he was quickly released and not charged.

But the desperate search for the Green River Killer did not touch Judith. She was very busy working at the daycare center, being Gary's wife, adjusting to being a step-mother to Gary's son, Matthew, and seeing her daughters and grandchildren when they came to visit. However, shortly into the marriage, Judith's daycare-worker career unexpectedly ended. She was bouncing a baby on one hip while she bent down to pick up a pacifier for a wailing toddler. When she twisted her torso in order to balance the baby on her hip while bending down, she felt a stabbing pain her lower back like she had never felt before. It took her breath away, and she was unable to call out for help. Taking in short pants of air, feeling herself being crushed in the vice grip of pain, she gently slid the baby to the floor and then let herself fall to the floor. Realizing that nobody on staff had seen her go down in the small room and being unable to push her voice up above the roar of the daycare noises, she slowly crawled to the door of the room and waved for help.

The doctors told her it was a "slipped disc" requiring immobility for possibly weeks. She laid in bed for almost three months while being treated with a mechanical contraption the doctors called "traction" and consuming a diet of muscle relaxants and painkillers. During the long weeks in bed, Judith had nightmares with ugly, graphic flashbacks of being a patient in the mental hospital. She had to take medication then too, and people told her what to do. All she wanted was to do was get well, get up, and get busy again. As she looked around the room, boring hour after hour, she gave silent thanks that she had her nice bed to lie in. *Lord, I'm so thankful Gary helped me get my own bed out of storage. It was a good thing because he had to give his bed back to that old girl-friend of his—Roxanne. I know this is bad to think, Lord, but I'm glad she broke up with Gary, because then I got to meet him and marry him.* Judith remembered Gary telling her about a woman that he was going to marry in 1984, the year before she met him, named Roxanne Theno. But Roxanne had abruptly and unexpectedly broken off the engagement. Judith remembered that after she had moved in with Gary, Roxanne occasionally called the house, asking to speak with Gary. Gary talked with Roxanne politely on the telephone while Judith sat nearby. She heard Gary agree to give Roxanne her bed back—the one she and Gary had been sleeping in. He also left the house a couple of times to go help her. One time, Gary said Roxanne needed her sewing machine fixed. So Gary went to fix it for her. But Judith hadn't felt any jealousy. That was simply the kind of man Gary was—kind and helpful to others. After all, look at all the ways he had helped her.

But Judith's perception of Gary's altruism would be violently ripped from her psyche fourteen years later when detectives explain to her that Gary got rid of his bed, maybe giving it to Roxanne, maybe destroying it, because he had murdered many of his victims in the early years of killing in that bed—the very bed that Gary had first made love to her in.

As Judith lay in her bed, she realized how much she missed her job at the daycare and worried that Gary might be upset with her for not working while she recuperated. But Gary completely halted her tormenting thoughts one day as he tended to her and they quietly talked in the bedroom. As if he had read her mind, he said, "Hey Judith, don't worry about working. Why don't you just quit and stay home now? I make enough money for both of us and you can get your fill of babies with your grandchildren." Gary acknowledged her love of holding babies and Judith was touched by his perception of her. She instantly let go of her

worries. Once again, her husband had shown her compassion and a willingness to take care of her. Life felt perfect again for Judith.

So she went back to being a full-time, stay at home housewife to Gary
like she had been with Lee, only this time around it was much more fun
because Gary didn't make all the demands that Lee had. There was no
reason to fear Gary. She easily created a new routine of housework—
housework that she could manage with her bad back that she would always have to protect—and partnering with Gary for weekend activities.

While Judith went about her household duties, another "phase" of
marriage building began taking form: Financial goal compatibility. One
day Judith picked up Gary's checkbook and studied it. She already knew
that Gary's mother had played a strong role in monitoring Gary's checkbook over the years prior to Gary marrying Judith. Mary made sure that
Gary's checkbook was properly reconciled with statements and that he
was paying bills on time while building up a savings. Judith noticed that
the checkbook needed some updating, so she sat down and started adding
and subtracting numbers. She noted that Gary had been faithful in making entries of deposits, childcare payments, attorney payments, and other
monthly bills, but he hadn't been updating the account balances. That
night over dinner Judith said, "Gary, you know, I'm home every day and
I have plenty of time, so how 'bout I keep your checkbook up to date? I
wasn't very good in school, but I like working with numbers."

"Fine with me," Gary said through a mouthful of food.

The couple began a system that would remain in place for their entire
marriage. Gary brought home paychecks and handed them to Judith who
would then make deposits, pay bills, and watch over the savings. She
made sure that any charges put on a credit card (sometimes Gary charged
gasoline when they traveled) were paid in full by month end. With amazingly similar core values in the financial arena, the couple experienced
endless discoveries about how they completely agreed on accumulating
and spending money. Not one argument took place over money during
fourteen years of marriage. A sensitive subject that has a reputation for
driving many couples straight in to divorce court, only brought a sense of
trust and satisfaction to the Ridgways as they saw their financial goals
manifest before their eyes.

The only subject connected to money that got Gary heated up was the
fact that he had to pay child support every month to a woman he did not
like, his second wife, Marcia. It was a recurring source of irritation to
Gary because he felt certain that she was wasting his hard-earned money.
He had no "say" about how she chose to spend the money. When he
complained to Judith about it, she tried to lighten his mood. "Well,
honey, this isn't forever. One day Matthew will turn eighteen and you

won't have to pay this anymore." On some occasions, Gary left the house to go meet with Matthew's mother to discuss matters about their son. Judith stayed behind.

Having both been raised by frugal parents, they understood how to really stretch a dollar—even a dime. Judith's stepfather had preached that only a fool would pay full price for something. "Everything should be bought on sale, Judith." He had done all of the shopping for the family as Judith's mother had never learned to drive a car, and he brought home discounted groceries—even free food that he had picked up at food banks. Why not? It was free. Judith's mother had learned to utilize food that she and her uncle Si had grown in their own gardens.

Gary's father had preached that nothing should be thrown away until every drop of function was squeezed out of it. He was a skillful hunter of useful goods at garage sales, thrift stores—even garbage dumpsters. He taught his boys that anything could be fixed and used again or sold for profit. Gary told Judith, "We would catch hell from dad if we ever threw something away that still had some use."

So Gary and Judith marched in synchronicity when it came to spending money. They typically bought all of their clothes, including underwear, at garage sales, swap meets, and thrift stores. The most thrilling clothes shopping Judith ever participated in was accompanying her mother-in-law to JC Penney's for special, invitation-only sales for employees of JC Penney and their family members. Mary worked as a salesclerk for many years at the SouthCenter Shopping Mall JC Penney store. When she invited Judith to after-hours store sales, Judith felt giddy with excitement. Not only did her attractive mother-in-law personally escort her through the lovely store, she was actually *encouraged* to cut loose and spend Gary's money. "Come on Judith, why don't you buy something? Pick out a new sweater for yourself!" Mary would bark.

"Oh no. I never spend this much on clothes for myself." Judith would answer as she stroked her hand over a stack of soft, new sweaters.

"Now, Judith, I won't hear of it. I know that Gary makes darn good money at Kenworth and I want you to buy something!" Because Mary told her to, and because Gary respected his mother so much, Judith would finally acquiesce and make a purchase. But the JC Penney sales were the only times that Judith bought new clothes.

They kept their food bill at a minimum using Gary's eating philosophy: "Judith, we eat to *live*, we don't live to *eat*." He explained to Judith that people eat too much, making them fat. He didn't need much to eat, and that's why he stayed so trim, he explained. Judith found it very easy to prepare meals for Gary. He wasn't picky at all. He only wanted some meat and potatoes, sometimes vegetables for dinner, (never dessert) and he didn't mind eating the same thing over and over. Leftovers were re-heated until they were gone. Many meals were simply heated canned soup. He discouraged Judith from buying packaged, snack foods. The only snack they indulged in was evening popcorn. Even then—sometimes Gary would wave it away as Judith offered him the bowl. "No, I don't need to eat any more food today," he would state.

Dining out was most definitely a treat for the Ridgways and it was only done with discount coupons, early-bird specials, and all-you-can-eat buffets. Once, when Judith burned their dinner and they had to go out for a hamburger, Judith asked Gary as they drove, "Gary, I was wondering, what does a prostitute look like? I mean, do I ever see one and not know it?"

As they drove along Highway 99 in Gary's truck he answered, "Well, let me find one for you."

"You mean, it's just that easy?"

Gary pointed his arm over the steering wheel. "Yep. Now look over at that woman standing there, you see—wearing the high heels and fishnet stockings? That's one."

"Oh, my *heavens*," Judith gasped. "You mean prostitutes are just out walking around, in the middle of the day, dressed like that?"

"Yep. Now you know what a prostitute looks like." He continued driving toward the hamburger stand.

Judith wondered what on earth had made her think about prostitutes when she was heading out for a hamburger with her husband.

Taking up his father's philosophy about re-using items, Gary brought things home to sell. Nearly every workday, after his shift was finished, he walked into the house, grinning as if he had just thought of the game for the first time, and stuck out two closed fists. Judith knew the game well. One fist would contain a "surprise" that he had brought home to her from work. Her part of the game was to tap on one fist—hopefully the correct fist—to find her surprise. If she tapped the fist containing the prize, Gary opened up his hand, and she would see a rubber band or pa-perclip or one set of foam earplugs resting on his open palm. Sometimes he brought home bigger surprises like a pair of coveralls or a pair of safety glasses. Everything came from his place of employment, Ken-worth Trucking. He told Judith, "You see—when a guy quits they need somebody to clean out his locker, so I do it and I get to take things home. I don't mind the extra work. I like helping out." Judith wouldn't know until years later that Gary was pilfering one item at a time, slipping it into his lunchbox or pocket to take home and sell at his garage sales. At times, the Ridgways had large boxes of safety glasses, rolls of masking tape, and coveralls stacked up in the garage, ready to sell. Earnings from the sales went right into savings. Paperclip by paperclip, the Ridgways were building wealth and getting ready to move up the ladder of success.

Gary always kept his eye open for ways to bring in more money. He gladly raised his hand at work whenever overtime was offered. Judith didn't mind him coming home late, as she supported his motivation to earn more money for their goals. She felt proud of him for working so hard. But he must have gotten very tired from working overtime because on some of the late nights getting home, Gary actually declined sex. Judith was in the habit of going to bed with her husband around 9:00 p.m. every night and having sex with him before he fell asleep. He liked to get to bed early because he rose early for work. Sometimes he left the house extra early to stop and have breakfast at Denny's and read the paper. After he'd fallen asleep she would get out of bed and go watch television in the living room, putting herself to bed much later. But on some late work nights, Gary would say, "No, Judith, not tonight. I have a headache." Or, "My sinuses are killing me tonight." Once, Judith thought she could try to entice Gary into changing his mind. She seductively pressed her body up against him and tried to kiss him, but he was firm when he said no. "I said, not tonight Judith." He gently pushed her away.

Even though Judith found her housewife duties to be fulfilling, there was something she was aching for: a pet to love. She asked Gary over dinner, "Would you care if I got a kitten? I would love to have a kitty here with me in the house and I would take care of it. You wouldn't have to do anything."

"Yeah. I guess I don't care." Gary answered, unruffled. "Let's pick a free one up at a garage sale or something."

They found their first pet, a white, longhair kitten, at the swap meet on Highway 99. Judith immediately named her "Fluffy." And, as Judith had promised, she primarily cared for Fluffy. Sometimes Gary would let Fluffy sleep on his lap while he watched television, and that gave Judith a tender feeling, but she knew that she probably loved the kitty more than Gary did.

In their second year of marriage, 1989, the Ridgways sold the small rambler and bought a house at 2139 S. 253rd in Des Moines. Gary put the equity he had gained from the small rambler into the purchase and Judith happily contributed her small settlement from her divorce with Lee. They would live in the house for eight years, doing exactly what they had planned: fix it up and increase the value. As they settled in, unpacking boxes, sorting through items they could sell, and making plans for the nicer, larger home, the first newspaper that was recklessly tossed onto their porch reported that another female body had been found in a shallow grave just south of the Sea-Tac Airport in a wooded area.

The Green River Killer was still at work.

Later in the year, a co-worker at Kenworth invited Judith and Gary to his house for a special evening. When Gary told Judith about it, she was excited to go socialize with people that Gary worked with. She wanted to be seen as Gary's wife. Later that evening they found out that the meeting was designed to introduce them to the Amway Products, and Gary's co-worker asked them to be sales representatives for the pyramid-like business structure. Judith wasn't sure she understood it at first, but Gary enthusiastically signed up. It was another way to make money!

Over the next several months, Gary became disappointed in his sales results. Their only customers were relatives, and they weren't showing a profit. Perhaps they weren't the "sales" type. But Judith didn't care much; she was having fun cleaning the house with all of the fancy cleaning products they got through Amway. But the side business fizzled out.

After the Amway attempt, the Ridgways tried selling a "cure-all" product containing tea-tree oil with the same results. Then it was on to therapeutic magnets. Again, the same results. It seemed the only kind of sales they were successful at was garage sales, so they decided to stick with what they were good at.

Meanwhile, Gary was winning "perfect attendance" awards at Kenworth year after year. Judith watched her husband accept gifts at award ceremonies such as Kenworth jackets and gift certificates to nice restaurants as her chest swelled with pride. She loved her husband so much.

Then a new sensation possessed Judith: déjà vu. Gary began attending regular union meetings after work. He had never applied for open management positions when they were posted at Kenworth, despite Judith's encouragement. Instead, he stuck with his painting position like a chef stays with a tried and true recipe. "Gary, honey, why don't you apply for a management position? You'd make more money."

"Aw, I don't know. I don't want the hassle of having to deal with people and all their problems. I just like painting trucks." But he did become active in the labor union that the Kenworth employees belonged to. That meant he had to attend regular union meetings—just like Lee had.

Once again, Judith heard herself saying through the telephone, "Okay, honey, I know you'll be home late tonight. You've got that union meeting. Remember to get yourself a hamburger before you go so you're not hungry. Yes, I'll be fine here with Fluffy. Don't worry about me." Judith watched television, sipping on inexpensive wine from a box she kept in the refrigerator.

On non-union meeting nights, Judith took delight in snuggling up close to her husband on the sofa while they watched television or a rental movie. She popped popcorn for them. Sometimes they drank her boxed wine, other times tap water. After watching dozens of movies over some years with her husband, Judith noticed something strange about him. When they watched movies containing scenes with a physical assault on a woman, or someone being killed, or a bloody military battle, she felt Gary wiggling and shifting in his seat next to her. Thinking he must have some sort of post-traumatic stress disorder from serving in the Vietnam War (she had heard about it on a television show anyway), she reassuringly put her hand over Gary's hand on his thigh to calm him. The violent scenes must have upset him, reminding him of the violence of war (though Gary had never admitted to being in actual combat). But her reassuring hand never helped. Gary would fidget more, taking in deeper breaths. When Judith glanced over and saw tears welling in his eyes, he jumped up and headed for the kitchen. "I gotta get a drink of water. Be right back." If Judith followed him into the kitchen, he would swipe away the tears and act like everything was fine. "Ah, I feel better now. I was really thirsty. Let's get back to the movie." Gary never acknowledged that he was crying during those times. Judith continued to note the pattern of tearing up during violent movie scenes, but she never talked about it. It was just something she knew about her husband. Part of being a wife, she reasoned.

Though Gary and Judith lived as true spendthrifts, Gary occasionally splurged on something he really wanted, completely blowing Judith away with surprise. One summer, Gary took Judith to the Enumclaw Suzuki dealership in Enumclaw, at the base of the path up to Crystal Mountain. "Judith, I'm going to teach you how to ride a motorbike." He paid cash for two, matching, blue Suzuki dirt bikes and then drove Judith and the motorcycles up into the wooded hills just east of Enumclaw.

"Whee-hee-hee. Look at me!" Judith cried as she steered the dirt bike and tried to remember how to shift with a clutch and brake with all of the levers Gary had shown her. "I can't believe it—one day I'm serving tea in a parlor in my long dress and the next I'm out riding a motorcycle in pants!" She threw her newly helmeted head back and giggled pure joy. Gary smiled at her and patiently gave instruction. She completely trusted him. If he said, "Give it more gas," she gave it more gas. In one-half hour she was able to ride along side him on the dirt logging roads. The motorbikes became part of their regular equipment on subsequent camping trips. Later, Gary sold their camper and bought a newer one featuring a compact bathroom with a toilet. Judith ceremoniously threw out the coffee can that had been their toilet for years in the old camper.

When the Ridgways weren't camping, they were selling goods at their own garage sales, relatives' garage sales, or at the Highway 99 swap meet. Gary was a patient teacher for Judith in that arena also. "Okay, Judith. If you mark something for twenty-five cents, people are gonna come up to you and say 'I'll give you five cents for that.' What you gotta do is say, 'no, how about fifteen cents.' That way they think they talked you down and you still got a sale. See?" Judith thoroughly enjoyed her time at the swap meets. It didn't resemble anything like work for her. She chatted with all the nice people who walked up to the Ridgway booth, a long table covered with a tarpaulin propped up by metal poles, part of the equipment they set up at each swap meet. They'd be covered if it rained. One sale that Judith would never forget happened at a Saturday swap meet. A woman approached Judith at their booth and said, "I simply must have that shirt you're wearing," pointing to the shirt Judith was wearing with "Days of our Lives" printed on it, one of her favorite daytime soap opera shows.

Trying to remember what Gary had taught her about negotiating prices, Judith thought for a few moments and said, "Well, how much will you give me for it?"

"Three dollars."

"Sold." Judith stood up, spun around on her feet, and said, "I'll be right back." She climbed up into their camper which was parked behind their booth, stripped off the shirt, replaced it with another she had inside, and walked back out to sell the shirt.

Her second favorite "score" at the swap meet was acquiring a particular wall decoration she had seen at a home interior party at one of her girlfriend's. Full retail price was fifty-nine dollars—an amount she would never dream of spending. But she had always admired the piece and when she spotted one at the swap meet she marched up to the seller and offered to trade a pair of baby shoes that were in top condition. Amazingly, the seller took the trade. Judith skipped back to her booth, wall hanging under her armpit, smiling like she had just won the lottery.

The practice of buying and selling goods was woven into the very fabric of Judith and Gary's life for the duration of their marriage. They never stopped collecting items that could be repaired or revamped and then sold. Gary took time to walk through thrift stores after work several times per month, looking for fixable items. They earned a reputation in their neighborhood as being downright professional garage sale coordinators. While some neighbors did not appreciate the constant activity around the Ridgway yard, other neighbors found it to be a convenient place to dump off unwanted clothes and household items.

The years clicked by, each year rather similar to the previous year in terms of way of life, activities, and relationships. Judith and Gary reverently acknowledged their wedding anniversary each year by re-using the original anniversary cards they had given one another. They pulled the old cards out and wrote new, personal notes to each other in the remaining blank spaces inside the cards. That way, they didn't have to buy new cards. And Judith thoroughly enjoyed pulling out the old cards, re-reading the previous declarations of love from her faithful husband. She spent a long while at the dining room table, reminiscing, thinking about what she wanted to write to her husband in the recycled cards.

On their tenth wedding anniversary in June of 1998, they threw a bittersweet party. Gary's father had died in January of that year, succumbing to years of effects from Alzheimer's disease and congestive heart failure. A bout of pneumonia finally took his life. Over the previous few years Judith and Gary had been visiting Tom and Mary's home more frequently, Gary mowing the lawn and Judith helping Mary care for bedridden Tom. Some weekends, while Judith went to stay with her parents, Gary went solo to help his parents. "Don't worry about nothing Judith. You go have a fun time with your parents and I'll take care of mom and dad. I'll go back to our house too and make sure the cat is fed." The tenth wedding anniversary seemed like a big deal to Judith and Gary—so big that they justified spending money on a party similar to their wedding day. They even had guests write names in an official guest book. Ten of the many people they invited attended: Mary Ridgway, Ed and Tina Ridgway, Greg and Dorene Ridgway, Kristen Ridgway, Dave and Thelma Gwinnett, Patty Scarsella, and Tina Robichean. Again, Judith and Gary felt surrounded by loving, supporting relatives and friends as they opened cards and gifts on the lawn of their neatly manicured yard.

During the fourteen-year marriage, Judith and Gary, precisely as they had planned, significantly upgraded their home and vehicles. (Interestingly, as the Ridgway couple became busier with their steps working toward the ultimate goal of retiring, the Green River Killer slowed down. Over the same period of time, the Killer snuffed out the lives of only 8 of the 48 victims he ultimately took credit for after his final arrest.) The camper with a bathroom was sold and they were able to purchase a small motorhome. A few years later, that motorhome was traded in on a class-A, bigger, almost new motorhome. The couple still managed to fit in camping trips between garage sales and checking on Gary's parents. Gary also upgraded his well-maintained trucks for newer ones. In 1997 the Ridgways sold their home in Des Moines and purchased their dream home in Auburn, near Lake Geneva, for $180,000. With ample equity to put down on the purchase price, they were able to secure reasonable monthly mortgage payments and be in a home that was far nicer than they had imagined they could acquire on Gary's Kenworth income. And it was this final home of the Ridgways where Judith really developed her life's epicenter. Through the home and its beautiful, park-like yard, she strengthened the relationships she cared about, she made the most magical love with her husband in the garden tub in the master bedroom suite and on the living room floor in front of the fireplace (though sometimes they had to take it easy because of her bad back), she nurtured her beloved pet family that had expanded to Poodles and Siamese cats, and she experienced true spirituality, alone in her yard. It was the place where the "pay-off" came after the many years of working and planning and saving. These were the best years.

When Mary came to visit, Judith and her mother-in-law strolled around the yard, listening to bird sounds and smelling flowers. "You know, Judith, with that green thumb of yours, everything you touch flourishes!" Judith, walking taller from the praise, cut starts of her favorite plants for Mary to take home and grow in her yard. Though it was never said, Judith sensed she was ranked the Most Favorite Daughter-in-law with Mary. After all, she had spent the most time with Mary, not having a career to attend to, and she took darn good care of her middle son. That surely pleased Mary.

The yard was a place in which to work side-by-side with her husband. While developing the yard was Judith's main passion, Gary diligently assisted her by trimming tree branches, pushing in wheelbarrow loads of bark and soil, and operating the lawn mower. If something was too heavy for Judith to lift, Gary was right there to help.

Over the years Judith and Gary had gotten in to raising Poodles which they fondly referred to as their "children." On nice days, when Judith suspected it was nearly time for Gary to get home from work, she would walk with the dogs down the driveway and down the dirt road to the main street where he would turn in and stop to check the mailbox. When the dogs spotted Gary's truck, they wagged tails and spun about, excited to climb up in the truck and get a ride back to the house.

The yard was safe for Judith's grandchildren to visit. They wrestled and played on the lawn, sometimes with "Grandpa Gary" mowing nearby. They told Judith about things that were going on in their lives.

Though Judith hadn't been raised in a necessarily religious home and had been confused by the different religions her mother had adopted, she felt closest to God when she was alone in her yard, when it was the most quiet. She stood still, scanning the yard and sky with her eyes and silently giving thanks for everything. *Dear Lord, you made me well. You took away my seizures. Then you brought me a good husband. I am so thankful, I can never stop thanking you for my blessings. When I look around this yard and see the beautiful colors and shapes of things that you created, I know that you are there. I feel peace in this yard.* As she went about her daily work in the yard while Gary was at work, she sang her favorite hymn aloud, "In the Garden," a hymn she'd heard as a child when her mother sang in the garden. "I come to the garden alone, while the dew is still on the roses, and the voice I hear falling on my ear…and He walks with me and He talks with me, and He tells me I am His own, and the joy we share as we tarry there, none other has known…"

Judith's faith was tested in 2001. She could hardly believe that God would want her to suffer that much. Why? Why did so many bad things have to happen in *one* year? The sadness moved in around her like a cold fog refusing to clear away and let her see the warm light of God again. First, in July, her beloved "Oscar," their smartest and most loved Poodle died in her arms after suffering a heart attack. When they buried him in the back yard, she cried and ached like she was burying her own child. That dog had brought laughter and affection that could never be substituted by another animal. They simply would not love an animal again on that level. Maybe they wouldn't get any more dogs. Judith and Gary held hands and said a little prayer for Oscar after he was buried. Judith set up a grave marker with artificial flowers pushed firmly in the dirt so that they would never blow away.

Then, on August 15th, only one month later, Judith and Gary walked into the house, just returning from a dinner out that had been an intimate celebration of Judith's birthday. Still feeling full and happy from the nice dinner, Judith walked over and hit the "play" button on the answering machine that was blinking. The recorded voice said, "Mom just died. You guys better get over here and say goodbye to her." Gary's mother had died on Judith's birthday, forever linking the memory of her death to Judith's birthday. Mary had been in medical treatment for cancer, but they were stunned by her death. *She died while we were laughing and eating!* Judith was overcome with guilt for not being there when her smart, sassy, mother-in-law passed.

Judith saw her husband grieve much more deeply for his mother than he had for his father. It was obvious to Judith that Mary had been the anchor for that family and her departure was devastating. Gary's older brother, Greg, was the executor of the will, so he took charge of business details. Judith helped plan a memorial that would be held in Mary's yard. After the ceremony, with tears still fresh in everyone's eyes, Judith pulled plants from Mary's yard, giving one to each family member to take home and grow something from Mary. How would they go on without Mary? She was the one they respected. She was the one they reported good news to. She was the one who raised the bar of expectations and urged the family to rise to those levels. She was the one who was proud of Gary when he had accomplishments. Somehow, Judith would have to try to give Gary what he had always gotten from his mother. It was a heavy baton to pick up and carry forward.

In the midst of the fog, another wicked finger reached through to poke Judith a third time that year. In November, right before the Thanksgiving holiday, she answered the phone and heard the voice of a police officer. "Are you Mrs. Ridgway?"

"Yes." Judith's heart was hammering in her chest.

"We have your husband, Gary Ridgway, here."

"No. Oh no. There must be some kind of mistake. Are you sure you called the right Mrs. Ridgway? There's probably more than one." Judith felt panic invading her body.

"Yes, I'm sure we have your husband here. He works at Kenworth?"

"Yes."

"You'll need to come pick him up. He will call you when he's ready."

Several agonizing hours later, Judith got a call from Gary. "Judith, I didn't do nothing wrong. I'll tell you about it later. Right now I need you to come pick me up at K-Mart in Kent. I'll meet you there."

Judith drove to the parking lot of K-Mart in Kent. Gary had jogged several blocks to it as soon as he was released from the Kent jail and was still catching his breath when Judith spotted him. He didn't want to be seen getting picked up in front of a jail he explained. "Judith, honey, all I was doing was, I pulled over on Highway 99 because I forgot to put my tailgate up." He bent forward, pressing his hands on his knees. "It was down. I pulled over to put it up and a cop stopped. Anyway, they took me in for questions, probably because they thought I was someone else. You know, it's crazy on Highway 99, people always getting stopped."

Gary smiled big and stared into Judith's eyes. His smile soaked up all of her hysterical thoughts like a big sponge. She believed him. One hundred percent. How could anyone smile like that if they had really done something wrong?

Standing up straight again he said, "Let's get home. They kept my truck. We'll have to come get it later."

They enjoyed Thanksgiving dinner with friends, and gave thanks for the blessings they still had. Judith gave silent thanks that Gary hadn't done anything wrong.

Then the fourth blow hit: Gary was arrested November 30th. He was accused of being the Green River Killer and this time he didn't come home.

Chapter 6
The Truth Comes Out

November 30, 2001:

Detectives Sue Peters and Matthew Haney were trying to get a handle on the chaos that was erupting in the Ridgway home. They had to keep Judith focused on the important interview for this case—the biggest case of their careers—while simultaneously swatting away the distractions coming at her. The house telephone rang nonstop as word swiftly spread that Gary Ridgway, the fifty-two-year-old Caucasian truck painter from Auburn, Washington, had been arrested earlier that day because of new evidence linking him to several of the Green River Killer victims. It was the biggest true crime story Washington State had known and high time the two-decade killer be caught.

Ridgway friends and family were frantically attempting to reach Judith. After she robotically stood up and went for the phone several times, Sue Peters, who looked like she might double as a physical education instructor with her short, muscular body and short-clipped black hair, announced, "We're unplugging it." Then there were the reporters at the front door, knocking with cameras rolling. Again, Judith slipped away from the detectives and opened the door just long enough for cameras to capture the image of her white, expressionless face (that would appear on the evening news that night) before Sue Peters rushed over, inserted her body between the door opening and Judith, and then slammed the door shut, effectively preventing the reporters from getting their exclusive, first-reaction-from-the-wife breaking news story.

It was a blessing for Judith that her body was in full battle mode. She had recognized the signs. With every cell in her body fighting off the impending seizure, her mind did not yet have to acknowledge the horrific news that the detectives had just delivered. Not yet.

Judith heard a muffled voice coming at her from the other end of a very long pipe: "Judith, let's get a bag packed for you now. We are going to take you to a hotel and check you in under a different name. Reporters won't know you're there. You are going to stay there for a few days while we search your home. Judith. Judith? Do you understand what I'm saying?" Sue Peters needed Judith to get moving.

Judith's brain began to register what she heard, "I can't—I can't."

"Yes you can, Judith. Let's get a bag packed."

"No, I can't be *alone*—alone in that hotel place. I want someone to go with me." Judith wailed.

"Okay, Judith, we'll have someone there to stay with you."

Detective Peters helped Judith collect the basics for a 2-3-night stay at the hotel: toothbrush, nightgown, a couple changes of clothing. "Can I take my box wine with me?" Judith asked.

"Go ahead." Detective Peters answered.

"What about my *animals*?" Judith shrieked, hysteria rising higher in her voice.

"I can assure you, someone will take care of your animals."

"They need to be fed. And don't—don't let them go outside—they'll get lost. Please don't lose my kitties." Judith's heart ached at the thought of leaving her two Siamese cats behind, not knowing if they would get fed.

Detective Matt Haney, standing six feet high and smartly dressed in khaki slacks, button-down shirt and tie, smiled warmly at Judith with his Homecoming King good looks, "Judith, detectives are going to search your home and yard while you are at the hotel. Is there anything that you want to show us now?" His long arms spread out on either side of him.

Judith led them to the backyard, straight to Oscar's grave that was marked with plastic flowers. "Right there." She pointed down at the earth. "That's where my Poodle Oscar is buried. He just died this past July. Whatever you do, don't dig him up—I'll be so mad!" Anger sensations felt good to Judith right then, making her extremities feel alive.

After assuring Judith her cats would not be lost, they returned to the house, picked up Judith's overnight bag, and escorted her to the car waiting in the driveway.

Judith recognized the hotel as they drove around to the backside of the Red Lion Inn, across the street from the Seattle-Tacoma Airport on Highway 99. It was a high-rise, fancy hotel that Judith had never thought she would stay in under normal circumstances, let alone be imprisoned there by police. The detectives explained that they needed to sneak her in the back so that nobody would know she was there. "Keep the reporters away from you," they explained as they hustled her into an unmarked, rear door.

They took Judith straight into a room where she discovered her sister-in-law, Tina, wide-eyed and pacing. Amazingly, the detectives had arranged to get Tina there ahead of Judith. Judith felt a moment of relief.

Tina had always been her favorite sister-in-law. She and Ed, Gary's younger brother, had seemed more like real people to Judith with their struggles and health challenges. Moreover, they had made some decisions in the past they weren't proud of, like Judith. Over the years, the three had intimately shared private jokes and confessions, all carefully disclosed away from Tom and Mary because they wouldn't have understood. They would have judged Judith, Tina, and Ed. But there was acceptance between Judith and especially Tina. Judith had even told her sister-in-law about her first husband, Lee, being homosexual. They had giggled together as Judith described some of the outrageous scenes in her first marriage.

"Oh my God, Judith." Sisters-in-law embraced. Judith cried.

"Okay, Judith, we're leaving now. Make sure you stay in this room and don't talk to anybody. Is that clear?" Sue Peters handed Judith a business card. "Now, you call me at this number if you need anything."

Judith and Tina were left alone in the silent hotel room. Judith sobbed into Tina's shoulder, trying to answer Tina's questions, but gurgled up more sobs than explanations.

After hours of crying, Judith finally collapsed onto the bed and fell into agitated sleep. The full-blown seizure never came. Tina clicked on the television and stared in absolute disbelief as the story about Gary—her husband's *brother*—was told again and again. She saw Judith's pale face on the television screen looking out from an opening at the front door while reporters peppered her with questions.

Judith existed in the purgatory-like hotel room with Tina, not knowing when she would leave or what she would find when she went back out in the world. Her only connection to the outside world was the television news and that was making her feel nauseous so she shut it off. She had fallen into a pattern of crying for two-hour stretches, then sleeping for about two hours, and then starting the crying again. She felt utterly exhausted.

After three days, Tina announced she had to go home. Judith hated to see her go, but she was thankful for her being there for those awful three days. Still terrified of being left alone, Judith phoned her oldest daughter and asked her to come to the hotel. Not long after the call, thirty-six year old Marie arrived, clutching a brown, paper sack containing hair dye—medium brown. "Mom, we need to color your hair. I don't want people recognizing you. We gotta make you look different. People saw you on the *news*." Marie stripped off her hooded sweatshirt, pushed her shoulder-length dark hair behind her ears, and got right to work in the bathroom, setting up her supplies.

Judith sat compliantly on the toilet seat while Marie worked the dye into her hair. "Marie, what am I going to do? I just can't *believe* it. They're saying all those things on the news about Gary."

"I know—I can't believe it either. People are saying it's really him. It's so creepy!" Marie's hands worked over Judith's head.

"I wonder how long I have to stay in this room? I'm so hungry and tired. I guess I haven't had much to eat in the last few days." She had been drinking her boxed wine and her head was pounding.

"Well, mom, did you order room service?" Marie flapped her tattooed arms against her stocky torso.

"No. I only have a little bit of cash with me, and these fancy hotels, things are so expensive."

"*Mother*. Don't you know? The police have to pay for everything here. You can order whatever you want!"

"Are you sure? I don't want to get a big bill."

"Hell yeah, I'm sure. I'm going to order us a bunch of stuff—make them police pay for what they're doing to you!" Marie picked up the telephone and placed an order for several appetizers, a variety of the most expensive entrees, and a couple of desserts. She picked up the phone again and ordered a movie.

Judith, with her new chocolate-brown hair and the same blank look in her red, swollen eyes, only poked at the food in front of her as Marie devoured the food that was delivered to the room, smacking lips and licking fingers. "Hey mom, let's watch the movie now."

"Okay."

After sitting through a movie that she wouldn't remember, Judith realized that she was out of clean clothes. She remembered the card that Detective Peters left for her and she scrambled around the room, trying to remember where she put it. Luckily, she found it on the floor between the nightstand and the bed. She called the detective and asked if she could go home and get more clothes. She asked, "How long am I gonna be here?

Detective Peters promised to come get her and take her home for more clothes, but, she warned, they weren't finished with the search yet. It could be a few more days at the hotel.

After seeing Marie boldly order all the fancy food, Judith decided to also be bold and leave her room. She just wanted to walk the halls for a while, get some exercise, maybe shake off her headache. Just after stepping out of her room, she spotted someone she knew well standing at the other end of the hallway: Matthew. Gary's son. She rushed to him and they embraced, holding each other for a long time with no words said. It registered in Judith's mind that, of course, Matthew must be going through the same shocking experience she was and that the police must have wanted to hide him from the media as well. Why hadn't she thought of Matthew before now? As she hugged Matthew's tall, muscled body, she realized that he really was a full-grown man now at twenty-six years of age. It seemed like yesterday that little Matthew came to stay with them on the weekends. She thought of the fun trip they had taken to Disneyland with Matthew and how she had gone on all the rides with him. But now, he was all grown up and developing a career in the military. She thought he had been stationed in California. Had the police brought him all the way back from California? She stood back and looked up at Matthew's face. He was so much like his dad—handsome, beautiful smile. For the first time since the detectives brought her to the hotel, Judith's heart was breaking for someone other than herself. She knew how much Matthew had looked up to his dad. What must he be thinking? His dad…a *killer*?

Judith then noticed Matthew's wife and her parents standing nearby, just watching. She had met them at Matthew's wedding. Nice people. Judith was happy to see that Matthew wasn't alone. They exchanged a few words of "good luck" and "take care of yourself now" and then returned to their respective rooms. Neither Matthew nor Judith said a word about Gary and the arrest. Anything they said had been only through body language.

Detective Peters picked up Judith and drove her back to the Ridgway house for more clothing. As they drove, Judith felt good to be going back to the house but knew that she could only go in for a few minutes and gather her things. She had to spend more time at the hotel while the detectives finished the search. But nothing had prepared Judith for what she saw when they arrived at the Auburn home: law enforcement people were everywhere, like an army of ants, in the yard, in the house, all busy with their intense inspection of the home. A canvas tent had been erected in the front yard under which a project command area was functioning. She heard the diesel engine sound of heavy equipment in the back yard, digging up the lawn, bushes, and earth. Bushes and trees that she and Gary had carefully planted, manicured, and watered were ripped out of the ground like big weeds, thrown on their sides in piles. Inside the house, cupboards and drawers were open in every room, with clothing and household items strewn about, some things stacked in piles. People were walking around in what looked like space suits of paper clothing and white booties, marking things on clipboards, taking photos. Judith felt like she had just walked onto the set of a CSI show.

Ms. Peters hurried Judith along. "Let's get what you need and get out of here." Judith had to put on rubber gloves and plastic booties before entering the house so she would not contaminate the investigation. *I have to put on gloves and booties to go into my own house? This is unbeliev-able. Wait 'til this is over. Somebody's gonna pay.* She remembered Gary's arrest in 1987 and how it had been a big mistake. And then there was the arrest just a couple of weeks ago when she had to drive to Kent and pick him up. Another mistake. Man, these people were really out to get her husband! *It's a good thing Mary isn't alive to see this mess. She would come unglued!*

A list was made of everything Judith was taking out of the house, and then she was returned to the hotel. After getting back into her room, she realized that she hadn't even looked for her cats back at the house. She had been too stunned by the disturbing scene to think of them. She felt awful.

Another thing she forgot was to grab her little telephone book. Now she wasn't going to be able to call people and tell them that she was safe and not to worry. She didn't have any of the numbers memorized. *Oh Lord, people are probably worried sick about me. I wish I could call them.* Judith massaged her temples with her fingertips.

The days blurred together, each the same, but at the end of the week, Matt Haney and Sue Peters came to visit Judith in the hotel room. They sat down with Judith and Marie, looking serious.

"Judith," Detective Peters began in her authoritative voice, "we're finished at the house, and we can take you back now."

"Well thank God!" Judith stood up with excitement.

"But wait—we need you to know that the house is a bit of a mess. Things are not in their original places. We know this will be upsetting to you."

"Okay." She sat down again.

"We'll leave you some paperwork. Fill that out and you can get some professional cleaners to help you, all paid for by the Task Force."

"Okay."

"And another thing you need to know. We had to impound all of your vehicles as evidence, so you will need to get yourself another car."

"Are you kidding me? You took my *car*? I want it back!" She was on her feet again.

"No, Judith. The car has 'evidence' in it that we need to study. You'll have to buy another car."

"That's a bunch of bullshit!" Marie shot at the detectives. "They can't just take your car Mom!" Her remark was ignored.

Judith and Marie packed up their things and got into the car with the detectives. Marie was the first to be dropped off at a friend's apartment, and then they took Judith home.

"Judith," Detective Peters asked in the driveway, "do you want to go in alone, or have me go in with you?"

Judith scanned the disastrous scene before her. "I—I think you should go in with me."

Together they entered the home. Judith slowly walked through the house, Ms. Peters close behind. She first saw actual holes where carpet samples had been excised in every room. All of the throw rugs had holes in them too. The contents of closets were thrown out onto the floor. Drawers, cupboards, boxes—all emptied onto the floor. When she got to their bedroom, Judith began crying. The bed covers were ripped off the mattress set and the bed was completely disassembled. The closet doors were left wide open like a bank vault just after a robbery, her blouses and dresses and bathrobes tossed about the room, in no order. Her jewelry was spread out on the dresser top. In fact, some of her favorite jewelry from her ex-husband's grandmother was missing. The police had taken many items out of the home and would keep them for an indefinite period of time. Her underwear was scattered about on the floor. Strangers had actually plundered through her most personal things. She felt an indignant outrage that was difficult to contain. What on earth had she done to deserve this kind of treatment? And why did they have to destroy her house this way?

When she went outside and saw the yard, Judith was more upset by what she saw in the yard than the inside of the house. She smashed a palm over her mouth, holding back a scream. Her yard, her sanctuary, the place where she had lovingly labored everyday, was ruined. Piles of dirt were mounded on the grass. Eight of her forty-two Rhododendron bushes were uprooted and tossed into piles. Careless feet had trampled flowers. The compost pile wasn't where it was before. What was once a park-like garden, now looked like a slipshod construction site. And the most sickening thing of all: Oscar had been dug up and reburied.

No. No way. I don't want professional cleaning people here. I don't want any more strangers in my house! I don't want anybody else touching my things! Judith shook with anger. *I will clean up everything myself!*

Fueled now by anger and a sense of victimization, Judith decided to work on getting her home back in order until Gary came home. And she began to wonder when she could talk to him. Despite the horrors of the past week and all of the shuffling to and from the secret hotel hideaway, she had a deep confidence that things would all work out and that there was going to be an end to this installment of the nightmare she had come to know as Gary Gets Arrested Now and Then. Because the police had always let him go! Gary had always explained to her that they had made a mistake. Didn't that happen all the time? Some people are unlucky that they resemble another person, or travel in the real criminal's territory.

Back in the house, faced with an overwhelming amount of work, Judith wondered how she could possibly get it all done. The answer came quickly: Her oldest granddaughter, Heather, arrived at the house. "Don't worry, Gramma," she said, getting right to work, "I'm gonna stay here with you and help you clean up this mess. Gramma, I love you. Oh, please don't cry." The seventeen-year-old angel sat cross-legged in the middle of the floor in the master bedroom and began neatly folding and stacking each piece of clothing that had been pulled out. While her granddaughter worked, Judith listened to the messages left on the answering machine. Her mother had called, out of her mind with worry. Her best friend and wife of one of Gary's co-workers at Kenworth, Linda Bailey, had left several, concerned messages. "Judith, where are you? Call us, honey, when you can...Judith, I'm trying to reach you...I'm worried sick about you. Please call me when you can." There were several calls from other friends and relatives.

Heather stayed with Judith for two days, working hard to first get Judith's bedroom back in order. But Judith wasn't much help. As much as she wanted to roll up her sleeves and get busy, her body felt heavy, her mind was fuzzy, and she could not focus on one task long enough to get it finished. Instead, she wandered about the house, drifting from room to room, grieving over the violation and realizing that her female cat was not coming back. The male Siamese came back in the house, but so far, no sign of the female cat. The police had probably scared her off with all their noisy equipment. *Liars! They promised nothing would happen to the cats, and look what happened.*

Judith had no appetite for food. When she felt weak enough to pass out, she popped a bag of microwave popcorn and washed it down with a glass of wine. She knew it probably wasn't good for her, but she couldn't gather enough strength to put together anything else. So she continued popping popcorn and drinking wine. Things got blurrier. She had difficulty remembering what day it was. How many days ago did they take Gary away? She couldn't remember. When Heather had to leave, she picked up the phone and called Linda. If anyone could help now, it would be Linda. "Linda...I need you."

"Judith, honey, where have you been? I've been calling and calling."

"They took me away to a hotel. But now... I'm back."

"Are you okay, Judith? What's goin'on?"

"Oh, Linda, you won't believe it. They tore up the house—and the yard—and they took all our vehicles. Our beautiful motor home is gone too. I don't have anything to drive. How am I supposed to get around?"

"You hold on, Judith, I'm coming over to help you." As Linda promised, she arrived shortly and took charge of the scene. Linda kept any opinions she might have had about Gary's guilt or innocence under wraps and simply focused on helping Judith clean up the house. She noticed her friend gulping down glasses of wine and mentally counted 6-8 glasses the first day.

"Judith, honey, I don't think that's good for you. Let's get you somethin' healthy to eat now." She fixed her friend a sandwich and took inventory of Judith's condition as she watched her eat the sandwich. She didn't like the vacant stare her friend's face held most of the time. Nor did she like hearing the bizarre mumbling that was coming out of her friend's mouth as she paced back and forth while Linda cleaned. Clearly, her friend was in a state of shock. And she understood why. It didn't look good for Gary. Oh, no. She had seen on the television news that detectives were in the midst of a massive search in connection with Gary including hunting down all of the vehicles Gary had ever owned and doing invasive searches in all of the homes he had ever lived in. Something big was going down.

Over the next week, Linda stayed with Judith. Judith wandered around the house like a toddler who had been abandoned in a department store, frightened, searching for a friendly face. She was still drinking wine, despite Linda's admonishments. And she had started taking sleeping pills at night that she kept in the medicine cabinet for use when her back pain flared up.

The first phone call from Gary came during that week. Judith answered.

"Hello Judith, I'm calling you from the King County Jail."

"How are you, Gary? When are you coming home?" Judith's voice sounded tired, like she hadn't been to bed in a week.

"Judith, you gotta believe me, I didn't do nothin' to those women." Gary sounded strong, just like before. Judith felt a burst of hope.

"I believe you, Gary."

"I know what they're saying, and all, but Judith, I didn't do nothin'."

"Gary, I talked to your brothers and we're gonna come visit you soon."

"Okay Judith. You take care of yourself."

"Bye, Gary."

I want some more wine. Where's my wine? Something about the way she felt in her stomach reminded her of the worst days in her first marriage.

At week's end, Linda told Judith she needed to get back to her family. "Judith, honey, are you gonna be okay here by yourself? I want you to stop drinking so much wine. You don't wanna go that route, believe me! Why don't you go to your doctor and ask for something to take for depression? There must be somethin' they can give you."

Judith thought about her friend's advice, arranged a ride, and went to see her family physician. During the office visit, Judith tried to tell her doctor everything that she was going through, how terribly frightened she had been, how she had been talking to Gary on the telephone at jail—"Shhhhsh." The doctor held up his hand to her face. "I don't think you want to tell me anything about Gary. Not a good idea."

"Huh?"

"Don't say anything to me that you might regret later. Let's just stick to medical talk." He quickly wrote out a prescription for something and left the exam room.

I might regret what I'm saying? I don't understand! Feeling alone and like she had just inflicted some toxic effect on her physician, she went to the pharmacy, filled the prescription, and then went home. She took a dose of the new medication, hoping it would do something for her.

For the next few days, Judith existed in the Ridgway house alone, thoroughly numbed by her combination of popcorn, wine, sleeping pills, and the newly acquired pills—whatever they were. During the day she tried to do more cleaning, but only managed a few small tasks. She couldn't organize her thoughts well enough to be effective. Evenings were passed in front of the television with her wine and popcorn. Linda called Judith each night to check on her.

"Judith, are you drinking wine?"

"No—Linda, I'm not drinking wine," Judith lied as she set her wine glass down. She was now lying to her best friend.

Gary continued calling Judith. One of his calls changed her life.

"Hi Judith, it's me."

"Hello, Gary."

"How's everything at the house? Are you getting things put back together? Is anybody helping you?" he questioned like the house was his main concern.

"Yeah, Linda was here and we cleaned things up pretty good."

"That's nice of Linda. Jim and Linda—they're good people. You listen to them. Judith, I need to tell you something. Something I should have told you a while ago, but, anyway, I didn't murder them women like they say I did. But I do have a *sex* problem. You see, it's like an addiction. Kind of like having a problem with alcohol, you know? A guy can't control it. I did see prostitutes...that part's true," he confessed with the right amount of penitence in his voice.

Judith was silent.

"Anyway, I didn't kill them women."

"I gotta go now. Goodbye, Gary." Judith hung up the phone, head and heart pounding to the same beat, unable to say anything to herself or anyone else.

She busied herself over the next couple of days, storing clothes away, re-packing boxes of craft items that had been dumped out, and throwing some old papers and cardboard into the trash as she cleaned. At least her house would get a good cleaning, if nothing else, while Gary was away. One day she carried a box of trash out to the garage, set it down, and then stood still in the haunting silence, looking around the garage, remembering how many times she had seen Gary working on their cars here. He had been adamant about changing the oil regularly and performing good preventive maintenance on their vehicles. "They last longer that way." She remembered all of the sounds he made with his tools. She remembered what it looked like when he cleaned his hands with shop rags. She walked over to his tool bench and ran her hand over the dusty surface. She remembered one time when Gary raised his voice to her—one of the only times he ever raised his voice to her—when they were in the driveway washing cars together in the driveway.

"Judith, why in the *hell* are you washing the lower part of the car before the top?"

"Well, why does it matter, as long as I wash the whole car?" Judith playfully sprayed water from the hose like she was writing her name in cursive with the water.

"Judith, I told you before! Always start with the top of the car and work your way down. That way, the dirt runs down. Why would you want dirt to run down over the clean parts?"

"Gary, it doesn't matter."

"Yes it *does* matter!" Gary shouted at her, clearly very angry.

"Okay, okay." Judith backed off, sensing that she had just royally pissed off her husband. When it came to cars, he sure was particular in his ways.

Judith slowly opened the drawers under the tool bench, one at a time, looking at supplies that Gary had used when he repaired picture frames and toys for her so she could sell them at the swap meet. She saw glue and string and little packs of nails and thumbtacks. She saw full rolls of masking tape and duct tape. She put her hand in the drawers and moved things around, taking some pleasure in touching Gary's things. She had always thought of the garage as Gary's area and had never paid much attention to how he had it arranged. As she poked around at car parts stored in a plastic rack mounted on the wall, she discovered something that made her blood turn to sand: condoms. Packs of condoms. And it looked like they had been intentionally hidden beneath everything else in the rack. *I-I don't understand! Why are there condoms out here? Gary and I never used a condom, not once! Why would he need condoms?* Her brain raced back over all the years she had been with Gary and still—no memory of ever seeing a condom. The finding sent new shock waves through her already hurting body. Gary had made that confession on the telephone a few days ago—something about being a sex addict, but she hadn't believed it. *Maybe somebody forced him to say that to me,* she had thought. But then, very slowly, like cold water seeping in through tiny cracks in a basement floor after consecutive days of rain, the realization entered her brain that Gary actually had been with prostitutes. The detectives were right! He had lied to her. Her perfect, smiling husband had *cheated* on her. *Bastard!* The man that she loved with every cell in her body was a liar!

Judith slowly backed away from the shelf hiding the horrifying evidence like she was backing away from the open mouth of a lion. She spotted an axe with a long, wood handle and grabbed it defensively. She hoisted it up over her head and brought it down on the tool bench, chopping at it over and over again with wild strokes, sometimes missing her target and bouncing the blade of the axe off the floor. She quit chopping for a few moments while her new rage escaped her body through a long scream. Then she raised the axe again and chopped randomly on everything around her, smashing boxes, shattering glass, until she was too weak to lift it anymore. Finally, she dropped it on the concrete floor and fell to her knees, sobbing into her hands. *How could you? How could you do this to me, Gary? Why? Why? Wasn't I enough for you? Didn't we make love all the time? That wasn't enough for you, huh, Gary? You had to go see filthy prostitutes?* She cried and cursed at the ceiling. This was the ultimate betrayal. Nothing could possibly hurt her more than this.

That evening, broken-hearted, Judith sat in front of the television, not really wanting to hear the sobering news reports about Gary yet again, but, at the same time, wanting to look at it again with her new perspective—now that she knew Gary was a liar and an adulterer—she watched, sipping boxed wine. She loaded up on anti-anxiety pills and muscle relaxants. Then she took double the recommended dose of sleeping pills so she could just go to sleep and feel peace for a little while anyway. Drowsiness came quicker than she expected. Around midnight she woke up and thought she'd better get to bed. She clicked off the television, shuffled over to the front door, made sure it was locked, flipped off a light switch, turned around and proceeded to wildly tumble down a full set of stairs, whacking her head on every step until she finally landed in a heap on the bottom floor of the tri-level.

Judith whimpered. She lay perfectly still for about five minutes. It was so dark. She didn't know if she dare move. Had she been taken down by a seizure? No, she remembered hitting her head on each step so she must have been conscious. Had she broken her back or neck? No, she could move her hands and feet. Cautiously, she got up into a crawl position and slowly climbed up the stairs, crying out in pain with each step. She crawled down the hallway to her bedroom and pulled herself up into the bed. She was sure that one of Gary's hammers from the garage was embedded in her head pounding away. After that, everything went completely dark.

Late the next morning, Judith woke up with a sore body and symptoms of a hangover. She remembered what had happened—the fall—and felt panic constricting her chest. She could have died! She could have paralyzed herself and perhaps nobody would have found her for days! Feeling like she was going to go insane with frightening thoughts, she reached over and grabbed the telephone off the nightstand. She called Linda and confessed everything. "Linda. I lied to you—I have been drinking wine. Too much wine! Last night I fell down the stairs and hit my head. I was so scared! I had to crawl all the way to bed. I'm so sorry I lied to you. You are my best friend and I *lied* to you."

"Jeez, Judith. You're scaring me to death. You gotta stop that wine."

"I know. I'll stop. And Linda—I don't want to live here anymore. Not alone. I gotta get *out* of here!"

"I know, Judith. I'll get back over there again as soon as I can and we'll figure somethin' out. Okay?"

"Okay," Judith whispered and hung up the phone. She hadn't told Linda what she found in the garage.

During the next phone call from Gary, Judith told him how scared she was. How she hated being in the house alone. And she told him about the terrible fall.

"Judith, you remember my friend, Rick? His wife babysat Matthew when he was small, remember? Well, anyway, he's a good man. You should call him if you need help. Listen to him." Even in jail, Gary was thinking of how to help his wife. Judith couldn't help but smile as she heard concern in his voice.

Judith did remember Rick. He had been an acquaintance of Gary's over the years, and she remembered him as being a nice man. She found his number and called him. He came over later that same day. As soon as he entered the house, she rushed up to him, trying to get words out as quickly as possible. "I'm so scared. I don't like being here alone." But her composure quickly fractured and she melted into his chest, crying. He firmly wrapped his arms around her and let her cry. When the sobbing ended, he gave her a little kiss on the forehead and assured her that she would get through it. It would just take some time. He didn't stay long, but a hug from a warm man had been better medicine than any of the pills.

The next day, another male stopped by unexpectedly. A man of about eighty-five years, a friend of the dear, elderly woman who had sold them their first poodle, had heard the news about Gary and came to see Judith. When she opened the front door, the man announced that he had come to pray with Judith. She led him to the living room and asked him to take a seat. Judith sat on the sofa and the man sat on her coffee table, facing Judith, knee to knee. He leaned forward, taking her hands in his and prayed aloud. Tears streamed down Judith's cheeks as she listened to his lovely prayer for her. Her heart was warmed by this man's concern, and she felt comforted by the prayer. Then, abruptly, shockingly, the man cupped her face in his hands and said, "I would like to kiss you now."

As he leaned in with puckered lips, she screamed "No! No, no, no! Get away!" She pushed his chest away from her. What was wrong with this man? He was in his eighties for gosh sake. And he was married! She told him he had to leave.

Judith was shaken by the strange visit. Again, she felt like she had to get away. Everything felt so strange. The life that she had known in this house was absolutely gone, replaced by some circus passing through.

Gary continued calling Judith daily. He asked the usual questions about how she was doing, how the house was, how the yard was, but they didn't speak again about him seeing prostitutes. She had gone into a cozy, safe den of denial and would stay there for the next two years.

After talking with Gary nearly every day since his arrest, Judith noticed that she had developed an aversion to the color green. She began throwing out clothing and items that were green. When she looked at the color it seemed to scream out, "Green River Killer. Green, green, green!" She had nightmares with the color green swirling around in front of her. For the first time, she began to dread phone calls from Gary. Thinking about his calls seemed to stir up the whole "green" thing. Besides, he had been calling "collect," and she worried about the phone bill getting too high.

So when the detectives came back to the house to "visit" (they had been back a few times since the search to ask follow up questions), she told them how very worried she was about money. Without Gary, she had no income. How would she pay the bills? She asked them to bring her Gary's wallet as it contained two, maybe three paychecks from Kenworth that hadn't yet been cashed. They said they would check in to it. Several days later, one of Gary's attorneys personally delivered the paychecks to Judith. She sat down and immediately paid a stack of bills.

When Christmas and New Year's Day quietly floated by her like an empty plastic bottle riding on a river's current, Judith realized she was facing a brand new year: 2002. And it was time to make a plan. She needed a car. She needed to figure out what to do with the house and all of their things (that hadn't been taken by police as evidence). And, she needed to know how she would support herself in the months to come.

During the past few weeks, phone calls with Gary had escalated to actual visits. She had visited Gary in jail several times and it didn't seem like he was coming home any time soon. The first visit had been devastatingly real. When Gary had been arrested in the past, she had never actually seen where he was. Didn't hear the sounds or smell the smells of a jail. He simply came home after a while. This arrest was so different from the times before. She felt it in her core but couldn't put words to the feeling.

The first time she went to see Gary, she traveled to the jail via public bus as their vehicles had all been confiscated. As Judith made her way to the bus, she looked back over her shoulders often to see if any of those media people were following her. After a long, anxious journey to downtown Seattle and a thorough screening before she entered the jail, when she was finally seated in a chair facing Gary, the first thing she noticed was a thick wall of clear glass separating her from her husband. It seemed so cruel. He was in there like some animal in a zoo. Seeing him triggered a storm of emotions, and she began sobbing. She pressed the palm of one hand on the glass, like she had seen in movies, hoping Gary would do the same. Through her tears she saw that her husband looked skinny and small in his one-piece jumpsuit. He wasn't eating it looked to her. And his face—it had aged years since the arrest. Gary sat still, composed, and eerily calm.

"Gary, honey, put your hand up on the glass," she pleaded, sniffing and heaving her chest for air. He slowly pressed his hand to the glass on the other side of hers. She sobbed harder. He didn't look comfortable with his hand on the glass, and he pulled it back down to his lap.

"How are you doing?" she asked her husband.

"Fine," he answered flatly. But he didn't look fine.

Judith noticed guards nearby looking at a television monitor and she saw a microphone near the glass. She felt certain they were listening to everything they said. "They steal things here. Don't send me anything because some guy will probably take it and try to sell it on E-bay or somethin'. They already stole a little picture I had of you." He looked down toward his lap and didn't say anything while Judith sobbed some more.

The visits always left Judith feeling cold, sad, and bewildered. She began traveling to the jail for weekly visits with Gary's older brother Greg and his wife, Dorene. After a few weeks they developed a routine: Judith would spend Saturday night with them, typically watching a movie with snacks in the living room, then Sunday morning they attended church services at Greg and Dorene's church (where the members were overtly supportive of the Ridgways), then they'd stop for breakfast at a local restaurant, and lastly, go visit Gary. On the way, Greg coached his sister in law. "Now Judith, we have to keep up these visits—show solidarity. We don't want people thinking we're not supporting Gary. We gotta keep doing this for him."

Judith wasn't sure what "solidarity" meant, but she guessed it must have meant something like showing family support. She felt too embarrassed to ask Greg what the word meant. She trusted him. He was college educated and all. A businessman. He had always been the one in the family to take charge in emergencies. He had done a good job as Executor for Tom and Mary's estate, following the wishes in Mary's will to the letter. Now, he was searching for the best defense attorney money could buy for his brother. He said it was going to be a long haul, and they needed to find their own "Perry Mason." The public defenders weren't going to do Gary justice he said.

The Sunday visits continued and Judith took comfort in being surrounded by Gary's kin. They seemed so confident that everything would turn out fine. Gary would be released. It was just a matter of time they told her.

For one visit, Linda went with Judith to see Gary. Linda explained that she had been tormented with wondering if he was or was not the Green River Killer. Wasn't getting any sleep. She needed to look him in the eyes, face to face, and form her own opinion. It was driving her crazy. Judith listened quietly as her friend grilled her husband.

"How are you doing, Gary?"

"Fine." Standard answer.

"Gary, I don't know what you did, and you're probably not gonna tell me right now, but all I can say is you better get right with God. Find God because he's the only one who can help you now. That's the only thing that's gonna save you, and I'll be prayin' for you."

Gary nodded his head toward the guards. "They listen to what we say."

"I'm sure they do. You better do it. Get right with God, Gary."

Gary hung his head, saying nothing.

That was the only time Linda went to see Gary, but subsequently, Gary began writing letters to Linda, thanking her for helping Judith, thanking her for everything. Linda didn't know it at the time, but she would receive letters from Gary Ridgway, a.k.a. The Green River Killer, for years to come.

Over the next few weeks, as detectives sorted and studied the voluminous evidence taken from the Ridgway home, they returned to the house to ask Judith more follow up questions. One time they dropped a bomb on Judith, telling her that they had reports that Gary had been seen with a tall, brown-haired woman at the Leisure Time Resort located at the end of Highway 18 where it intersects with Interstate-90. Reportedly, he was camping there recently with the mystery woman in the Ridgway motorhome. He had happily introduced her as "Mrs. Ridgway" to fellow campers. They didn't believe it had been Judith as she stood barely five feet tall with blonde hair. Did she know anything about that? Did she have any idea who that woman might have been? Judith was quietly dying on the inside as she imagined her husband with another woman *in their motorhome,* the motorhome they had made love in on so many wonderful trips together.

"No. I don't know anyone who looks like that. I guess he might have had time to do that when I went to stay with my parents for the weekend. He told me he was going to work on a car all weekend."

On another visit, the detectives further devastated Judith when they asked her if she remembered camping with Gary at a place called Bear Creek.

"Oh yes, we loved camping at Bear Creek. I remember it was near a place where people practiced search and rescue stuff."

"And do you remember meeting a couple there that you became friendly with?" asked Sue Peters as she jotted something on a notepad in her typical business manner.

"Oh yes. We made friends with a lovely couple. Can't remember their names right now, but I remember them because they had an arts and crafts table set up and they were selling things. We got to talkin' with them and found out we like doing the same things we do—traveling and selling things."

"And did you stay in contact with the couple after you got back home?"

"No. But I did write down their phone number and address when we were there. You know, you say you're gonna get together again sometime, but we never did."

"Yes, we found their name and address in some of your papers. Do you think that Gary ever saw them after your camping trip?"

"No. No we never saw them again. Why?"

"The woman was found dead, lying along side a country road, not long after you all met." Sue Peters stared right into Judith's eyes.

"Oh my God! No! She was such a lovely woman." Judith pushed her hands flat against her chest.

"Do you think that Gary had anything to do with her death?"

"No! The people were lovely. We talked about camping with them again sometime. That's just horrible. Oh my God..."

But the visit that most upset Judith was when they presented ugly details about Gary picking up prostitutes on Highway 99. They explained how undercover officers had tailed Gary for months prior to his arrest. It was all she could do to keep from running out of the house screaming.

"...and he would drive up to one and wave forty dollars at her...forty dollars...and he would pick them up and have sex...did you know that Judith? That your husband had sex with prostitutes?" Detective Peters pounded Judith hard with her words.

"No—no, never!"

"Did you know that he was a regular visitor to Highway 99, that we saw him before and after work cruising the strip?"

"Well, I know he went to Denny's for breakfast before work, and he liked to read the paper. One time the nice people at Denny's called me and said that Gary had dropped his wallet on the ground in their parking lot. Anyway, I had to drive over there and get it because Gary was at work—."

"Your husband *routinely* stopped and talked to prostitutes. He paid them for *sex*. Did you know that?"

"Please—please stop. I don't want to hear this. Just stop!" She clapped her hands over her ears.

Every time the detectives came to the house, it ended this way for Judith. Shaken, further wounded, alone. She wished they would stop tormenting her.

During the next Sunday visit with Gary at the jail, Judith asked him what she was supposed to do for money. She had bills to pay. The septic tank needed a $400 service. And she had repairs to make to the house and yard as a result of the extensive search by the police.

Gary had a solution. "I know, Judith. You can cash out that IRA we have. Bring me the papers, I'll sign them, and you can use that money to get yourself a car and get the house fixed."

"Okay, Gary."

Judith cashed their IRA for $22,000 at the bank, speaking in low whispers to the bank teller, looking left and right, feeling certain that everyone in the bank was staring at her. Did everyone know that her husband was in jail, accused of being the Green River Killer? What were they saying about her? Were they laughing? Did they think she was a horrible person for being his wife? A new feeling of shame covered her like sticky, wet paint that wouldn't wash off, beginning what would be a several-year term of avoiding public places. Even though she eventually purchased a small, used car with some of the IRA money, she would rarely use it, fearing that she would be recognized.

That night Gary dealt her another blow. Over the phone, from jail, he said bluntly, "Judith, we need to get a divorce."

"Why, Gary?" She asked, heartsick, but knowing he was not coming home this time.

"Because. We need to protect you. We need to change your name. I don't want you to get hurt any more because of this—thing." There he went again, trying to protect her. No matter how hard she tried to imagine it, Judith could not see Gary killing women. He was just too compassionate for killing.

"Okay, Gary. I'll talk to Jim and Linda about it. Maybe they can help me."

When she phoned Jim and Linda, Jim supported what Gary had said, "I agree, Judith. You need to start a divorce right away. You gotta start thinking about your life and what's going to happen to you."

The only attorney Judith had ever known was a character from her past life, from the medieval parties with Lee, Rebecca the real estate attorney. Judith called her, explained what she needed, and, even though divorce wasn't her specialty, Rebecca promised to help. Judith thanked her and cried a good long time after the call. She had actually just asked someone to help her start a divorce from Gary—her Prince Gary. The one who had given her hope. The one who had given her safety. The one who loved her like a man should love a woman. The pain was overwhelming.

When the $22,000 was nearly depleted, Judith knew she had to sell the house. She called a woman who had attended her 10th wedding anniversary party, a real estate agent, and asked for help listing the house. She had helped Gary and Judith sell their previous home so Judith trusted her. There was much work to be done, and it wouldn't be easy to sell the "Green River Killer's house," but the friend agreed to take on the challenge.

Judith set to work cleaning the house and, per the suggestion of the real estate agent, began thinning out possessions, throwing out some items and selling others. Gary's aunt and uncle came to buy their wood chipper one weekend. As they stood in the yard, looking down at the piece of equipment, Gary's aunt, a sister to his deceased mother, said, "Well, you know, Judith. It doesn't surprise me that Gary did those awful things. You know he's a lot like his father. That Tom—I never did like him. Mary was too good for him. He was nothin' but a womanizer—seeing prostitutes back when he was a truck driver and all..."

Judith listened silently as Gary's aunt rambled on and on about Tom. After a while, Judith tuned her voice out. Her mind filled with memories of Tom Ridgway, her father-in-law. He had always seemed pleasant enough, rather quiet, but, now that she thought about it, she hadn't exactly been comfortable being alone in a room with him. His humor struck her as kind of, well, odd. And there was that one time she walked alone with him to the mail box and back. He told her some raunchy jokes that she really didn't understand. She laughed along with him, but couldn't wait to get back to the others. Was Gary's aunt telling the truth? Maybe that's why Mary had seemed so angry with Tom at times, especially when he began showing symptoms of Alzheimer's. Mary had been so impatient with him. She yelled at him and called him names. One time Judith had to drive over to her in-law's house and help Mary lift him back into bed after he had fallen to the floor. Mary was fit to be tied that day. Ultimately, Tom had to be transferred to an assisted living facility when Mary could no longer care for him.

The Ridgway dream house went on the market in March of 2002. Judith wondered if anybody would buy a house that the so-called "Green River Killer" had lived in. She doubted it. Maybe it would never sell. Then what would she do? She had to continue making mortgage and insurance payments until it sold.

As Judith started her transition into a new life without her husband, others were planning a new life for Gary. March 28th, 2002, King County Superior Court Judge Richard Jones was selected to hear the complicated Ridgway case. Then April 12th, Judge Jones appointed a special master whose sole responsibility would be to oversee costs for the Ridgway trial that were expected to snowball into unimaginable figures. April 15th, seasoned King County Prosecutor, Norm Maleng, made his announcement at a news conference that he planned to seek the death penalty for Gary Ridgway should he be found guilty.

But Judith was too busy selling the Ridgway possessions to catch the news about any death penalty. And the Baileys, who had been closely monitoring the news, didn't mention it as they helped her organize a huge garage sale. As the sale day progressed, Judith felt certain that the majority of the people came just to get a look at where the "Green River Killer" had lived, the way they were gawking around. Those damn news people had shown their house so many times on the news, especially the view from the helicopter looking down on their house and yard, and that only added to her fears. Who knew what kind of kook would show up?

She urgently wanted to get out of the house. She was keeping all the doors and windows locked, curtains closed on all the windows, and she refused to answer the doorbell. There had even been some vandalism to her front yard. Little statues tipped over. Kids who took a dare to approach the "Green River Killer's" yard, most likely.

Gary's nice friend, Rick, kindly suggested that she rent a room in his house. He had plenty of space since his wife had passed away and all. He helped Judith move the furniture she wanted to keep for herself into a storage unit and then helped her move into his house. But it wouldn't be a peaceful place to live. In the beginning, Rick's mother greeted Judith with a welcoming spirit. But then—overnight it seemed—she told Judith that no woman was going to take the place of her deceased daughter-in-law. She flat told Judith, "You have no business living here with Rick. It's not right. You need to get the *hell* out."

Just like her doctor, this woman appeared to be negatively affected by Judith's mere presence. What was going on? People were judging her! Why was she a bad person?

Rick seemed a bit intimidated by his mother, a strange reminder of how Gary had reacted to Mary's strong opinions when she was alive. In a short time, Judith knew she would need to find another place to live. Meanwhile, Rick was a source of comfort and strength. He was a live body to describe her feelings to and when he held her—like he did more often these days—it felt good. Yes, there was guilt, being a married woman and all, but his arms still felt good around her. It was hard to be strong all the time. And she felt like she was comforting him in his grief. His wife had died of cancer not long ago. For the moment, they were good for each other.

When the tension became too strong between Rick and his mother, Judith put her bedroom furnishings into the storage unit and kept only her clothes and hygiene supplies in her car. Where would she live now? Greg and Dorene said she was welcome to visit them on weekends, but it would be too hard to have her live with them. Since Gary's arrest, Greg and Dorene had been arguing over the case and attorneys and everything else. Having Judith in the house full time, they said, would only add to the stress. Tina and Ed had enough troubles of their own and couldn't take in Judith. Jim and Linda were in the middle of moving themselves, and didn't have anything to offer Judith. And Judith's daughters were each struggling to make ends meet with their children in tiny apartments. No room for mom. Miraculously, a 92-year-old woman, a member of Greg and Dorene's church offered Judith a room in her house. Judith gratefully moved in and struck up a friendship with the sweet woman. Judith had her mail delivered to Greg and Dorene's where she could pick it up when she went for visits. After only two weeks at the elderly woman's home, she was told to get out. The woman's granddaughter was coming to live with her and needed the bedroom that Judith was occupying.

Judith became officially homeless, living out of her car. She drove around during the daytime, pulling over when the crying jags were too intense. She didn't eat much. Then she drove herself to the storage unit when she needed to go inside and change her clothes. As she stood in the musty, damp, dark storage unit, surrounded by boxes filled with her former life, she nearly lost her will to live. She took a mental inventory of where she was: She was alone with no means of supporting herself, she was still responsible for the house until it sold—and the offers weren't coming in—she would run out of money soon, she had no place to live, and she had no hope. She simply could not see a future for herself. Anywhere. It was as if her life were being canceled, deleted like a message on her old answering machine.

Days passed. Judith changed her clothes in the storage unit. She cried in the storage unit. She begged God to help her again in the storage unit. She was getting to the point where she thought she might lie down on the cold floor and never get up when another elderly woman referred to as "Grandma M" heard about Judith's situation and took her in to her home. Judith gratefully stayed with her for three months, enjoying the gentle, nurturing spirit this woman had. They talked about dogs and hairstyles and watched daytime soap operas on television together. Judith began to feel hope again. She was laughing again. She could see that she was bringing some joy to this woman's life as well.

Then one day Judith got an alarming phone call from her mother. "Judith, your father has cancer, and he can't drive. We need you to come live with us and help us. Won't you come, Judith? Please?"

Judith had not considered burdening her parents when she needed a place to live. They were getting older and they were already housing her disabled brother on a very limited income. But her mother didn't drive, and if her father could no longer drive, she would have to go help them. With a disappointed heart, she said goodbye to Grandma M. and moved in with her parents in their doublewide mobile home, in a remote, quiet neighborhood south of Tacoma. Her mother and father moved out of the master bedroom, offering it to Judith as a sign of their appreciation. Awkwardly, they all avoided the subject of Gary and the whole Green River Killer subject. It was just easier that way.

Judith stayed with her parents for the remainder of the year. Except for necessary business calls, she had essentially cut off communication with

Gary. She had accepted in her mind that he was a liar and a cheat. That was fact. And, as a result of that fact, he had broken her heart. But she was still in denial about the killing thing. Gary admitted having a sex addition, but he still vehemently denied being a murderer. And she tended to believe him. Where was the proof that he killed anyone? There was nothing in her history with Gary that, in retrospect, hinted at killer compulsions. Who would know Gary better than his wife? No, dammit, not Gary! This was a guy who loved their Poodles. This was a guy who gently held her grandbabies while she watched Rachel graduate from alternative high school. And this was a guy who had no interest in hunting or fishing. He didn't even want to kill animals for heaven's sake! No. They had to be wrong. She'd wait and see what came out of the trial, but for now, she was certain Gary was no killer.

In September, her divorce was finalized with Gary. She was no longer "Mrs. Gary Ridgway." Judith decided to take her maiden name again: Mawson. That way, she could live with some privacy. Wouldn't have to explain the "Ridgway" thing time and time again.

For now, all she had to do was drive her parents to medical appointments and wait for a phone call from the real estate agent with the news that their home sold. She finally got that call in November, exactly one year from Gary's arrest. The house sold to a couple that moved in from out of state. Apparently they weren't all that concerned about the Green River Killer thing. They loved the house. The sale price was $250,000. According to the divorce agreement, after the mortgage balance was paid, she would receive 60% of the proceeds, with 40% going to Gary (actually Gary's attorneys). After paying the approximately $40,000 mortgage balance and fees, Judith received a check for $104,000. Gary got the remaining $80,000. But his money went straight to his team of attorneys to cover a fraction of what his legal fees would end up being. Greg had hired that well-known defense attorney, Mr. Savage, and he charged big bucks. Greg had told Judith that this guy was their "Perry Mason," and if he couldn't get Gary out of jail, nobody could.

The money brought huge relief to Judith. She had been making the mortgage payments and paying the utilities with money she got from selling their possessions and a check she got from their homeowners insurance. Now she could finally make a move forward. The house was gone. But, quite unexpectedly, the money started a battle between herself and the Ridgways. The first time they asked the question, Judith thought her ears were playing tricks on her.

"Judith," Dorene began matter-of-factly, "you *are* going to donate your house money to Gary's defense fund, right?"

"Huh?" Judith thought she heard wrong. "Yeah," Greg and Dorene's young, blonde daughter chimed in, the granddaughter who had been most favored by Tom and Mary in Judith's opinion, "you're gonna give your money to Uncle Gary, right?" Gary's niece looked at Judith with innocent wonder.

"Wha…what? Why would I do that?"

"Because," Greg said as he authoritatively took control of the conversation, "Gary is going to need all the money we can get to pay for his attorneys. These defense attorneys—they're not cheap. And we've got the best—Savage. Now, I'm sure you'll do the right thing and put your share of the house money in."

"Na-uh. I mean *no*." Judith was still having her mail sent to Greg and Dorene's, just to throw off pranksters. She wasn't expecting this kind of affront when she dropped by to get her mail. "Don't you see? I have to take care *of me* now. Who's gonna take care of *me*?" Anger was choking her throat. She cleared her throat and started again. "My mom and dad don't have no money, I don't have no work skills, I don't have no education, and I have no house now, what do you expect me to *do?*"

"Calm down, Judith. Maybe you can give some of the money and keep some," Greg proposed.

"*No!* I said no! This is not my problem. Why should I have to pay for Gary's lawyers?"

"Because you're his wife," Greg countered.

"No, I'm not—not anymore!"

The next time Judith stopped by for her mail, she was dumbfounded when she discovered that they had changed the locks on their house. The key she had been using no longer fit. Later, she called Greg and Dorene. Dorene answered.

"Why did you change the locks? How am I supposed to get my mail?" Judith was outraged.

"Judith," Dorene began in a patronizing tone, "we can't have you coming here anymore. It's just too upsetting to all of us. Greg told me that if you keep coming around here, we're headed for divorce!"

What was this curse? Why did she have an ill effect on people just by being near them? Divorce? Just from her being around them?

The Ridgways had turned their backs on her apparently because she wouldn't give up her share of the house money. It hurt so much. She didn't understand anything anymore. She felt herself falling down inside a dark, slippery well where stone walls would only echo her terrifying thoughts in a tortuous reverberation. Judith was descending into a deep depression. And nobody was reaching down to help her.

Chapter 7
A Future For Judith

Naked anguish. That's what Linda Bailey saw in her best friend's eyes each time she visited. A dark depression had swallowed up her friend and she wondered how Judith would ever climb out of it.

It was November, 2003, two long years since Gary left the house and never returned. Gary had just pleaded guilty to the murders of 48 women. After he was charged in the beginning of 2003 with aggravated first-degree murder for the deaths of three early Green River Killer victims, he subsequently admitted to his attorneys that he was, in fact, the Green River Killer. King County Prosecutor, Norm Maleng, had already announced the previous year that he intended to seek the death penalty for Gary if he were found guilty. A storm of meetings began between the Prosecutor and Gary's team of attorneys. Then, a surprising and controversial deal was made: Gary Ridgway, a.k.a. The Green River Killer, would be released from the high-security unit of the King County Jail in Seattle and put in the custody of the King County Sheriff's Office. If Gary could take detectives to the places where he had dumped other bodies, and that led to identification of more victims, the Prosecutor's office would negotiate life sentences for Gary instead of death. Families of missing victims suddenly had fresh hope for identification of loved ones. Others were outraged at the weakness shown by the Prosecutor. Nothing short of death would be appropriate for the heartless Green River Killer. Lengthy articles about the Prosecutor's unusual deal with Gary appeared in Seattle newspapers, sparking conversations across Washington State and beyond.

Amazingly, Gary's new location was kept secret from everyone except for those directly involved in questioning and guarding him. Five months later, the public would learn that he had been housed in a small room at the Task Force office headquarters near Boeing Field. Detectives questioned Gary for weeks and finally put him in a van and told him to take them to other places he had dumped bodies. Gary first directed them to Highway 410 near Enumclaw, where he and Judith had gone camping and motorcycle riding many times. Pammy Avent's remains were found. In the same month, Gary calmly led detectives to the Snoqualmie Pass, East of Seattle, just off Interstate 90, where the remains of April Dawn Buttram still lay, twenty years after her disappearance. The next month, Gary delivered again when he directed his guards to Auburn's West Hill, near his and Judith's dream home, and pointed out the remains of Marie Malvar at the bottom of a very steep ravine.

The drama played out, day by day, on the Seattle television news. Where would they take the killer next? How many more bodies would be found? Judith watched her television in horror as she saw her ex-husband, dressed in one-piece coveralls and a baseball cap on his head, shackles on his wrists and ankles, stepping out of an unmarked, window-less van, surrounded by detectives, heading into wooded areas to find yet another set of remains.

"How could that *guy* be the same man I was married to for fourteen years?" she asked Linda again and again as they sat together, holding hands and watching the television news. "I mean—this man held my lit-tle grandbabies on his lap as we watched my daughter graduate from high school. And when I told him I might have to fight for custody of my older daughter's children when she was going through a bad time, he was all for it. He would've let my grandchildren *come live* with us!"

Linda nodded sympathetically as her friend went on, jumping from memory to memory in no special order.

"And that time at the KMPS picnic for country music listeners—out there at the King County Fairgrounds in Enumclaw—we sat there in the warm sun together, so happy, clapping and listening to country music—our favorite—and how could I know that man was a killer?"

"I know honey, you had no way of knowing." Linda patted the back of Judith's hand.

"This is the same man who offered to *vacuum* for me when my back was hurting too bad." Tears returned again. "Linda, I—I—remember when we made love, it was so special. He made me feel like a new bride every time. And now—I find out he's a killer! *That bastard!*" Judith shrieked as Linda moved in close to hug her. Linda held her as she sobbed and released the turbulent emotions that had been building over the past months.

"I know honey, I know." Linda cooed.

"That awful man—the one who killed all those poor girls—he was my hero! He was *everything* to me." More sobbing. "Linda, I never told you this before, but one day when I was cleaning out the garage in our old house, I found some condoms that Gary hid out there. I totally lost it! I just took an axe and started chopping on everything around me."

"Oh, Judith, no."

"All I could think about was my husband out having sex with those prostitutes and I hated him! I chopped and chopped until I couldn't do it anymore." Judith sobbed hysterically into her hands. After several moments she raised her head and looked into Linda's face and said with a voice nearly drained of energy, "When I realized he really was seeing prostitutes all those years, that was the worst pain I *ever* felt. But now, hearing Gary admit that he killed women...so...many women...I don't know how to live." Judith pressed her hands against both sides of her head. "My brain can't understand how the man I loved could be the *same* man who did those things."

Linda figured she would be holding her friend for a long time that night.

She had been making regular visits to Judith, hoping each time to see some improvement in the debilitating effects of the depression. Linda racked her brain for ideas to help her suffering friend.

Judith had moved in with her parents in 2002 in order to help her stepfather during a medical crisis. At the same time, the Ridgway dream home had been emptied and put up for sale. After her stepfather's medical situation improved, her parents vacated their doublewide mobile home in Pierce County and left it for Judith to use.

She had been living alone in the musty, dark-paneled mobile home with curtains closed and doors locked for the past year, and inside this structure is where she met the depths of her depression. Nights had been fraught with terrifying nightmares. Days had been cold, silent, and lonely. At times she felt like she was losing her mind to paranoid thoughts. *I wonder what people are saying about me? What if they find out where I live? Would they want to harm me?* As Judith stared out a crack in the curtains, wondering if any of the neighbors knew who she was, she thought *how strange, I'm a prisoner too — like Gary. I can't go anywhere.*

She tried to explain her feelings to Linda.

"But why do you care if somebody sees you?" Linda had asked pointedly.

"Because, Linda, don't you *get* it? People probably think I'm bad too — like Gary. People must think that I should have known what he was doing — that I should have done something to stop him."

"Oh honey, it's not your fault. You're talking crazy now. You didn't do anything!"

"I know, but I feel so bad. I feel so bad for all those families..." And that's the way all of their conversations had ended lately. Judith had assumed she was judged as being equally as horrible as her husband, and if she dared to go out, surely someone would spot her and curse at her for not stopping the monster earlier.

Judith saw the monster's face for the last time on television when he was in court on November 5th of 2003, pleading "guilty" 48 times for 48 murders in King County (he had admitted to detectives that there were probably more but he couldn't remember them) in a low, soft-spoken voice. Judge Richard Jones allowed ten minutes each for any family members of victims who wished to address the Green River Killer in court. Judith was gripped by the different tones that family members used when speaking to Gary. He sat still during the entire process, turning his head sharply and looking over his right shoulder to better see the people talking to him. As they read from prepared statements, most threw curses of damnation toward Gary, telling him they hoped he would rot in Hell and suffer as much as their loved ones had. Judith watched Gary's face remain firm, expressionless, as he listened again and again as people described how he had devastated their family. When one father of a victim told Gary that he had forgiven him for what he'd done, Gary's composure crumbled. His lips trembled, tears leaked out of his eyes and ran down his cheeks, and he wiped his dripping nose.

When it was over, Gary was escorted out of the courtroom. He was back again on December 18th when Judge Jones sentenced him to 48 life sentences to be served in Walla Walla State Penitentiary, a high security prison in central Washington, about three hours from Seattle. No possibility of parole for the Green River Killer.

Judith believed she would never hear from Gary again as she struggled to see some future in her life. But Gary wasn't ready to let go. He regularly wrote letters to Judith in pencil on lined paper. When the first one showed up in her mailbox, she carried it in the house and laid it on the dining room table. She took a few steps backward and stared at it. Dozens of conflicting feelings were whizzing through her. *Gary, honey, I miss you. I wonder how you are. Are you eating?* Then, *You creep!! You killed innocent girls and women. I hate you for what you've done and for ruining my life!* For days Judith left the unopened envelope on her table, glancing at it each time she walked by, sickened.

When the unopened letter became a stack of unopened letters, she decided to open one and try to read some. She was curious about what he might have written. Still, she wasn't sure she could do it. She was feeling spooked by recent phone calls from local reporters and producers for national magazine shows. The calls were so similar they blurred in her memory. "Hello, Mrs. Ridgway? I'm so-and-so from something-something news. Mrs. Ridgway, I understand how traumatic these past few years have been for you, but I'm wondering if I could do a story about you?"

How did they find me? "Uh-umm, no. I'm not ready to talk to anybody." She quickly ended the connections before they had a chance to say more.

One day she heard footsteps on the front porch followed by a doorbell ring. *Who in the world could that be?* Her heart was racing. She waited until the footsteps left and a car backed out of the driveway. She waited a few more minutes, just to be sure. Slowly she opened the front door and gasped when she saw a large, colorful, expensive bouquet of flowers on her front porch? *Oh, how sweet! Somebody sent me flowers.* Immediately she stiffened her body and felt cold. *Nobody knows I'm living here except for Linda and a few others.* She opened the card with the flowers, read it, and covered her mouth with the other hand. She recognized the name of the television show—one that specialized in gossipy, scandalous stories about celebrities. They sent her flowers. The card read, "When you're feeling better, maybe we can talk." *How did they find me?*

Judith raced for the phone and called Linda, babbling her terror in one, never-ending sentence that was incomprehensible at the other end.

"Judith, now settle down," Linda coaxed.

More panicked babble.

"Judith, listen to me. Okay, hold on. Jim and I are coming over."

That was the pattern for months: Jim and Linda racing over to see Judith and calm her hysteria as different events upset her. Sometimes it was something she saw on the TV news. Other times it was a phone message left on her answering machine. She began to turn over any paperwork that needed attention to Jim. Anything beyond eating and sleeping was overwhelming to her. If there was any kind of decision to make, she was on the phone to Jim and Linda for advice.

Linda noticed that Judith's hands shook when she tried to explain what had upset her. She also noticed little wounds all over her hands where she had apparently been picking at her flesh. She wondered if Judith had been abusing wine.

"Judith, honey. How about seeing your doctor again? See if he can give you something for your nerves?"

"Yeah, maybe I should." Judith promised to make an appointment.

In the car on the way home, Jim remarked to Linda, "I think it could go either way. Either she'll get it together, or she'll completely go off the deep end."

"I know. When I went to the refrigerator to get Judith a bottle of water, I saw a box of wine in there." They agreed to keep Judith in their nightly prayers. She was going to need all the help she could get to recover from the disgusting truth about Gary and losing the love of her life.

Jim and Linda stayed in close touch with Judith, giving encouragement, advice, and, inasmuch as possible, hope. Finally, in early 2004, entering the third year since her husband was taken away, Judith worked up the courage to read a letter from Gary. She opened the oldest letter according to post-marks on the envelopes. She was only able to read a portion of it before tears blurred her vision:

"1-1-04.

Dear Judith,

I am very sorry for hurting you. I didn't mean to. I'm sorry I lied to you so many times.

I was told by Sue Peters (they taped it) that you weren't going to wright to me. I was told by Dave Reichert (they taped that to) you had meet someone you cared for. I don't want to stand in your way of starting new. I don't want you to be sad anymore.

The day of me pleading Guilty. They arranged a meeting with _____. That Saturday I sat with them in a room and we hugged. I needed you there so much. I cried most of the time. I did some bad things. I hurt a lot of people. Most of all I hurt you, I'm sorry. 1985? I made a prayer to God, I will stop killing if I don't get caught. I had to live with all that in me all those years. I couldn't tell you. I was like a alcoholic dry for a time. Then fell of the wagon. I miss you so much.

Why did God let me do these things. Why didn't he kill me.

I asked Sue Petters if I could see you. I had to see you, hug you just one more time. I don't think she ever tried. Ask for your forgiveness. All I got from her was a cold shoulder.

Judith I needed you there to know I was doing the right thing. I feel I let a lot of people down.

God had to be there to get me through that. They call me evil, the devil, mad, monster, satin and others.

Right before my sentencing they arranged a meeting with _____ again. I was so mad I couldn't see you. I cried so much. I would have been able to kiss and hug you, for the last time of our life."

Judith placed the partially-read letter on the table, visualizing Gary's face, warm tears falling down her face. She imagined Gary sobbing for her, wanting her—just like she had sobbed for him so many nights. *He still loves me.* After a few minutes she read more:

"Why didn't Sue Petters ask you to come. I think it because of punishing me. They think I'm holding back or something. But I am not. It means so much to me. Judith I'm sorry. Sense the 18th they have me on suicide watch. They come by every fifteen minutes to monetor me. Everyday they have a head shrink come ask me if I am going to hurt myself, or others. Why am I here. I long to hold you, look in your face to say goodbye. I well never touch, kiss, or hug you. It hurts so much.

Do you think God will forgive me. I don't even forgive myself.

You were the best wife, lover, and mother I ever had. I blow it. I needed help and couldn't find any. I'm sorry for what I did, it was wrong. But I had you and didn't want to lose you. Maybe I am evil, a madman, the devil, and a monster. I prayed so much for the ladies I killed. I prayed for you. To find someone who could take care of you. I did a bad job of that.

Why can't I quit cring. I have a part of my heart missing. I can't seam to keep it together. Judith why didn't Sue Petter get you to see me. Just one last time.

Is it better to have loved and lost it. Than to have never love.

God forgives sinner. Will he ever forgive me.

Love You, Gary L. Ridgway"

Judith sat on a chair at the dining room table, looking at the remaining unopened letters in the pile. *I'm so confused. I hate him and I love him.* She pushed back from the table with her arms and walked away, vowing to not read any more letters. It was too hard.   Curiosity   brought   her back to the table only a few days later. She opened several more letters. They were similar in terms of Gary missing her, Gary being apologetic, and Gary describing his new life in prison. But some passages jumped up off the paper and had the effect of slapping in her in the face:

"Before going to bed, put a little aftershave on my pillow. Hold it close to you heart. I love you. It well help you sleep better…when you mail me a letter, please put a little perfume on it. It well remind me of you. I will keep it close, and smell it before going to bed at night. When my emotions are down it will bring back good memories of how much you mean to me…Find out did I get fired or terminated from Kenworth? With 30 plus years of service you would think they would have a thank you letter…"

I guess I could write back to him. Maybe it would be good for me—tell him what I've been going through. Judith wrote a letter to Gary in slow, deliberate cursive. But, as she wrote, she found herself editing, telling him only about how she was dealing with money and disposing of his things. A thick wall had grown around her heart, not allowing any deep, personal feelings escape into the letter.

Gary quickly wrote back:

"1-30-04

Hi. I just received your letter last night. Thank you for getting the will power to write me.

I sent all your photos back to you. They would have gotten misplaced if the jail had them, to send me here. I had to tear up all phone numbers and addresses. I didn't want any inmate any chance to get anything…Judith, I just love you so much. I don't want any more hurt for you. What's going to happen in one or two years. You fall in love with some other person. It seems to me it will tear your heart out more. Do you really want to write anymore. I read your letter. It looks to me you are happy with your self. By writing me doesn't it hurt to know all the hell I put you through…Judith I married you for life. I am so sorry I broke your heart. Judith we <u>had</u> a real good life.

I love you always,

Gary L. Ridgway"

A few weeks later, Judith wrote him back. Again, she was guarded in her writing. Very quickly Gary returned a letter:

"2-14-04

I just received one letter from you. Just think in a couple of days I will be double nickels (code for age 55)…I did not push you away when I said we needed a devorce. It was to protect you. I did not want to disown you for changing your name. I did it because I loved you and wanted you safe. You mean the world to me…"

Judith ferociously plucked at the skin of one hand with the fingernails of her other hand. *What do I do? What do I do? He still loves me and he always tries to protect me. Idiot! He's the Green River Killer.*

"2-8-04. Hi Judith. How are you doing? I hope you are fine. Did you get my last letter?"

This is too hard.

"2-26-04. Dear Judith. I am sorry for the last letter I wrote to you. I will not stop writing to you until you stop me..."

He's going to keep writing to me. Judith ignored his letters for a while.

"4-2-04 Hi Judith. I have not received any letters this week. I was praying I could get one letter every week or every other week. I should be just happy with what I got..."

It feels like he's pressuring me to write back. What if I don't want to?

"4-24-04 Hi Judith. How are you doing. Have you sent any letters in the mail. I haven't received any from you or anybody else either...Have you written me this month. Because I have not received any mail from you. Maybe someone is taken my mail or put it in the trash can. Judith I ask this a while ago. Do you forgive me for all the hurt I caused people. I am sorry for all the hurt, pain and emotion problems I caused you. I gave you some time to think about it. I am not saying it will be like before all this happened. Because it would not be. Forgiving me does not mean forgetting what I did. It is not excusing me for what I did. In Matthew 6:14 For if you forgive men their sins, your heavenly Father will also forgive you. But if you do not forgive their sins, neither will your Father forgive your sins..."

He's telling me I have to forgive him now. Well, maybe I'm not ready to do that!

"4-26-04 Hi Judith. I Just received your letter. Thank you very much for writing back to me. Is that the only one you mailed me. I haven't been getting any mail for about 2 ½ weeks...Judith what type of Church would you like to go to. Try to get dressed up, find out what time there services are. And go set in the back. Maybe try that for one or two times. Its kind of like going to the mall and watching people...take courses in music or something you always wanted to do. How about teach some young children how to read and right. Kids need a role model. Judith you have talents. How about doing income taxes. Its only at this time of the year. Help out with a little extra money..."

I think he wants me to move on. Do something. Judith noticed that Gary's letters were getting longer. Several pages now, front and back. And, recently all his letters included Bible quotes.

"5-9-05. Judith please read Luke 12:22-34. It will help you about stress and worrying about your life. You are in the right time place to grow closer to God...Always make God #1 in your life. "Happy Mothers Day.""

June 2004. Dear Judith. How are you doing. I hope the sun is shinning on you. It has calmed down here. I have all new Offenders except l and 3 cells. They are calm must of the time.
I hear Linda wants to take you on a small vacation this summer. That sounds good. I think if they still have Leisure Time that would be great too. Like a week at Cascade Resort or Paradise Resort...I will send you a Positive Thinking pamphelet by Norman Vincent Peale. You can also visit their website. This one is on You Can Start Over Again. It is real nice so I thought you might like it. It should help you get closer to God..."

"6-17-04. Hi Judith. Judith when we had it all it wasn't enough. I am very sorry for us. We built our future on sand. We needed Jesus Christ in our hearts more. With a strong Christian life, Church, people, prayer and fellow ship with God. I know we would have been better off. Strong to go through this.
Now we are like strangers living day to day. I hear and see the loneliness here. Its hard to really fell love and other fellings.
I can see your moods in your writings to me. It brings sadness to my soul. That I am the cause of all the pain I inflicked on you.
I am sorry for all those letters I write to you asking for Forgiveness. You may never say it to me. I know life is hard on you. Forgiveness comes from your heart..."

Judith began leaving the house, driving directly to Jim and Linda's house, often staying with them for several days in the guest room, and then driving straight home. It felt good to be with people who cared about her. It felt good to get out of that depressing house.

"7-24-04. Hi Judith. I hear the temperture is pretty hot over there. How hot does it get in your home. Do you have A/C in there or do you need it. How is your car doing. All cars have to turn on their

A/C's a couple times a year to get it to work. I think it says that in the owners manual. I'm sending you some Bible verses…"

He still worries about me and the car. As the Seattle air warmed with the longer summer days, so did Judith's heart. She noticed that she was feeling more cheerful. She made more visits to Jim and Linda's house.

In August Judith received a real birthday card from Gary. He had told her in a previous letter that they pass out cards for the inmates to use.

"Happy Birthday Judith. Peace for your soul. Joy for your spirit. Love for your heart. Hope for your future. Gary L. Ridgway."

That was nice of him to send me a birthday card! And it was a pretty fun birthday. I think I'm doing better, feeling stronger. And it sounds like Gary is getting comfort from the Bible. Good for him.

"8-28-04 Emergency Phone Numbers. When in sorrow call John 14. When people fail you call Psalm 27. When you want to be fruitful call John 15. When you have sinned call Psalm 51…" It went on to be a four page letter.

You know, if I keep writing to Gary, it's like we're staying connected. I don't think that's good for me. He's never getting out of there. As long as I stay connected, I'm stuck with him in the past.

The last letter from Gary was dated 12-4-04:

"Dear Judith. This letter is long overdue. I have spent a lot of time on this. I read books to get words to say to you. I prayed ask all kinds of questions. The answers are not in books. It comes from the heart. No book has it and never will. Mat 5:23, 24.
I am sorry for all the hurt I caused you.
I am sorry for killing all those young women.
I am sorry for ruining so many victims families and their friends lives.
I am sorry for all the wrong paths I took in my life, hurting Matthew so much. I am sorry I lied so much to you. Causing so much pain and health problems in your life. For betraying you and losing your trust. I am sorry for blaming all my problems on other people in my life. Hurting family. I am sorry for the tax payers paying for all the bills during all the years. All the Police, Prosecutors, Attorneys, Psychologists and everbody else involved.

I hurt and killed a lot of Gods children. I have sinned against the Creator. I hope someday you can forgive me. I am sorry for not getting this letter out to you before this time. I pray I did not leave out anything. I hope you will know this comes from my heart.
God Bless you take care,
Gary"

Judith neatly re-folded the letter, tucked it in the envelope, and put the envelope with the other dozens of letters she had bundled together with rubber bands, sorted by month and year.

It's still hard for me to get through each day. But I am getting out of the house a bit now, going to the store and to the bank, and I have some nice people who care about me. I think it's time to let go. Think about it— he's never gonna get out of there. Even if he did, we wouldn't be the same. He killed people. I would be afraid of him. But I'll always love him.

When Judith made the decision to let go of Gary in her heart, she tapped into a new well of strength. Now she was a single woman. Suddenly, she realized she had important matters to take care of. Business things. Papers to fill out. Letters and calls to answer. Bills to pay. She sat up straight and felt energized just thinking about all the things she had to do. As she looked around her mobile home she thought *time to paint over this dark paneling with some nice, bright paint. And I could move that piece of furniture over there to open up that wall, and I could put up some new pictures on the wall, and—I know! How about some new throws over the living room sofa? That would be nice.*

I need to learn how to use a computer, start eating better, lose some weight...

Chapter 8
Best Friends of The Ridgways

A note from the author:

In my earliest conversations with Judith, it quickly came to my attention that Mr. and Mrs. Ridgway had a close relationship with another couple—the kind of relationship people commonly refer to as "best friends." These best friends, Jim and Linda Bailey, were among the few who had attended the Ridgway wedding on the front lawn of Gary's next-door neighbors, had remained friends throughout the entire marriage, stood firmly by Judith's side after the arrest in 2001, and, perhaps longer than anyone else, believed in Gary's innocence until his stunning confession in 2003.

I spent a day with Jim and Linda, asking them questions that stirred up feelings of shock, pain, anger, and disappointment in humankind on the deepest level.

Jim and Linda welcomed me into their home in Maple Valley, Washington. The reason I remember the day so clearly is because it was one those treasured, blue-sky, hot summer days that are rare in the Seattle area. With cool drinks arranged on the dining room table, the Baileys' well-fed Cocker Spaniel, "Serenity," watched intently from the floor, and their disabled, adult son, "Timmy," observed curiously from his wheelchair as we all sat down to talk about a painful subject.

Jim and Linda first took a few minutes to explain how they had been holding their feelings about Gary inside for a very long time, and that they believed they were finally ready to talk. They hadn't been able to before. Linda emanated the energy of a nurse who had seen much in her life—the kind of nurse who wouldn't tolerate any nonsense from her patients. She crossed her strong arms in a defensive pose across her stocky torso and waited for her turn to speak. Jim struck me as the more sensitive one. With a quiet countenance, he stared down at his clasped hands that were resting on the table as he slowly shook his head side to side, as if to say he still couldn't believe what Gary had done.

I waited. Finally, Jim and Linda looked nervously at one another, cleared their throats, took several sips of water, and then began:

Author: Jim, Linda, today I'd like to ask you about how you met Judith and Gary Ridgway and what your relationship was like with them. Please tell me how you met.

Jim: The first time I met Gary Ridgway was back in 1980 when I went to work for Kenworth at the Seattle location. At that time, I didn't know him well at all. I just knew who Gary Ridgway was. They always called him "Wrongway Ridgway." Usually the other people who were in the tape design area where he was. They said he always did tape designs the "wrong way," but I always found him to be doing them the right way and they were the ones who were wrong. They said it behind his back. It was like everybody knew that Gary was just a little bit off the bubble, but he always did his job.

I was a painter's helper at that time. I got laid off in the first part of 1981 (from Kenworth) and didn't go back to work there until late '82. At that time, I started back in the plastic shop. I started painting back there and moved up front in 1983. That's when I really got to know Gary because that's when I worked next to him. I was going through a training program. He taught me how to tape, do layout design, and sometimes painting. He spent some time painting but he was usually the layout design person who did most of the taping and painting of designs on the trucks.

Author: So, he was in a more senior position than you were at Kenworth?

Jim: Yes. I was working under him.

Author: How long do you think he'd been working at Kenworth at that point?

Jim: About fourteen years, probably. It was about 1969 when he first started there. Then he went into the service. Then he came out and went back to work for Kenworth.

Author: What was Gary like to work with? Was he loud or quiet?

Jim: He was okay. He was always telling jokes. They were kind of 'off-color' jokes, strange, little jokes. They were one-liners.

Author: Were they sexual jokes?

Jim: No. No. I don't ever remember him saying...I've never heard Gary cuss...not once.

Author: Not even among guys at work?

Jim: I was never around him when he did. If he did, it was with other people. I've never heard it. His language was clean and he told silly jokes, you know, one-line jokes. Like 'do you know why…' then he'd give you the punch line.

Author: Kind of like 'do you know why the chicken crossed the road'?

Jim: Yes, that's it! It would always be some kind of dufey answer.

Author: Did Gary strike you as a smart man?

Jim: He had a memory that amazed me. His memory impressed me because he could remember designs that he had taped 5-6 years ago and nobody else could! And he'd remember the measurements on them. You have a particular measurement on the hood to lay out a design and he would always remember that and somebody else would say, "No, you're wrong" and he'd say, "Well go get the blueprint," and they'd get the blueprint and Gary was right.

Author: Most people, when they go to lay out a design to paint a truck, do they typically have to refer to blueprints?

Jim: Yes.

Author: That sort of impressed you?

Jim: Yes and no. Anybody who had been doing that job for a long period of time was pretty good at that. He wasn't the only one. But Les Stevens was the only guy who had it on Gary when it came to taping and remembering. But Gary was the 'go-to' guy for everyone. When they wanted to know something about a design on a truck, they would go ask him. That's where they always sent me. "Go work with Gary if you need anything…ask him."

Author: So, he had a reputation as having a good memory?

Jim: Yes. And hard working. Dependable. Always there. On time. Never smoked. I've never seen him…I can't remember him taking a day off work for anything. He used to get perfect attendance awards. I never knew him to be sick. They gave away perfect attendance awards down there for 1 year without missing a day and every year he was getting them. I think he had 4-5 years in a row perfect attendance.

Author: What was the award?

Jim: Jacket or dinner or…yes…several years in a row.

Author: Did you like Gary?

Jim: Sure. Him and I together would turn out more production than most people so we worked well together.

Author: Did Gary talk about anything other than work?

Jim: Camping…umm…retirement…that's about all. Contracts … because we both got involved in union stuff … only I became shop steward and he started going to union meetings, maybe because of me, I don't know. He started going to meetings about that time in 1985. That's when I became shop steward and he went to meetings and that's the way it stayed until about 1988-89. But during the time when he was taken in for questioning in, I think, 1987?—it was a pretty trying time. That's when a lot of people at Kenworth saw him as being guilty before he was ever pronounced guilty. I was a shop steward at that time and had to go around and tell everyone that he wasn't guilty, not yet, and so don't pronounce him that way. So when he came back to work, everybody just thought, fine, nothing to it. Went along for another year or two and nothing happened, so we figured great.

Author: Tell me everything you remember about that day when you said police came to work in 1987.

Jim: I was working out back, there's a place called "touch up" in back, and Gary was up front. It wasn't too long before quitting time, it might have been about 2:00 in the afternoon, and someone called me and told me. By the time I got up front, Gary was gone, cops were gone. They'd opened up his locker and took everything out of it, and I went into Personnel to see what was going on, and they told me Gary had been taken in for questioning.

Author: At that time you were the shop steward?

Jim: Yes, in addition to my regular duties.

Author: That's not like a job all of its own?

Jim: No, no. That's just an intermediate union type position, union representative. I think it was like a week later, maybe 4 days, when they released his truck, and I took him to get his truck. He asked me. Nobody else. He asked me.

Author: Took him where?

Jim: To the impound area. The police impound area. They had damaged his truck. They dropped a hook and chains on it when they towed it in.

Author: What kind of truck?

Jim: Ford pickup. It was brown at that time and it had been painted from green to brown, half-ton pickup, and on the way to get that truck I asked Gary—point-blank—at that time if he had anything to do with any of these murders or any of these women and he said no. I said o.k. I believed him a hundred percent.

Author: He seemed believable?

Jim: Yes.

Author: Did you think they had the wrong guy?

Jim: Well, you know, I knew they had taken in that other guy, that taxi driver, and I knew there was another guy they were looking at and I said, "Sounds to me like it's a case where they can't know who did it because they're looking at so many different people and they had been for a period of time." I took him at his word. I figured it must be one of those other people, or they'll find out. Well, as time went on, and they never did find out, I figured it couldn't possibly have been him (Gary).

Author: So, you think from that day forward the co-workers at Kenworth came to their own conclusions?

Jim: Yeah. Absolutely.

Author: Did you consider that harassment?

Jim: Sure, sure. Saying untrue things, something that hasn't been proven, sure. They could lose their jobs over it. I wouldn't want anyone to get to that point.

Author: Did any workers receive warnings?

Jim: No, just from me verbally.

Author: Everyone just sort of cooled it after you went around and said their talk wasn't appropriate?

Jim: Right.

Author: Do you think that people treated Gary differently anyway?

Jim: Umm...I couldn't tell. I still maintained my position in the back, so I didn't get to work up front around Gary anymore. Matter of fact, for the next three years I didn't work up front much anymore. And for all intents and purposes, he'd come back every once in a while or I'd go up front. We'd talk and we'd go through details about trucks that had been painted or laid out wrong or whatever, just to get to the bottom of how it really needed to be done. It was problem-solving stuff, probably 2-3 times per week, like one-half hour, but then every third Thursday of the month we would go to the union meetings together. That's about it. After he and Judith got married, we'd go out and eat a couple of times but it wasn't like if was an every month thing.

Author: So, when you were working together, before you knew Judith and Gary as a couple, would you call him just a co-worker, or would you call him a friend?

Jim: He was a co-worker. I don't know about the friend thing until probably 1985 or '86 when I really started to think we would go places and do things together if it ever came up. But we didn't. No, it wasn't like we rode to work together.

Author: You never commuted to work together. Did you eat lunch together?

Jim: Not very often. He usually brought his lunch to work. Didn't stop off after work. I never did that. I went straight home after work.

Author: What shift were you working then?

Jim: Day shift. 6:00 am to 3:00 pm. The next one is second shift, 3-12. They very seldom had a third shift down there.

Author: Did you go home and talk to Linda about this guy that was on the news?

Jim: Oh, sure. Well, I know I mentioned about people at work who would say certain things. A couple of them in particular I would tell her that they go with the wind anyway. Whichever way the tree blows, that's the way they're going to go, so, you know, I didn't put much stock in that. I remember one time she asked me, "Well, what if he is guilty?" I said, "Well, then I imagine they would arrest him."

Author: Jim, when did you first meet Judith? At their wedding?

Jim: I met Judith before Gary did. That was back in 1984? At the hospital. My mother was in the hospital (Valley Medical Center, Renton, Washington) and Judith was in the same hospital visiting her daughter, Marie, because her husband or boyfriend had roughed her up. And then he threw her off a balcony. The elevator door opened up and she (Judith) just fell into my arms. My mother was there because of a car accident and I was standing there at the elevator door. The door opened, and I see a woman standing there and, man, she looked awful! I just put my arms out and caught her. We went out and sat around the water fountain and talked for about 30 minutes probably. She was a wreck.

Then, years later, I met Judith at the Kenworth union dinners and open houses, between 1985 and 1988. Gary introduced her to everybody. He introduced her to Linda and me. I didn't recognize her right at that time. You know, I don't know when I actually remembered her from the hospital. But I said, "That's the same lady I saw on the elevator!" I had to tell Judith that I was that guy on the elevator. I know if was after they got married that I told her. But I'm certain I realized it before that.

There was this time we went to dinner at Coco's Restaurant with Gary and Judith and at that time, a car followed us. Gary says, "Do you know who they are?" He told me the police were following him when the ladies weren't listening.

That's when we talked about, later in life, we'd travel around, after we retired, and do all that RV stuff. He knew the police were following him. I believed him because the guys sat in that car the whole time we were eating.

Author: Did you feel creepy hanging out with him if you knew police were following him?

Jim: Yes, I did. And eventually they quit doing it. So I said, "There you go, he's innocent." Kenworth built a new plant in Renton in 1993. Gary went to the new plant. They laid off certain workers and sent some to Renton.

Author: You went to Renton too?

Jim: No, I was in the business representative job in 1990. I quit working for Kenworth in 1990 and went to the business rep's job. In 1991 or 1992, during that period of time, Gary was my shop steward and at one time or another and then he got on the Executive Board in 1992 or 1993 for the union and he came to every meeting, went to all the functions. He and Judith would go to the Christmas dinners and whatever else we had. There were times when we had trustees meetings that Gary came to because he was a trustee on the board. Those meetings, none of the women came.

Author: Do you think he went home late after those meetings?

Jim: Union meetings didn't normally start until 7:00 pm. So he would get off work at 3:00 pm. He had all that time. Meetings were usually at the Labor Temple, lst Avenue in Seattle.

Author: He had a good attendance record at the meetings?

Jim: Oh yeah, never missed a meeting. Always had a good, positive input. Was always part of the team.

Author: So, when did your relationship with Gary go from co-worker to friends?

Jim: That's probably 1989, right? Not too long after they got married. I was his best man as I was kind of the only one he talked to. Other people at work weren't very polite to him.

Author: Tell me about the wedding.

Linda speaking for the first time: I remember somebody saying something like they felt sorry for Gary and Judith because not very many people showed up that were invited from Kenworth.

Jim: Yeah, he invited everybody at work in the paint shop and that's like sixty people, and only a tiny percentage came.

Author: Did Gary make any comments about that?

Jim: No.

Author: What was your involvement in the wedding?

Linda: Jim was the best man. I just kind of watched. It was nice and everybody seemed to be happy and talking to everybody. It was real nice outside. June 12th. It was a nice, warm day outdoors. I loved the color of her dress. Pretty color. They acted happy. Judith was the one who was more affectionate. You could tell, with Gary, she would always go up to him and put her arms around him and, you know, like she does. At that time I had in the back of my head all the things that had happened (the arrest) and I watched him and really observed him to see how affectionate he was with her. And he wasn't very mushy, he never got mushy.

Even when we'd go to dinners or something she'd get up and be all excited and he would tell her to calm down.

He was real quiet. He wasn't affectionate. Even then he would tell jokes. He's always havin' those little, quick, quacky jokes. He had me laughin' at the dinners because he'd come off with the jokes. Every time I was around him, he'd always pull out the chair for me and for Judith and he was always very polite. It was fresh in my mind when they got married. Later it wasn't bad. I noticed how he didn't like public displays of affection.

Jim: He never talked about sports, not once. He had a week off for the honeymoon, I remember that. I think they went down to the ocean?

Author: After they were married, how often did you see them?

Linda: We'd go to their garage sales and they'd come to our garage sales.

Jim: Every couple of months or so, we'd have something going on. Linda had those home interior parties and Judith would come.

You know, I just got this flashback about the night that I was...this had to be 1983 or 1984...me and this friend of mine had a little mechanics business, and I was delivering a car at the cemetery, they owned a flower shop right there up on Highway 99, right down from the airport and Gary saw me that night. Well, I had come around the back way past the cemetery, and that's where he was at. I delivered that car and picked up mine that I had left there and, yeah, he said, "What were you doing up there last night?" I didn't ask him, I just thought, it was dark, he saw me and I didn't see him, it wasn't a union meeting.

Author: Did you think that was weird?

Jim: Yeah, because, you know, I wasn't up there for anything other than delivering a car and I wasn't there long enough for anyone to see me, so I think he actually saw me on 99 which is where he used to do all his pick-up's. I didn't make the connection until later on. I think he said he was up there helping a friend. I thought that was strange (at a cemetery). And I remember the time that he came to work with a bandage on his arm. At that time he said somebody's transmission hose busted and he got hot fluid on it, but later on the reason was that he'd been scratched by a victim.

He told Judith that a car had caught on fire that he was working on.

Author: He told you that he was fixing someone's car?

Jim: Yes, well, they were stopped along a road and the transmission broke and when he stuck his arm up under there, the fluid ran down his arm and burned him.

Author: Like he was a good Samaritan helping?

Jim: Yes, exactly. It was all bandaged up. He still came to work though.

Author: So, you saw each other every couple of months to go to garage sales, go out to meals, and you went to union meetings and sort of special things and award ceremonies?

Jim: Every three months we had a trustee's meeting which he would come to, or every quarter... and then any special meetings that were called. Sometimes in July we'd cancel regular meetings if they were close to the 4th or on a holiday or something like that so we wouldn't have them, but we'd have the executive board meeting. Everybody might come at 6:30 pm and then it's all over.

Judith said he'd get home those nights between 10:00 pm and midnight, saying he'd gone out for something to eat after the meeting. I never went out with him before or after meetings.

Author: Gary had a history with you of being good at his job, reliable, dependable, someone you could count on, and the thing with the police...nothing else after that. How would you sum up your opinion of him?

Jim: Before his arrest...he was someone that I probably would have run around with after we retired. We had plans to go camping together. It just never happened. Him and I talked about that a lot. Oregon, Northern California, in that area and he said he'd like to go down there. He never talked about going back east anywhere.

Author: And, Linda, what did you think about Gary?

Linda: Weird. I just thought he was strange. I mean—he was comical and he never hurt your feelings or nothing but I'd say to Jim, "He's weird."

Jim: Yes, she has said that to me.

Linda: Because his personality wasn't real upbeat. He wasn't...he was just different. He just...some of his jokes he would tell...he turned on and off real fast. He'd be up one minute and then the next he's off. He never mistreated me. I never really thought too much about going on trips with him. That was more the guys.

I remember Gary and Judith saying they picked up little things when they went camping, arts and crafts.

Jim: Gary could have retired at age 55. When he was arrested in 2001, he only had 3 more years to go. He was 52 when he was arrested.

Linda: Judith told me sometimes when her and him would go camping they loved to go out in the woods and make love. And they loved the Greenwater area. I can't imagine him being like that and then doing the things he did. That's the difference. I guess he treated her (Judith) with compassion and then he was another way with those other women.

Author: When did you guys find out that Gary was arrested and they thought he was the Green River Killer?

Linda: It come on the tv news and Jim and I were just shocked!

Jim: The first thing I did was call Kenworth to make sure it was right. Linda Robinson was working at the time and she said yes, it was true.

Linda: I tried to call Judith.

Author: He was arrested at work?

Jim: Yeah. He just walked out from work and they told him he was under arrest. Gary gave no struggle. He was at the end of his shift.

Linda: We were just shocked.

Jim: That's when she said (pointing at Linda) I gotta call Judith, and I said yes, call right now. We knew that they were getting him, so someone was probably getting her. And then we saw her face on TV.

Linda: We couldn't get through! Then after a couple of days I helped her get her house put back together.

Jim: We actually got a phone call from a sergeant from the Task Force. He wanted to come interview us and I said, "Nope." At that time, I was still trying to deny it.

Author: You still thought this was an outrageous mistake?

Jim: Yes. I said to myself, "So, they took all that stuff from him and they had him in there in 1987, and now they're using it because they can't find anybody else." When they came back with matching DNA on that third girl, that's when I finally changed my mind. That's when I told her (pointing at Linda), "He's gotta be guilty."

I couldn't talk to Judith about it. I was too uncomfortable. I said Judith should get a divorce, file for a separation for now, and then get a divorce.

Author: The DNA connection was proof for you?

Jim: That was it, yes.

Linda: Judith was in denial when she went to visit Gary.

Jim: Gary's family…they kept telling Judith don't give up, it will look bad. You've got to be supportive for Gary's sake.

I never went to visit him.

Linda: I went to visit him. I went with Judith one time. I was numb. Just really…I watched him with Judith and, of course, again Judith was the emotional one, crying and trying to hold hands with him. But he was…he just…I asked him how he was doing and he said fine. I said, "Gary, I'm sorry this happened," and, you know, he just kind of looked at me and I said, "The only advice I can give you is you'd better get right with God. Find God. That's the only thing that will save you now and we'll all be praying for you."

Jim: After the fact, one of the statements he's made is he couldn't admit to anything or he would have gotten the death penalty. I'm guessing he probably would have confessed to them (Judith and Linda)…but he…there was always a tv up there and they were on tape.

Linda: Yes, cops sitting right there and an intercom there, they can see right over you, so you know they're listening.

Jim: He knew he was done. The run was over. He was just playing his cards to not get the death penalty I think.

Linda: He didn't say nothing like that because the cops were listening. He said the police were listening when we visited. He just said that, I told him I was sorry, he didn't say nothing, he just kind of hung his head. He really didn't say anything. I did most of the talking. The only thing he said was, "They listen to the conversation."

Jim, shaking his head: He wasn't going to confess to guilt at that time.

Linda: They read his letters that came in. He said they went through his mail. Some people at the jail tried to steal things. They stole Judith's picture, one of the inmates, and he would write and say he couldn't have anything because they were stealing from him. He always thought it was because they wanted to make a buck. He said don't send any pictures.

Author: Did you think he was guilty?

Linda: Yes.

Jim: I had a hard time sleeping for a long time. I was a mess. I've always been what I consider to be perceptive about people and things about their lives, public, whatever...and in this particular instance, it was like there was a brick wall and I just did not see it. Not one sign.

Author: You felt like you were duped by Gary?

Jim: Yes. Well, if I could explain it in spiritual terms, I'd say God didn't want me to see it (the truth) and there's a reason and I think the reason was Judith. I think if more people had seen him for what he really was, there would have been less chance of getting him in the end. I think he would have taken off. If he thought everybody knew he was guilty, he would've been gone. But he thought he had everybody fooled.

Author: You sort of felt like a fool?

Jim: Yes.

Linda: He wouldn't listen to nothing about Gary on the news, and he wouldn't read the letters I got from Gary. Didn't want to talk about it.

Jim: Every time I'd go around someone we knew mutually, like people from Kenworth, that's the first thing they wanted to talk about. So, I quit going around them.

Author: So you withdrew?

Jim: It's like a form of betrayal. It's like a husband and a wife, they have that bond and when someone does something like that, well...I trusted you! When I look at the bigger picture, it's like, why should I be worried about it? It wasn't me! But at the time I was hurt, tricked.

Linda: Let's face it here—there wasn't too many people that really even would talk to Gary. They didn't say anything positive about Gary because everybody thought he was different.

Author: And you stood up for him and defended his honor, more than once, so you probably felt like a fool in the eyes of your co-workers too?

Jim: Sure I did. Absolutely.

Author: Linda, Gary stayed in touch with you by writing letters?

Linda: Yes, because I always wrote to him. When he writes, he always says Jim and Linda on them and at the end of the letters, he puts "Love Gary."

Author: Even though he knows that you guys know he's guilty, on some level he still feels like you care?

Linda: Yes.

Author: Do you remember the last thing you said to Gary?

Jim: I was visiting down at Kenworth after I retired and he and I talked a little while. He was doing a tape job on a truck and I asked him how Judith was doing. I can't remember anything other than that. That was it. It seems like it was about Thanksgiving, like a week before he was arrested. I used to go to Kenworth around Thanksgiving and Christmas to visit, but I can't remember for sure.

Linda: When he was in jail, that's the last time I talked to him. Yeah, he looked skinny. He didn't look good. He looked bad. You could see age on him already. He was stressed but always put on a calm face. I'll never forget that. He put on a calmness about him. It was like he just…

Jim: It's like he worked hard at his good qualities to cover up the bad. That's why we saw so many positives about him and never really got into the negative.

Author: What would you say to him today if you saw him?

Linda jumps in first: I'd sit down and talk to him…man…I would want to know what was his thinking when he killed these young girls. What satisfaction did he get out of it? You know, I want to know all of that. What happened? Did the two ex-wives hurt him? I want to know what happened. I guess because I was sexually molested as a child so then I look at a man who's killed women and I want to know why. What was in his mind? Did he realize what he was doing?

Jim, quietly: I wouldn't have anything to say to Gary. That's between him and God now. And I still don't believe that he's accepted what he did. I don't think he's been forgiven yet. I just don't believe him.

Chapter 9
Gary's Comments From Prison

The arrest on November 30, 2001, ended the Green River Killer's twenty-year career. After the arrest, Gary Ridgway spent nearly two years in a King County Jail in downtown Seattle while the massive case was investigated and his team of attorneys, headed by the prominent defense attorney, Tony Savage, maneuvered with the Prosecuting Attorney, Norm Maleng. After steadfastly denying murder accusations for eighteen months, Gary finally confessed to being the Green River Killer and agreed to give details about the forty-eight known (and possibly more) victims, how they were killed, why he killed, and where some of the still-missing bodies were located.

On June 13, 2003, —"Friday the 13th"—Gary signed a plea agreement. It stated that if Gary would truthfully disclose the location of bodies he had killed in King County (he may have killed in other counties, but this agreement was specifically for King County), the Prosecuting Attorney would withdraw his notice to seek the death penalty. Gary spent the next six months in an ultra-secret location near Boeing Field confessing the shocking details of his murdering vocation and assisting detectives with recovering bodies that remained in his "dump sites."

During hundreds of hours of recorded sessions, Gary described how he regularly "dated" prostitutes that worked along Highway 99, known as the "strip" to locals, south of Seattle. He had sex with many prostitutes that he did not kill. He said he actually cared for some and didn't want to hurt them. But some he killed—the ones that made him mad for various reasons.

He typically negotiated an agreement to have sex for twenty dollars. He felt anything higher than twenty dollars was ridiculous. After paying the fee, he had sex with the "dates." Gary described how he could only climax if he got "behind the woman." Face-to-face turned him off. Then, if they made him mad, he killed them by strangulation. He used socks, pants, wires, cords, and other items to rig up tourniquet-like killing weapons. He sometimes stood on their backs and violently yanked back on the tourniquet. Sometimes during the struggle, he broke one of their arms or legs. He sometimes bit the women on their breasts. After the victim was dead, he removed all clothing and jewelry, took back his twenty dollars, and dumped the body.

He killed in his house (when he was single), in his truck, and in the outdoors. After dumping a body, he casually tossed the victim's clothing and jewelry out the window of his truck as he drove home, some distance from the body.

As Gary progressed in his confessions with investigators and attorneys, he gave them a sickening shock: He had engaged in necrophilia. He actually returned to the bodies to have sex with them—*if* the maggots weren't too bad yet. He could have sex as much as he wanted and, best of all, it didn't cost him anything.

Gary told the interrogators that he thought of the bodies as his prizes and that he had control over them. He enjoyed going back to "visit" them. In one case, he returned to a dumpsite near the Leisure Time Camp Resort where Highway 18 and Interstate-90 intersect east of Seattle to retrieve a skull from one of his victims. His plan was to transport it and plant it in an area far away from that dumpsite as a ploy to confuse the police. It's not clear if he followed through with that.

Finally, Gary admitted to posing the bodies to make it appear that several killers were at work. He was aware that killers often left a "signature" on bodies and at crime scenes, and he wanted to confuse the police by creating different signatures. With some bodies, he inserted small rocks into their vaginal cavities. For others, he placed random items on top of their bodies. And for others, he arranged the limbs of the bodies in strange positions. He once lit a victim's hair on fire. Some were buried. Some were not. But, all of his cunning attempts to fool investigators failed. In the end, it was DNA and tiny particles of truck paint found on some victims matching DNA and paint particles unique to Gary that made the case against him stick.

When the confessions were finally finished, the authorities had asked all the questions they could think of, and after Gary faced victims' families in court and admitted his guilt, he was sent to live the rest of his life, serving forty-eight life sentences, instead of being put to death per the plea deal, in Washington State Penitentiary. He settled in to his new quarters January 6, 2004.

Washington State Penitentiary, often referred to as "Walla Walla State Pen," shares a city of 29,000 people with two colleges, Walla Walla Community College and Whitman College. The penitentiary is positioned on 540 acres of level ground, which is surrounded by rich farmland famous for producing the "Walla Walla Sweet Onion," wine, wheat, and other crops. Walla Walla is located in Eastern Washington, about a four-hour drive east from Seattle.

With a foreboding address of: 1313 North 13th, the superstitious are sure to be spooked. Incoming inmates are appointed to one of four buildings on the grounds, depending on the level of security they require. Gary was placed in the IMU or Intensive Management Unit where he was closely monitored and would never be allowed to come in contact with another inmate. He would not be allowed to eat in the cafeteria, work at a job, or mingle with inmates in the "big yard." Prison officials had reason to believe Gary would not survive in the general population.

In letters that Gary wrote to his ex-wife, Judith, and friend, Linda Bailey, he described what daily life is like for him at Walla Walla State Pen. He exists in a tiny, single-person cell with a bed, toilet, and sink twenty-four hours per day, leaving the cell only one or two hours per week to go outside into a pen for solitary "yard" time. The yard is barren with four walls and the total size being about the size of a living room in an average house. If he chooses to forfeit yard time, he may use the payphone to make an outgoing, collect call. Gary reports that he tries to go outside no matter how severe the weather is to see the sky and breathe some fresh air. Meals are shoved in to his cell through a narrow slot in the door. In the beginning, prison food disagreed with him and he complained to the Chaplain who was successful in requesting a change in Gary's meals. Gary now claims to be a vegetarian and feeling much more healthy. When he first arrived, he earned the right to have a small radio in his cell. After a lengthy period of good behavior, he traded up for a small television. He claims he watches sentimental movies that make him cry.

Today Gary spends his hours writing letters and copying passages from the Bible. He claims to be a student of the Bible and has long talks with the prison Chaplain. Gary's brother, Greg, deposits money into Gary's inmate account so that he can purchase paper, pencils, postage stamps, and toiletries that are not standard issue. Gary claims he writes so much that he can use up two pencils in a week.

Through letter communication, Gary agreed to let me interview him via phone. I would be the first person, other than law enforcement, to interview him since incarceration despite numerous requests. On the day that I interviewed him, he gave up his "yard time" and called me collect:

Chapter 10
Interview with Gary
12/18/06

When the call came in, I asked Gary how he was doing, and he said, "Oh great, just great," in a tone of voice that could have been from a guy luxuriating on a sunny beach, enjoying a lengthy vacation. I had imagined that he might sound more distressed. Then he told me that he had completely shaved his head, and now he looks like "Coach Holmgren of the Seattle Seahawks." It struck me as an odd, random way to begin our interview. I got right to the many questions I had for him.

Author: Judith told me that she felt like her life was destroyed on November 30th, 2001, the day that you were arrested and you didn't come back to her. She said you got up early that day to go to work at Kenworth, like any other day. Did you have any sense that the police were closing in on you at that time?

Gary: Uh, no I didn't. Just a regular day. Except for at 11:00 when they (detectives) came by and grabbed me to talk to the officers, um, in that room, yeah when they came in there and asked me some questions about, um, some of the stuff, you know.

Author: Did you think something big was going down?

Gary: It was just a little bit rude how they came by and picked me up, the-the uh, the uh, manager came over and took me over to this room, and the-uh detectives were in there. I was kind of more irritated than anything.

Author: Judith told me there were a couple of other times that you were questioned by the police like in 1987 when your house was searched and other times. Did this arrest feel any differently than the other ones?

Gary: Uh, it did in a way, but, um, you know, it didn't seem, um, real to me in a way, you know. It took a day for me to settle in and realize I did get arrested, you know.

Author: You were kind of stunned at first?

Gary: First stunned, yeah, a little bit stunned, and not knowing what to say and when the detectives talked to me they kept on asking me questions and I kept on asking for a lawyer and they slammed me with all these questions and they arrested me on a Friday night and I couldn't get a lawyer, you know, I didn't know any lawyers other than one guy and I forgot his name, you know.

Author: Now, you were kind of stunned and wondering what was going on. Were you able to think about what Judith might be going through at the very time you were arrested?

Gary: Yeah, I was, uh, I was in a fear because I knew that Judith was going to have a hard time taking all this stuff by herself because, you know, nobody's there to help her, you know. She was left out on the street by herself, you know, she didn't get much help from my family, you know.

Author: You were concerned about what was happening with her then?

Gary: Yeah, I was really concerned because she didn't have my, uh, uh, she-she was more emotional. Women are more emotional than I am, you know, in a way, you know. They care more-women care more than a man does.

Author: I want to go back to February, 1985, when you first met Judith at the White Shutters Tavern at a Parents Without Partners dance. Do you remember that night?

Gary: Yeah, I remember it really well. And, uh, I remember her because when I met her I was at one end of the table, or something like that, and there was an argument between another woman, I forget what it was about, you know, and, uh, that was the first time I ever met Judith.

Author: What was your impression of Judith the first time you met her?

Gary: I really did like her! She was, uh, kind of, um, not too forward, she was kind of laid back a little bit and she was curious and there was just something about her that was different than other women, you know.

Author: And when the evening ended, she said that you and your friend wanted to continue on with the evening and you went to your friend's house and what were you hoping would happen that evening?

Gary: I think that was a friend of Judith's, I forget what her name was, but she found this other guy and, because I think she knew the woman from the White Center area and, um, it was not, I didn't know any of them, basically, you know.

Author: Were you hoping to spend more time with Judith that night?

Gary: Yeah, in a way. We stayed up all night and I think we had breakfast the next morning, you know. And I thought it was really nice to have somebody that's-it was the weekend too, I forget what day it was.

Judith: Judith said that initially she felt really concerned that she was nearly five years older than you. Did that ever bother you?

Gary: No, it didn't bother me at all. No. The age didn't bother me at all. I was kind of proud of having somebody smart, you know.

Author: The public knows from all the reporting that you were married two previous times, and what do you think was different about Judith as a wife, compared to the other two?

Gary: Well, for one thing she was more dependent. She needed somebody. And with my first wife, it was a Navy wedding and I went for her with five or six years but then when we got married it just fell apart when she was away from her parents, you know. The second marriage was with Marcia, and actually, Judith knew Marcia before she knew me. I don't know if she told you that or not.

Author: Yes. She said she met Marcia when she played in a band. So, how do you think Judith was different or more special?

Gary: Well, she was more, she was more caring than Marcia or Claudia. She cared and because when we first got married we both had checking accounts and she did hers and I did mine and finally I let her have both of them, you know, it worked out better that way to keep her busy doing something, you know.

Author: You must have trusted her?

Gary: I trusted her and it didn't matter if she worked or not. She liked to work and liked to be busy so, you know, doing working the daycare and she was happy with that.

Author: So when you and Judith began dating, did you think that being in a relationship with her would sort of help your sexual urges and perhaps not need to date the prostitutes as often?

Gary: Well, I basically had a, um, you know, to open up to anybody, you know, there's no programs out there for people that go out there to have a sexual problem like that. It's like the same thing as gambling, you know. You gamble and you can't control the urge. And to a point there I could control it but then I dropped back in to the urge of it, like alcohol, in a way, you know. It controlled me. That's why I wanted to retire early with Judith because I think we were going to retire at about fifty-eight and have a place away from the strip so we could do some traveling and things like that so I wouldn't be around it.

Author: You thought that would help if you got away from the strip (Highway 99)

Gary: And I think it helps anybody if they have an addiction, you know, they need to have more places that will help people with problems, you know.

Author: I was curious if your happy relationship with Judith helped to calm that down at all or if it was just sort of always there?

Gary: For a while it helped a lot and, uh, I guess it might have been a little bit of the, uh, you know, I guess some people say there's a little thrill in it, you know and, um, I just wanted to, uh, get the house sold because we were getting ready to sell it and, uh, start plans with being some place where I wouldn't be around that stuff and have to drive back and forth, you know, around the strip and everything like that where it bothers me, you know. If there was some kind of help out there I would have got into it, you know.

Author: Would you say that your sex life with Judith was satisfying?

Gary: Yeah, it was satisfying, yes.

Author: How do you think having sex with Judith, your wife, was different than with a prostitute?

Gary: Well, uh, I guess it was, um, I think it was because of the little thrill of, you know, getting away with it, and I don't really know why, you know like on the weekends I spent all the time with Judith and we never, uh, we went most every place after work and everything like this so I didn't have any problem with that, but just to and from work.

Author: It was trouble for you because that's the way you drove back and forth to work?

Gary: That was the way I drove back and forth to work, yeah.

Author: Did you ever try to purposely drive a different way to avoid the strip?

Gary: Well, the thing is, I did try driving a different way a couple of times, but like one time I had a blow out on my truck and I had to try to change it on the-on the 167 (highway) you know. Whenever I had car troubles or something like that, truck troubles, you could always pull off on 99 (highway) or something like that and fix it and be on my way or something like that, but taking the freeway—I didn't like taking the freeway. No place to pull over or anything and also that accident I had in, with my pickup, right after I met Judith when I had, uh—matter of fact, before I met her, I had an accident with my other truck and totaled it out.

Author: Did you ever feel afraid of passing a sexually transmitted disease on to Judith?

Gary: Well I tried to use a rubber whenever I could, you know, and protect us. And, uh—I washed myself with alcohol to, if there any bugs, you know. So I wouldn't catch anything, you know.

Author: So you cared. You didn't want to give anything to Judith?

Gary: Judith said that there were sometimes when she wanted to have sex with you at bedtime and you did not. Sometimes you said your sinuses were bothering you or you were too tired. Was that really the case, or do you think you had just been on a date with a prostitute?

Gary: No. I think my sinuses did bother me all the time. They still bother me now. I always have, uh—there's another guy down there at Kenworth by the name of _____. He worked with me all the time and we always had sinus problems. Any time I've put a mask on, my nose would be running all the time, you know. And I'd run around where I work, a lot of times I would go out there and blow my nose. Every time I got a chance to take a break, I went out and blew my nose. It was just running like it was going out of style.

Author: From the materials you worked with, the chemicals?

Gary: The chemicals and, uh, allergy problems. The task force kept on thinking I was, because you constantly have a sinus problem, and you're always swallowing all that mucous, you know, down your throat, and every time I made a sentence, no matter what I talked about, I would just make a big swallow, no matter what I was saying, even if I was telling them names and addresses.

Author: What was the thing you liked the very most about Judith?

Gary: Uh, her ability to create things. She did a lot of creating things like making dolls and jewelry.

Author: Good with crafts?

Gary: Good with crafts, and stuff, yeah, and making dresses for dolls and some of that, she was real good at that.

Author: What did you least like about Judith?

Gary: Uh, uh, she was a little bit, one time we were going to this, uh, I guess this thing for making money. You ever been to one of those things where they, uh, you take piece of dowel and put up next to your neck and push it against each other and break it?

Author: No, I have not done that.

Gary: That was like at the Sea-Tac Red Lion, or something like that, seminar on things like that but, um, sticking her neck out, the little bit might have been a little bit that, any problems I had, but that would be about it.

Author: What about that bothered you?

Gary: Uh, everybody else went through it, like fifty people, uh, she was the only one that dropped out of it. It's important to build your courage up.

Author: Did you think she was a little bit weak?

Gary: Well, a little bit, but you know, I don't like sticking my neck out either, you know. But I was a little bit braver than she is a little bit on things, you know. Manly, you know. You don't want, as a man, goes into something, he doesn't want to look like a wuss, you know. When I played a game of pool with her, I think it was 50/50 on our pools. She won 50% and I won 50% and, uh, you know, if she won more, it takes the manly away from me, you know.

Author: That bothered you?

Gary: No, it didn't bother me that much, you know. It would for some people, you know. Most of the time we played pool it was just her and me and nobody else around.

Author: Did you like it better when you won?

Gary: It didn't matter. Nobody fussed about it, you know.

Author: Did you enjoy it more when it was just you and Judith out?

Gary: Yeah, I enjoyed just her and I all the time. Every time we went to Seaside, you know, and up in the mountains, you know. If we had somebody to do something with, nothing else, we just walked the dogs around, you know, by ourselves. It didn't bother us. Being together, yeah. We always did everything together. Except maybe I would go take a shower up in the place, or something like that, but that's when I always was done before she was so, it might take longer to get showers done at the campgrounds and stuff like that, so I would be waiting for her.

Author: What did you think about Judith's two daughters from her first marriage? Did you have any opinion about Marie and Rachel?

Gary: I got along with them okay, you know, when we had problems with them was when we had problems, they wanted to move, and we would help them move, but we would always try to get them to get things boxed up before they moved and it was kind of hard for us to move everything for them and plus doing all the work and they're doing, you know, not half of it, you know.

Author: Not helping so much?

Gary: Not helping so much. I think that they needed to respect us more than what they did, you know?

Author: What did you think about Judith's first husband, Lee, and the sort of strange lifestyle that they had?

Gary: Well, I kind of resented it, you know. I, um, didn't, ah, care to go over there (Lee's house) like when she wanted to go over there, a lot of times there was something else I could do to get out from going over there, and she'd go over there on a Friday night which I would be doing something, I don't know, uh, she's leaving in the afternoon to go out there so I would go with her, you know. Or meet her there or something like that. I didn't care for the lifestyle of, you know, him.

Author: Was that before you were married to Judith?

Gary: It was before marriage and after marriage. She went over there a few times, you know. Go to birthday parties and birthday parties for the kids and stuff like that. It didn't matter. I went over there one time when her car broke down and fixed the car and drove it home, but, um, if I was doing something else or working on Saturday or something like that, I wouldn't go and she'd go and I didn't hesitate to let her go, you know.

Author: But something about it made you uncomfortable?

Gary: It just, the other guys, you know, made you uncomfortable. It probably made her uncomfortable because she did it for the love of her kids, you know.

Author: So, she told you about the parties they did and the medieval times and the homosexuality? You knew all about that?

Gary: I knew all about that. That didn't bother me because I knew she wasn't going back in that stuff, you know, like her husband does.

Author: Now Judith believes that you made her life better in all ways, and that you were a wonderful husband.

Gary: Uh, I tried to, I learned from the first mistake and the second mistake of trying to maybe be bossy. Marcia said I was always bossy with her and everything. With Judith, I went along with 90% of, you know, I tried to do what she wanted, and I talked her into something that we wanted to do, but in the way that she could, you know, not bother her back because she had some problems with her back, so I tried to make everything possible. I didn't force into work and stuff like that. If she wanted to work, she did. If she didn't, that was fine with me.

Author: Do you think she made your life better in any way?

Gary: Oh, I think she made it 100% better, yeah.

Author: How so?

Gary: Well, because of, uh, not, uh, watching what I spent money on and, uh, people that we were around, you know, we weren't around any rowdy people that I hung around before, you know. And she brought me out where we could talk to people and we tried the Amway, we tried the other multi-level marketing things, you know, and she did the paperwork and she did a lot of talking. She could talk you into just about anything, you know. When were out camping or something like that she'd talk to somebody. If she didn't know Jim and Linda and she was looking at your motor home, she'd come over and talk to them, and eventually they were bringing her in and showing her their motor home. She was that, you know.

Author: So you were a good team?

Gary: Yeah, we were a real good team, yes.

Author: At any time in your fourteen-year marriage, did you ever want to hurt Judith or kill her?

Gary: No, I didn't. Never even thought about it. She was the best I could ever get, so there wasn't nothing I wanted to do to hurt her.

Author: You did lie to Judith sometimes about where you would be before and after work. She said there were times when you went to browse thrift stores and junkyards and things of that nature. Were those the times that you were having dates with the prostitutes?

Gary: Those—those were probably on the, uh, probably on the uh, on probably working on a Saturday I might stop by and see a prostitute once in a while, but that's about it, you know. If I went to a junkyard I went there to get something, you know, and always come back with a bunch of stuff, you know.

Author: She was guessing that those were the times you were maybe seeing prostitutes.

Gary: No. I didn't try to do that much, you know. Plus the prostitutes were not in that area like the Kent Valley is where the junkyards were. That's where I usually went, you know. And no prostitutes down there.

Author: Did you ever feel guilty when you told a lie to Judith?

Gary: I did, but after a while, I guess it's like anything—you get away with it and, you know, I guess a lot of times I guess Judith probably knew.

Author: So you think there were times that she had a suspicion that you were lying to her?

Gary: I think a few times, yeah.

Author: Did she ever confront you or question you?

Gary: Uh, no she let it go by. She wouldn't bring it up anymore, you know.

Author: Of all the people that you know, whom do you think you hurt the most?

Gary: Uh, Judith. Definitely Judith.

Author: And when you were doing those bad things, did you ever think that it would affect Judith?

Gary: Uh, I think, I think I had, when I, when I first, before I met Judith, I didn't have any confidence in myself. I was, I didn't, I couldn't love anybody and going through the divorce I had with Marcia, she kinda took advantage of me several times, you know, so that caused, uh, it's kind of like starting out with a pyramid, you know, not a pyramid, but uh, you worked your way, do small things, and work up to worse things and, um, I believe, what was the question again?

Author: Did you ever think that what you were doing wrong would affect Judith someday?

Gary: I didn't think I would ever get caught for one thing. And, if I did, in a way I knew that I wouldn't get the death penalty because of what I knew was worth more than what they wanted to give me the death penalty, you know.

Author: During your whole marriage to Judith, did you believe in God?

Gary: I believed in God off and on and I, uh, more because of, you know, doing what I was doing less, and like the one (murder) in, uh, '88, that was a complete accident, you know, that one didn't have to happen, you know. Uh, I was trying to get completely out of that, hurting people, you know.

Author: I'm not sure what you meant by that.

Gary: I think it comes down to—I was in a long break between there and my dad died in 1999, I think it was, and sometime after that, or something like that, I—I killed a woman but it wasn't planned. It just happened, you know.

Author: Did you ever pray to God or read the Bible during your marriage?

Gary: Uh, I read the Bible several times, but there was so much in there, reading, and I have a problem with emotions. Like I read something and it makes me cry because there's certain things in here like, uh, I still cry a lot of times when I read where Mary says in the Bible, "where did you hide my Jesus?" You know, sometimes that bothers me and it makes me tear up a little bit, you know.

Author: Judith said that you and she spent a lot of weekends and vacations with your son, Matthew. She said you had many fun trips. What would say your relationship was like with Matthew?

Gary: My relationship with Matthew was, is pretty good, I guess real good, you know. The best we ever had, and then, uh, but he didn't go to our wedding and he didn't go to, uh, his mother's wedding, you know. Uh, I don't know why he didn't, I forget, just doing something he wanted, or.

Author: Did you ever worry that your son would find out what you were doing?

Gary: Uh, no. No I didn't think he would ever find out, you know, like it did happen.

Author: Do you have any kind of relationship with Matthew today?

Gary: No, we don't talk at all, no.

Author: Out of all the trips and activities and things you did with Judith, what was the all-time favorite?

Gary: The—the best thing I think was the camping and stuff and going to swap-meet and working together, you know, working together at the swap-meet or selling things, that was good, you know. We enjoyed it.

Author: She said that too. She said that you two rarely had an argument. Do you remember a particular argument that you had with Judith?

Gary: Uh, let's see, the argument might have been, uh, I think more over her kids. You know, her and I used to loan money to the daughters and the daughters not paying it back, that was basically the only argument I ever can think of. It wasn't anything about Judith. I wasn't arguing, you know, about her back or anything like this. You know, I knew she had problems and I'd listen to her on the back and I think most of it was about her kids. Her love for the kids was more overpowering. She had so much love for them, you know. (Gary's voice breaks and he begins to cry, sniffing.)

Author: You and Judith had many garage sales and you spent time preparing for them. What did you like about doing those garage sales?

Gary: Well, I liked a lot about it, spending the weekend with Judith and around the house, like we had garage sales and I'd be out doing yard work, and the, um, coffee and the liqueur, you know, we put that in our coffee, and you know that day before we might buy a box of donuts and, then for dinner so she wouldn't have to cook, we usually ordered a pizza or something like that.

Author: So it was a fun activity?

Gary: Yeah, it was really fun. Sometimes we didn't make anything but we, we got rid of stuff and we spent some time together, you know.

Author: Judith said that sometimes when you sat down to watch a movie together in the living room, if there was a scene with violence or maybe a woman being hurt, she thought that she saw tears in your eyes. Is that true?

Gary: Uh, that is true. I still have tears now. I watched, uh, let's see, what movie, there was a movie on yesterday on Channel 7, uh, Christmas movie, and I still have tears come out of my eyes a lot of times, you know. I'm very emotional.

Author: From everything I've heard, it sounds like you were an excellent employee at Kenworth. You had perfect attendance awards, you worked with the union, you were an excellent truck painter. How did you feel about your job?

Gary: I felt that I was doing a real good job. I put in a lot of over-time in. Back in the '82 and '83 when I had all the trouble with women, I felt that a lot of times I was getting used and that's why it caused a lot of my problems is because the women there, they would, they would get over on other people and it bothered me more than it bothered most other people, I guess.

Author: Do you think you had friends there at Kenworth?

Gary: I think I had friends but we didn't do too much with them, you know. Sometimes we went out for a beer, you know, but that was about it, you know.

Author: You were friends with Jim and Linda Bailey, right?

Gary: Yeah, friends with Jim and Linda Bailey. We'd go to union meetings and go out to dinner sometimes, you know.

Author: In 2001 when you were arrested, you were just a couple of years away from retiring. Judith said you had plans for selling your home and traveling in your motor home. If you hadn't been caught, what do you think you'd be doing today?

Gary: Uh, I'd be, the ideal would be into a smaller house and probably traveling more and, uh, because we had a lot of stuff in the paper, you know, because Judith told you about all the stuff we had to sell, making money on the side, and, uh, I think we'd be, uh, probably down in Seaside this time of year for, you know, a week or two down there, doing, making money on the side, making crafts and stuff like that.

Author: What was your relationship like with your father? I know he's passed away.

Gary: Uh, in one way, I think we're both a little bit—he had Alzheimer's toward the end and I have troubles with memory a lot. I can remember some things but I couldn't remember the very first person (killed) you know and, um, I have trouble remembering like trying to remember Bible quotes and stuff like that, they're hard to remember.

Author: You think your father had memory problems too?

Gary: I think he had a little bit. Toward the end he had more, I think he was more of a, he liked to come over and help, but he liked to just jump in and do it all for you, you know.

Author: What was your relationship like with your mother? I know she's passed away as well.

Gary: Uh, she, uh, I spent, I'd go over there in the evening and we'd have a cup of coffee and, you know, eat a lot of times. I'd spent about two nights, three nights a week drop by the house, and, um, see her. I think we spent more time with my parents than we did with Judith's parents.

Author: Your mother and father were deceased when the world found out you were the Green River Killer. If they had been alive, how do you think they would have reacted?

Gary: I don't know how my mother and father would have reacted.

Author: If you could wish for anything for Judith now, what would that be?

Gary: Uh, happiness and peace, um, love, um, I guess move on, I guess.

Author: If you could go back and live your life over again, what would you do differently?

Gary: I would do, uh, uh, all that different, you know, I wouldn't be a criminal, you know. Do it all over differently, yes.

Chapter 11
Professional Analysis of Gary's Handwriting

For a graphologist, one who is specially trained to analyze handwriting, the very idea of obtaining an authentic, first-generation handwriting specimen from the serial killer who yielded the most kills in United States history—Gary Ridgway a.k.a. The Green River Killer to study and possibly write about is exciting. To have this sample unexpectedly offered up by an individual close to the Ridgways is extraordinarily exciting, and it happened to me.

At a social function in early 2002, an acquaintance walked over to me and matter-of-factly said, "I understand you do handwriting analysis."

"That's right," I answered.

"Well," my acquaintance said as she nervously looked around and lowered her voice, "I have a friend, and she'd like you to take a look at her *husband's* handwriting."

"Does your friend's husband know that she wants his handwriting looked at?" I questioned as I began my usual, professional disclaimer.

"No, he doesn't. He's in jail. He's Gary Ridgway."

Dazed, I stared in silence, trying to absorb what she had just said.

The acquaintance was Linda Bailey, close friend of Gary and Judith Ridgway. Gary had been arrested in November, 2001, and was sitting in jail in Seattle, charged with being *the* Green River Killer, the one who had eluded capture for over twenty years, the one who had murdered several dozen women and underage girls by strangulation after having sex with them and then typically dumped the bodies on and around the banks of the Green River in Western Washington. I had been following the riveting news reports closely because I had lived in the killer's community for his entire killing career, and I had often wondered what kind of person would be clever enough to avoid getting caught for so *many* years. Had I ever stood next to him in a bank or grocery store check out line? Looked over at him while sitting at a traffic light? Over two decades, as I graduated school, married, raised children, and started my career, I had even imagined specific profiles of men as the killer: Perhaps he was a long-distance truck driver who killed only when he was in the Seattle area. I shuddered when I imagined some local creep impersonating a police officer, putting the women "under arrest," and then transporting his new prisoners to a wooded area to carry out his demented fantasies. Or, perhaps there was an original killer who committed only the first few murders and then several nut cases followed with copycat-style murders. But no matter what profession the killer was based in, I was certain the killer had to possess an I.Q. at ceiling height—the genius type. Who else could find a way to murder repeatedly and dispose of bodies without ever being seen? Who else would have the intelligence to manage the clues left on murder victims so as to outsmart forensic experts? And who else but a genius could deftly answer questions during police interrogation if he had in fact been arrested, released, and placed on the Green River Task Force suspect list? It was common knowledge that the suspect list was lengthy. Imagine my astonishment when I discovered the Green River Killer turned out to be a quiet, slender, polite, clean-cut, married man, father of one son, loyal employee of Kenworth, and close friend with *people I knew!*

Gary Ridgway wouldn't admit to being the killer until Spring of 2003, so when Linda brought me the handwriting samples in 2002, she and her husband, Jim, and Judith Ridgway, Gary's wife of fourteen years, hoped that I might analyze Gary's handwriting and tell them whether or not he really had committed the murders. The Bailey's weren't convinced yet that he was guilty. Gary had been nothing but a faithful friend over the years. Mrs. Ridgway, Linda told me, absolutely supported her husband's innocence—the part about murder, anyway—believing he had been falsely accused. Yet they wanted me to examine Gary's handwriting. How very interesting.

"Right now, we're just all in a state of shock," Linda explained. "We thought maybe you could tell us somethin' about Gary from his handwriting."

"Gosh, Linda," I gently offered, "Handwriting analysis does not determine specific information like whether or not an individual committed acts of murder," I began to explain, "but I would like to study the handwriting and see what kind of clues it offers about his basic personality." And, naturally, I wanted it for my collection of interesting handwriting samples.

"Sure. Do what you can. We can talk later."

Graphology (most refer to it as "handwriting analysis"): Dictionaries define it as "the study of handwriting as a clue to character." But, frustratingly, when I typically begin conversations with most folks about handwriting analysis, I hear comments such as, "Oh yeah, handwriting analysis. I've heard of it. Isn't that like fortune telling? Here—look at my handwriting and tell me my future." So I end up taking a deep breath and giving a mini-history lecture on graphology before handwriting conversations really take off.

First, I explain that graphology has been used for a very, very long time. Fascinatingly, the first ones to write about the correlation between handwriting styles and various personalities were physicians. Aristotle, first a court physician to the Macedonian Royal Family and later going on to study philosophy with Plato, wrote in 330 B.C., "Speech is the expression of ideas or thoughts or desires. Handwriting is the visible form of speech. Just as speech can have inflections of emotions, somewhere in handwriting is an expression of the emotions underlying the writer's thoughts, ideas, or desires." Then, in the early 17th century, Camillo Baldi, an Italian physician, wrote his treatise on handwriting and character. He wrote in part, "Handwriting, being a manifestation of the one who writes, somehow reproduces something of its writer's temperament, personality, or character."

The father of *modern graphology* is French monk, Jean Hippolyte Michon. In the late 1800's he created the first formal system for studying handwriting, and he is credited for creating the actual term, "graphologie." Today's graphological techniques have roots in Michon's work. He designed a system of analysis that looked at each, individual stroke in a body of handwriting, sort of like looking at each bone in a skeleton to imagine how the parts work and move together as a whole structure. He believed that the parts of handwriting, when put together, told a story about the individual's mind.

One of Michon's students, Jules Crepieux-Jamin, took handwriting analysis in a slightly different direction. His focus was looking at handwriting as one whole body, rather than as a collection of individual pieces. Today graphologists refer to this style of analysis as the "holistic" view of handwriting. Crepieux-Jamin persuaded Alfred Binet, creator of the well-known Stanford-Binet I.Q. test, to test the reliability of handwriting analysis and was pleased with Binet's findings.

Graphology finally found its legs. The universities of Europe embraced handwriting analysis and helped put it to work. Soon European businesses began regularly employing handwriting analysts to screen job applicants. Handwriting analysis was accepted as another psychometric examination, similar to personality tests that various psychologists had already developed.

In the early 1900's, one famous psychologist, Carl Jung, had a French student named Anna Teillard who studied graphology extensively and wrote a book relating handwriting to depth psychology.

Around the same time, a Swiss man, Max Pulver, was applying handwriting analysis to the field of psychoanalysis, and his big contribution to graphology was classifying three areas or what graphologists refer to as "zones" of handwriting that paralleled Freud's theory about id, ego, and superego.

The 1900's found another busy handwriting analyst in Germany: Ludwig Klages. Unfortunately, Klages would earn a reputation for being a bully in the field of graphology, and he is credited with blowing a big hiccup into the credibility of graphology—a hiccup that graphology is unfortunately still trying to recover from today. Klages established what he called the "Gestalt Method" of handwriting analysis and published many textbooks on the subject. But his method was flawed because he based his principles for analyzing handwriting on his personal philosophies instead of a more universal standard. His interpretations of handwriting were completely subjective, based on his own personal feelings. He either liked or disliked handwriting samples and made reports based upon his impressions and feelings about handwriting. Now, that on its own did not damage the reputation of handwriting analysis. It was when he teamed up with his pal, Adolf Hitler, that the trouble began. Klages told Hitler he needed to outlaw all forms of handwriting analysis except for his Gestalt Method. Hitler did so, essentially snuffing the growth and development of handwriting analysis in Europe for the next fifty years. Handwriting analysis, at that point, had a negative connotation with mystics who claimed they could simply look at a piece of handwriting and know about the writer.

Graphology came to the United States in dribs and drabs starting in the 1920's when Louise Rice, an American journalist, brought information about graphology home with her after working in Europe. Her 1927 book, *Character Reading from Handwriting*, is still in print today. June Downey did extensive research at the University of Iowa, publishing a study called *Graphology and the Psychology of Handwriting* in the early 1900's. Harvard psychologists Gordon Allport and P.E. Vernon supported handwriting analysis in their book, *Studies in Expression of Movement*. In 1939 Hans Jacoby came to the United States and published a book called *Analysis of Handwriting*.

Graphologists across Europe, along with new graphologists in the United States, studied in concert for the next several decades to revive the field to where it stands today.

Graphology, in my opinion, never fully recovered after the Klages hiccup. It still faces criticism from traditional scientists because its techniques do not meet the very strict definition of empirical science, and the foundation of scientific studies upon which graphology was built is weaker than the more traditional fields of science. But that doesn't stop graphologists from making beneficial contributions to a wide variety of professions with their skills. The reason most people are not familiar with its reliability and usefulness today is because handwriting analysts, especially in the U.S., are typically employed "behind the scenes," and the public misses most of the interesting discussion. Occasionally, we see handwriting analysts interviewed on television for their opinions on a piece of handwriting linked to a sensational crime case. One example is the Jon-Benet Ramsey "ransom note" found in the Boulder, Colorado, home wherein the adorable, blonde, six-year-old Jon-Benet was brutally murdered on Christmas Eve, 1996, and hidden in the basement of her family's luxurious home. The sensational story got national and international attention. Some graphologists believed that the handwriting in the ransom note matched the handwriting of Mrs. Ramsey, Jon-Benet's mother. The case remains unsolved and Mrs. Ramsey is now deceased.

"Oooo-kay, I didn't realize that handwriting analysis has been around for so long." is what I typically hear next from folks. Then its, "So, where do handwriting analysts actually work?" I go on to explain that handwriting analysts usually specialize in one area within the field of graphology and act as consultants to others, typically working out of a home office. For example, some handwriting analysts get additional training to qualify them as "Questioned Document Examiners." This means that they use techniques to determine whether or not a piece of handwriting is authentic to the intended writer, and they are qualified to give testimony in court. Banks work with graphologists in their unending battle with forgery—that is, checks, contracts, and other official documents signed by someone imitating the handwriting of the real signature. Individuals turn to graphologists in cases of contested wills. Sadly, there are occasions when Aunt Susan re-writes Grandma's Last Will and Testament (shortly before Grandma passes away) to include more for Aunt Susan, signed by Aunt Susan imitating Grandma's lovely signature. Other family members become suspicious and hire a handwriting analyst to make a determination. Aunt Susan gets busted because there are unique strokes in her own handwriting that show up in the forged signature, even though she practiced signing like Grandma for hours on scrap paper. The various components of our body language such as tone of voice, body gestures, facial expressions, and intensity of energy is evident in our handwriting through nuances, angles, strokes, letter spacing, pen pressure, etc. It is impossible to completely imitate another's handwriting because one's neurological system is not identical to anyone else's.

"Do handwriting experts work with the police then?" I'm asked. In fact, yes, I continue. Law enforcement is a big arena wherein handwriting analysts can be of service. In the 1930's the United States' FBI (Federal Bureau of Investigation) began using forensic handwriting analysis in their technical laboratory. Today the FBI technical laboratory employs many experts in areas such as ballistics, fingerprinting, blood typing, DNA matching, voice analysis, and more, along with graphologists who analyze the content and style of writing as well as utilizing state-of-the-art equipment to trace sources of ink and paper for notes linked to criminal cases. Confessions, ransom notes, threatening notes, blackmail notes, suicide notes, etc., are brought to analysts for investigation. Often, the handwriting analysis can make or break a case. Some recent, high profile cases requiring handwriting analysis that come to mind are: Jon-Benet Ramsey ransom note, Theodore Kaczynski's (a.k.a. The Unabomber) manifesto, Washington D.C. Snipers John Allen Muhammad and John Lee Malvo, and the Anthrax letters sent to television anchor Tom Brokaw and U.S. Senator Tom Daschle. Handwriting experts analyzed all of these suspicious, handwritten notes.

In addition to forgery, questioned documents, and crime cases, handwriting analysts work with businesses in the hiring process. Handwriting samples can be legally obtained in the application process and sent to graphologists for analysis. Company owners and hiring managers who use graphologists are highly interested in hiring personalities that are a good fit for the position they are filling and matching new personalities with established team members. They know how difficult and costly it can be to terminate an employee once hired, and hope to make the right decision the first time around. Again, graphologists typically work behind the scenes for this kind of screening.

Working with businesses to hire strategically and build harmonious teams of people is the area of graphology that I most enjoy. Over the years, I have specialized in hiring staff for medical and dental practices. It is highly rewarding, for example, to help physicians and dentists choose new associates to join their practices and receive feedback such as how well the new associate blended in, and how positively the patients responded to the new practitioner. So, when the handwriting samples from The Green River Killer were handed to me, the focus was different than what I typically worked with in my specialty, but I felt compelled to study the samples because a friend had asked me to do it, and I wanted to see if the handwriting indicated the kind of *genius personality* I had imagined the killer would need.

I couldn't have been more surprised when I found the opposite to be true in Ridgway's handwriting.

As I began to analyze Gary's handwriting specimens, I first took a *holistic* look at the entire body of writing. Imagining that the blank piece of paper represents his world and his personal space, I looked at how his writing—his energy—used up the space on the paper. Where did he position his writing on the paper? Was it concentrated in the upper space of the paper? Middle? Lower? Did he use up every available bit of space on the paper, or leave open spaces for margins, headers, footers, and spaces between lines of writing? I taped a page of his handwriting on the wall and stood back several feet, seeing the writing as one blob of energy, not individual words. How did the arrangement of the writing look overall? Was it neatly, consistently uniform, or did it have a messy, chaotic look? Was the body of writing expressing a bold voice or a gentle whisper? Did the body come across as aggressive or timid? Did the writing appear to be flowing in a harmonious rhythm, or was it erratic and disturbed? How did it look when turned upside down?

Sample 1.

In this sample, Gary's handwriting covers most of the paper, using up the top and bottom margins, and he even turned the paper sideways to cram in additional writing on the left side of the page. This is consistent with other writers who fill their day with activities, staying busy with tasks from the time they rise in the morning until the time they retire to bed at night. All of their time is occupied with something to do. These people are commonly referred to as "worker-bees." Another characteristic of writers who fill up their paper with writing is having an attraction to clutter—that is, having many possessions around them in their home and workspace. (Recall that Gary and Judith always had boxes of items to sell at garage sales stacked up in their garage and house.) But, even though the page is mostly filled with writing, there is open space between the lines of writing and between the letters and words, and an overall neatness and balance to the body of writing suggesting that Gary used a logical, systematic approach to his work, and that he had a way of arranging his time and things that could be considered organized. In other words, he neatly arranged his clutter!

Sample 2.

Still in the holistic view, I looked at the *baselines* or imaginary lines that run under lines of handwriting. They appeared to be steady, slightly rising and falling, consistent with others who experience up's and down's in life but possess enough emotional control to bounce back quickly from emotional upset. These are not people who exhibit extreme outbursts. They give the impression of being controlled and self-disciplined. They are sensitive to what's going on around them, and they can adapt quickly to different people and situations.

Sample 3.

> Standing up for my rights, It has hurt me in all kinds of ways. Always in my mind just let it go. Do what they say and don't ask questions. Some around me are miserable and they do everything they can to make you miserable to. I try to do the best, and follow the rules. Some inmates look up to me and wonder how I can take it.

Next, I looked at the *speed* of Gary's handwriting. When we study handwriting, it is possible to determine if the writer's hand moved swiftly or slowly across the page when forming letters and words on the paper. The speed or pace of handwriting indicates how quickly the writer can imagine a thought, transfer the thought to his hand, grip the writing instrument, press the instrument to the paper, and write letters and words. We all remember learning how to write in the earliest school years—how we watched the teacher slowly and deliberately write one letter on the chalkboard and then we slowly, deliberately imitated her example on our own paper. In the beginning, we had to consciously focus on bringing our pencil upward on the page, make a hump, and drag it down to the line again. After we had practiced making one letter many times, it became more automatic and we could do it faster. Our thought-to-hand processing had picked up speed. In the typical writer, we see very slow, deliberate handwriting or printing when the writer first learns to write. Then, we see a pattern of steady increases in speed that correlate with the writer's increasing biological age and mental processing. Handwriting samples from grade school look slower than samples from middle school, and high school samples are faster than middle school. Individuals typically reach their *graphic maturity* in high school—the point when one can fluidly write sentences without having to stop and think about how to write a letter or word.

Sample 4

> Judith this 30 days. I can't write to anybody. Please think pray go deep down inside whats left of your heart. Ask your self. What do I get out of writing to me. Am I going to start living my own life. Is there a future. What does Judith want. Where does Judith want to be. What are Judith needs. Set

Notice that Gary's speed appears to be slow. If one traces over his handwriting, one can get a sense of how slowly and carefully he created his letters on the paper. Slower handwriting correlates with slower speech and verbal responsiveness. This writing is consistent with others who speak and write hesitantly, starting and stopping repeatedly before they are able to completely express what they want to say. If a person with faster writing verbally challenges them, they will become flustered and have difficulty defending themselves. Their thoughts don't come quickly enough for effective debate. (Recall that Gary had poor academic achievement throughout school, especially with reading and writing, and that he graduated high school two years after his class.)

At this point in the analysis, I knew the *genius-type* was not represented in Gary's handwriting. My theory about the killer was wrong.

Next, I studied the *size* of Gary's handwriting.

Sample 5.

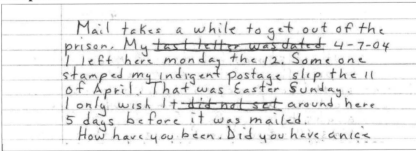

> Mail takes a while to get out of the prison. My ~~last letter was dated~~ 4-7-04 I left here monday the 12. Some one stamped my indigent postage slip the 11 of April. That was Easter Sunday. I only wish it ~~did not set~~ around here 5 days before it was mailed. How have you been. Did you have a nice

Size of handwriting is measured with a special tool, and we measure the middle zone, or bubble portion of letters such as "b" that rests on the baseline. The size of the middle zone and whether or not the size changes throughout the writing has meaning. In Gary's handwriting, I found his size to be consistently *average,* suggesting that he functions well within familiar territory, but may feel overwhelmed when responsibilities become larger than what he feels qualified for. He seeks approval for his performance in a practical environment. (Recall that Gary worked for one company for thirty years where he painted trucks in an assembly line format. Judith encouraged him to apply for higher-level positions, but Gary stubbornly refused. He enjoyed painting trucks and enjoyed his reputation for being a good painter. He felt comfortable in his environment where he knew exactly what was expected of him and how to do it.)

Graphologists are also very interested in the *slant* of handwriting. Again, we use a special tool to measure the degree of slant with the handwriting tipping from left to right. The slant that handwriting takes on paper (having nothing to do with left-handedness or right-handedness) gives many clues about the writer's style of expressing emotions and willingness to express emotions. The more extreme the slant rightward, the more extreme emotions are expressed from the writer. For example, handwriting with a far-right slant, in the 150-180 degree range, correlates with individuals who are openly demonstrative with their emotions. They are interested in the feelings of others, and they want to connect emotionally with others. They tend to be extremely outgoing, passionate, affectionate, sensitive, and willing to laugh, cry, and show anger openly. The opposite, the far-left slant in the range of 40-60 degrees, correlates with individuals who have introverted tendencies and dislike expressing emotion in front of others. They are private, inhibited, often repressed, and highly selective in choosing friends. This can become confusing to analyze as some left slant writers come across as extremely gregarious. Some people develop facades or "public faces" they have developed over time to be able to blend in with society more easily and behave the way they think they are expected to behave in a group of people. But, we know that the slant in handwriting indicates the true nature of one's willingness to express emotions.

Sample 6.

think I'm holding back on something But I am not. It means so much to me. Judith I'm sorry. Sense the 18th they have me on suicide watch, they come by every fifteen minutes to monitor me. Every day theyhave a head shrink come ask me. if I am going to hurt myself, or others. Why am I here

Gary's slant measures in the 90-100 degree range, slightly right of vertical, suggesting that he keeps his emotions under strict control. Other writers with this slant are described as "cool, calm, and collected." No matter what they are feeling, they keep their emotions under strict control, never revealing their true feelings to others. Few, if any, witness emotional outbursts from these writers. With the tight emotional control in place, others find it difficult to have an emotional relationship with this type. Their energy is self-oriented and conservative. They really don't want to connect emotionally with others. In fact, they recoil from emotional displays. The best way to win an argument with this type of individual is to appeal to their sense of logic using only facts and figures.

Another major component of handwriting we study is called the *zones*. These are the three areas of the human psyche that Sigmund Freud referred to as "id, ego, and superego." With handwriting, we divide the letters into "upper zone, middle zone, and lower zone" to find where the majority of the writer's id, ego, and superego energy is directed. The lower zone is the portion of handwriting that dips below the baseline. For example, the letter "y" has a tail that drops down below the baseline typically. That area is referred to as the "lower zone" or id. This is the area where subconscious urges drive the individual to grab what he or she craves, wants, and needs—survival instincts. The urges for social interaction, sex drive, exercise, and acquiring materials possessions are related to this lower zone. The "middle zone" or the ego is where the middle portion of a letter resides. For example, in the letter "b," the bubbly, round portion of the letter is in the middle zone. This is where the conscious, present, daily thoughts and activities reside. And in the "upper zone" or the superego area, abstract thinking, philosophical analysis, and spiritual beliefs are managed. In the letter "b," the stem that rises above the bubbly, middle zone is the upper zone. So, in handwriting analysis, we look at the balance and ratios between the three areas. The most balanced individual will have writing proportioned over these three areas. However, some writers push the majority of their writing into mostly the upper zone, which tells us that most of their thoughts and energy are in sort of an imaginary, abstract realm, farther away from daily reality. Visionaries. When the middle zone is emphasized in handwriting, most of the writer's energy is funneled into everything that occurs in the present, or daily activities. There is much more interest in accomplishing what's on today's checklist than thinking about future projects. These people are more literal and hands-on in their approach to life. And when handwriting is lower zone dominated or id driven, we find individuals who direct most of their energy into the socio-sexual part of life. They respond more to primitive urges for sex, money, possessions, food, drink, travel, and excitement.

Sample 7.

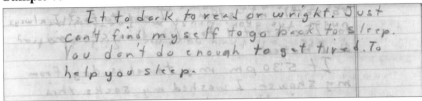

Gary's handwriting has middle zone emphasis. I interpret this to mean that he put conscious focus on everything that happened in his daily schedule and short-term goals. Lacking an inner harmony and maturity, he achieved a more secure sense of balance by applying focused energy toward completing all of his tasks at work, organizing the plan for each day, meticulously arranging items in his garage, preparing for and executing yard sales, and doing chores around the home. With less energy in the upper and lower zones, his spiritual and physical health were more likely to suffer. Lacking the ability to process complex, imaginative thoughts including high-level studies, he preferred to stick with mundane duties and work and home.

Getting into a bit of *trait analysis*, looking at individual letters and strokes, I want to point out the letter "k" in Gary's handwriting.

Sample 8.

Notice that the "k" is larger than the surrounding letters in his words. And notice that the arm on the k-buckle rises up and higher to the right. The letter is taller and wider than other letters in his text. This is what we call the *defiant K*. It represents a rebellious attitude toward authority figures. Such writers typically resent being controlled by others, being in subordinate positions, being mocked, challenged, and pushed. At the same time, these people are not typically strong leaders, and they depend upon the structure and guidelines that they resent and rebel against. This is a constant source of irritation.

Continuing on with trait stroke analysis, notice the tails on the lower case "g" and "y."

Sample 9.

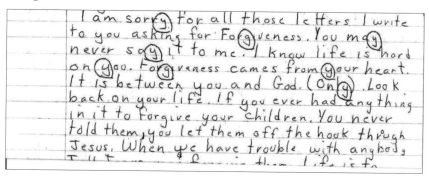

Notice how the tails of these letters come down into the lower zone, point left, and then stop, failing to make a loop and return back up to the baseline. Graphologists refer to these tails as symbols of "socio-sexual shame." This trait correlates with writers who are experiencing a sense of guilt or shame in the area of sex and social actions. The writer is frequently dwelling on or repressing a painful issue in the past that hasn't been resolved. This corroborates Gary's overall sense of frustration.

After studying many other trait strokes in Gary's handwriting, including ones that enhance or reduce other traits, I finally arrived at the following summary:

(It is not possible to describe the entire analytical process used on Gary's handwriting in the space of this chapter. Please note that the above examples, of how Gary's handwriting was analyzed, are incomplete, and readers should not extrapolate portions of the analysis and apply it to their own handwriting or that of people they know to arrive at the same conclusions given here.)

Gary Ridgway's handwriting presents as being from a man who is simple, modest, soft-spoken, polite, and seeking recognition for his compliance and good work. Fascinatingly, Gary's handwriting has a benign gentleness to it—nothing like I had imagined for a serial killer.

Sample 10.

Look at this sample of Charles Manson's (hippie-era cult leader and murderer) handwriting, taken from *Crime & Penmanship, A Graphological Rogues Gallery,* by Ted Widmer. This handwriting is more like what we imagine for a serial killer. It's unbalanced, aggressive, irregular, chaotic, muddy (thick blobs of ink), varying in size, slant and pressure. Look at Charles Manson's handwriting next to Gary's— a striking difference. We notice the more gentle lucid, organized form in Gary's handwriting. It's non-threatening, simple. Manson's handwriting makes us want to pull away. It's completely disturbing.

Sample 11.

I long to hold you, look in your face
to say good bye. I well never touch, kiss
or hug you. It hurts so much.
Do you think God will forgive me.
I don't even forgive myself.
You were the best wife, Lover and
mother I ever had. I blow it. I needed

But the fact is, Gary Ridgway is a long-term, aggressive killer. And, just as his attorneys and investigators had their doubts about this slight, polite, agreeable man being capable of all that he was accused of until his full confession, I too felt puzzled by the incongruence between the handwriting and his savage actions.

Charles Manson's handwriting appears crazy and unbalanced every time he writes. Gary Ridgway's handwriting appears controlled and organized every time he writes. I believe the difference between these two killers is Manson is *in* a pathological state of mind continuously. Ridgway, on the other hand, lived in the energy of a normal, working man who demonstrated accountability and reliability—thirty years at one job and fourteen years with his wife, Judith. But then at times, he *switched* into a completely other energy mode—when he killed—and, unfortunately, we weren't able to approach him in the midst of a kill and ask him for a handwriting sample. Had that been possible, I think we would have seen a wildly different piece of handwriting.

So, Gary led a double life. He fooled his wife, family, friends, and co-workers. I believe that his aw-shucks, everyday-guy energy actually helped him to blend in as just another john on the Strip and perpetuate his killing career. His looks were average. He drove an average looking truck. He worked at a blue-collar job and went home to his wife. Nothing stood out about him to cause alarm with prostitutes. Even when he was picked up and questioned by police over the years leading up to his final arrest, his controlled, unflappable, bland affect lowered suspicion with investigators. He even agreed to do a polygraph test during one arrest and passed! The strong emotional control that I see in the neatness, spacing, and slant in his handwriting worked in his favor as a killer.

Another incongruence is the lack of sexual aggression in the lower zone of his handwriting. One would think that a man as sexually obsessed as Gary would have long loops and tails on his letters dipping far down into the lower zone. But we don't see that in his writing. Recall that the letters "g" and "y" in Gary's writing are short and have incomplete tails that we call socio-sexual shame. I believe that Gary continuously struggled to sublimate his sexual compulsions with prostitutes into the everyday, accepting world of work and family. Recall in my interview with Gary that he said he really wanted to quit seeing prostitutes and killing. He thought he had finished killing and then "accidentally" killed another one late in his marriage with Judith. He went on to say that he was looking forward to retiring from Kenworth and moving away from the Strip because he thought that getting away from the tempting region would reduce and maybe stop his urges. I believe he knew that what he was doing was wrong in the eyes of others—and getting the approval from others was important to him so he tried to show people what he thought they wanted to see. However, I do not believe he thought what he did was wrong for himself, and I'll explain why shortly. The strict family values that were impressed upon him by his parents gave Gary a framework of what society expected from him, and he endeavored to fulfill those expectations. He claims that he loved his parents very much and, according to Judith, he was a devoted son. He visited his parents several times each week and made himself available if they needed help with anything. Judith reports that Gary insisted they spend all holidays with his parents. Because of Gary's understanding of what kind of a man his parents and society expected him to be, he felt he had to hide his sexual urges because they didn't fit in with the expectation. In other words, he was trying to shift his lower zone energy into the middle zone. I believe he agonized about it everyday and tried to keep himself very busy in the mundane activities of daily life, hoping that he could avoid giving in to his urges.

But, unfortunately for every one of his victims and their families, his urges won the war. Time and time again he returned to the Strip to hunt for his next victim, each time swearing to himself that that was the last one.

Let's take a final look at Gary's handwriting.

Sample 12.

> What would happen if tomorrow. Someone
> came forward to prove 100 percent I didn't
> do it. And not go to trial. Would my
> so called friends do then.
>   Work on getting the house ready for Sale.
> Find homes for all stuff.
>   Get a update picture of you for me. I love
> the past. But I love you, I need a newer
> picture

If Kenworth had hired me to screen Gary's handwriting during his application process, I would have submitted that Gary was an excellent match for the position of truck painter for several reasons. His strong emotional control and disinterest in expressing emotion with co-workers enabled him to spend time alone with trucks. He did not require interaction with people, so working with inanimate objects was a good fit for him. His desire to perform his duties well and receive recognition pushed him to earn perfect attendance awards and praise from superiors about the quality of his work. And his slow, deliberate handwriting with wide, slow humps on his "m" and "n" letters indicated that he learned new information through visual and tactile opportunities. He was good with constructing with his hands, and he enjoyed seeing the visual results of his creations—supportive qualities for truck painting. And, while observers have reported Gary as being "slow" and "academically challenged" for most of his life, at least one co-worker at Kenworth was amazed by Gary's accurate memory. Recall that Jim Bailey described Gary's memory for blueprint details on trucks he had painted years prior as simply amazing. It was like Gary could see the blueprints in his mind and read the measurements.

I think the most fascinating fact about Gary's handwriting is that in all of his samples, spanning many years, his handwriting remained the same: always the same printing with space between every letter of every word. I spent many hours sifting through birthday cards, anniversary cards, notes and letters that Judith saved from Gary (recall that Judith and Gary saved everything). In every case, his writing style remained the same.

This struck me as highly unusual, because for most folks, our handwriting is influenced by the moods and events happening in our lives. For example, an individual's handwriting may change for a period of time during an illness by looking weaker, lighter, and smaller. Sad handwriting can have a falling baseline that makes the lines of writing appear to run downhill, matching the writer's mood. The same thing goes for an incredibly happy event such as winning a lottery. The handwriting will appear larger, bolder, more energized.

As I studied his writings further, it occurred to me that Gary had no connectors in his handwriting—a stroke joining one letter to the next one. Not one anywhere. Not even in his signature! His handwriting, as I stared at it longer, reminded me of typewriter letters. Whack, whack, whack. I saw how his letters hit the paper almost mechanically, and this brought me to my final thought on Gary's handwriting.

Connectors are strokes or ligatures that bind one letter to another within a word. It is a visual symbol of how people are connected by joining hands, sharing their energy with one another. Gary, even though he pretended to be connected to his wife, and pretended to be connected to his parents, son, and co-workers, really wasn't connected to anyone. (Recall that Gary said in his interview with me that he really never could love anyone.) He stood alone in his world with no true emotional connections to anyone. And, just as his letters stood alone, side-by-side but not touching, so did his emotions. I believe that Gary used an extreme form of *compartmentalization* to line up bins of feelings and experiences in his psyche, each separated by space, never allowed to touch, allowing him to avoid *integration* of his feelings for his entire life. Every lie, assault, and murder was stored in its own bin, separate and away from the others. Everything isolated. No feeling. No emotion. No connectedness to the victims. The final incongruence: Gary said in his interview that he is very emotional and cries over sad movies. I believe that tears may fall from his eyes, but he has absolutely no idea which bin the tears belong to.

Photos, Cards, and Letters

1.Kenworth Trucking Plant–Renton, Washington–where Gary worked for 32 years.

2. Gary Ridgway's High School Graduation Photo–20 years old 1969.

3. Judith holding "Oscar" in front of new motor home 2001.

4. Gary holding "Oscar" in front of new motor home.

5. Gary and Judith with poodle, Oscar, five
months before his final arrest.

6. Gary and Judith camping in dream motor home in Seaside, Oregon.

7. Judith and Gary celebrating his birthday
Feb 18, 2000 one year before final arrest.

8. Gary enjoying a beer on a hot day

9. Judith and Gary just started dating and he proudly
showed her trucks he painted at Kenworth Trucking
Plant.

10. Gary took Judith to Expo `86, Vancouver,
BC Canada. 1986.

11. 21859 32nd Pl South
Kent, Sea Tac, Washington.
Judith lived with Gary in this house
where he killed many women.

12. Gary and Judith just began
dating in 1985.

13. Gary and Judith 1987
Lake Sammamish, Washington

14. Judith and Gary holding two of her
grandchildren in 1987

15. Uncle Si–1953

16. From left: Helen Downing, baby Judith, Uncle Si –Vader, Washington

17. Judith's father Wesley Mawson, 17 yrs old. Only photo Judith has of her biological father.

18. Judith and Gary on vacation in the Bahamas 1993.

19. Gary on the beach in Ft. Lauderdale, Florida.

20. Mary Ridgway at her Retirement party, J.C.Penney Dept Store, South Center Mall Tukwila, Washington– Early 1990's.

21. Judith and Gary enjoying a summer afternoon at the KMPS country music radio picnic. Enumclaw, Washington.

22 Gary relaxing at home in Des Moines with poodles–early 1990.

23. Gary holding one of Judith's grand-children–1990's.

24. Judith and Gary frequently went camping in the Washington Mountains–1988

25. Matching motorcycles Gary bought for the couple at Enumclaw Suzuki for camping trips–late 1980's.

26. Mr. and Mrs. Gary Ridgway toasting.

27. Gary and Judith's wedding day June 12, 1988.

28. Judith and Gary on a Washington beach vacation 1988.

29. Judith, early teens, posing in her bathing suit for a neighbor man.

30. Judith, 16 years old, 1960.

31. Gary Ridgway, 16 years old, 1965.

32. Lee's dream house today–2006.

33. Judith, 16 years old, 1960, Ryther Child Care Center.

34. Judith, 8 years old, 1952.

35. Judith holding her first-born daughter, Marie, 1966.

36. (No caption)

37. Young Judith, Renton, Washington, when a traveling photographer came to the door.

38. Judith, 4 years old in 1948.

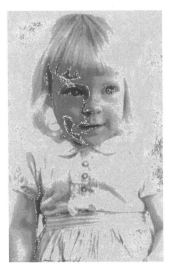

39. Judith, 2 years old in 1946.

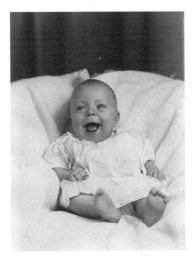

40. Judith, 7 months old.

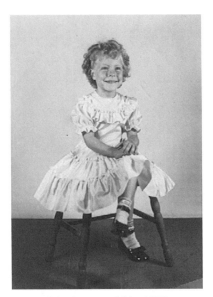

41. Judith, 6 years old in 1950.

42. Helen Downing holding 1 year old Judith, 1945.

43. Judith and Gary at Kenworth Trucking Open House
1980's.

44. Judith, one year after Gary's final
arrest in 2002.

45. Judith, 21 years old, wedding day
1965.

46. Dinners with Lee and Judith were always formal. Late 1960.

47. Judith camping at a medieval festival.

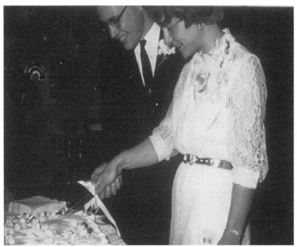

48. The happy Mr. and Mrs. Lynch.

49. Lee's dream house, 6205 Latona Ave, N.E.
Seattle, WA.

50. A kiss for "luck." Lee and new wife,
Judith, in 1965.

51. Judith, 1965, young wife to Lee Lynch

52. Lee and Judith posing in their Victorian-style home.

53. Judith, 20 years old, all dressed up in her mother's clothing for a Dance with Lee Lynch in 1964.

54.Lee insisted that Judith wear long gowns. 1969.

55. Judith and Lee. Judith hand sewed these purple velvet costumes.

56. Judith and Lee drank plenty of wine.

57. Judith dancing at Medieval Festival.

58. Judith and Lee in medieval costumes 1970's.

59. Top: Judith and Lee
Bottom: Daughters Rachel and Marie in
early 1970's in Seattle.

60.Judith and Gary 1996.

61.Judith standing outside Western State Mental
Hospital where she was a patient during her teens.

62. Lee and Judith moved to this house, 4407
Sunnyside Ave. Seattle, WA 1966.

63. First home for Lee and Judith.
917 B, 72nd Street Seattle, WA 1965.

64. Gary and Judith's dream home.
4633 S. 348th St., Auburn, WA.

65. First motor home for Ridgway couple. 1995.

66. Park-like grounds of Ridgway yard, 2001.

67. Ferry ride, Seattle, Judith and Gary 1995.

68. Judith and Gary 1998..

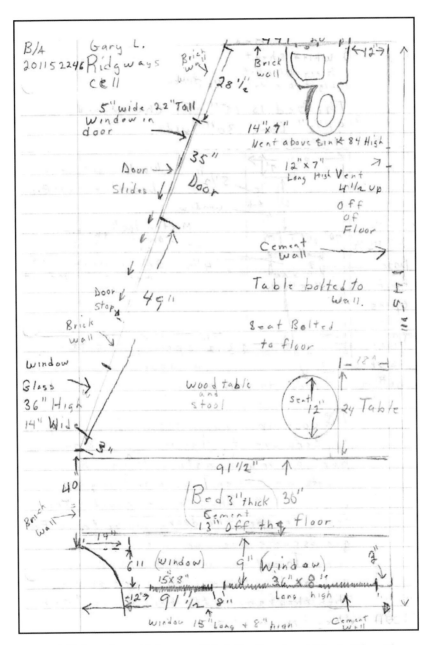

69. **TEXT** Gary drew this layout of his jail cell and sent it to Judith not long
after his arrest.

Bed
2 white sheet
1 Heavy blanket
1 Light blanket   No pillow

The bed is 15" off the ground.
91½" long 30" wide.

← 34" →   7"

5½"
2?
window

Walls light Biege
Door & trim Light Brown

Master lock on all the time
exept for Food
or to hand cuff
me to take me out.

4½"x15½   70"   8⅕"   15"
Door
for Food
Opens
out
Hinge
is on
bottom

4½

23½" opening on bottom
of door
Floor to door opening.

The door opening is where I back up
to. Bend over to slide my hands and
part of my arms thru. To get hand
cuffs on. Then I go over to my bed
neel on it. They tell the guard in the
tower to open the door. Two or three-Four
guards come over while my back is to
them. To put on Leg chains on and arm
chains like the ones you see on me.
Then they remove the hand cuffs. Then
they tranport me.

70. **TEXT:** Letter from Gary page 2.

02-27-02

Dear Judith.

Its hard for me to wright, There is so much
I want to say and can't say. I mis you so much.
You dont Know how much you do, till something
like this happens. I love you.

Give the people a hug and thank you for all
the help they give you. Judith you have a
fighting spirit in side of you, dont give
up. As long as you got hope, friends and
family you well do fine. Take care of yourself
think positive, your body well heal. Pray,
believe is the best attitude you can have.

You have a great smile, a great personalsty
and a great body. Look through my eyes
you are beautifull person. See what I see,
and what other people see. Deep down
in side you are strong, you have to be.
Pray and hope for the best to happer.

How am I ever going to find out what
I did 18 years ago. How is any body ever
going to figure out what they did then.
I don't have the answers. Friends and co-
works are not there for me. It eats me
inside I guess I know who my true friends
are.   OVER

71. **TEXT:** Letter from Gary 2-27-02 page 1.

What would happen if tomorrow. Someone
come forward to prove 100 percent I didn't
do it. And not go to trial. Would my
so called friends do then.

Work on getting the house ready for sale.
Find homes for all stuff.

Get a update picture of you for me. I love
the past. But I love you, I need a new end
picture

I read books and do crossword puzzels
I am sorry I can't answer some questions
about the house, or what to do with
the things in the house, Like my
cloths, pack them up and make a
decision later. Ask Greg and Darene

Ask Mildred. if she would sell her
house to you, when she died.

I love you. I dont want to sound cold
to you, but all I can do is suggest things.
You have to do whats right for you. I
alway wanted to spend my life with
you. For 17 years its been great. This future
scares me. We had a lot of dreams of
retirement, I do care very much what happens
I love you. All these books on me and
news media how do I get a far trial.

Love you always, Gary

72. **TEXT:** Letter from Gary 2-27-02 page 2.

4-23-02

Hi

Just thought about you. This letter is to just let you no, I'm thinking of you, always. I well not let jail destroy me. It all depends on my attitude and what I'm made of. I've always walked away from not standing up for my rights, It has hurt me in all kinds of ways. Always in my mind just let it go. Do what they say and don't ask questions.

Some around me are miserable and they do everything they can to make you miserable to. I try to do the best, and follow the rules. Some inmates look up to me and wonder how I can take it.

It seams some people out there have a gripe with me. Now that I'm in here all hell brakes lose. I being accused of all sorts of other crimes.

May 2, is going to be a big day we are asking the Judge to get the Prosecuting Attorney to set times to get more material to the Defence. By way of a court order The document is about 29 pages. Its been almost 4 months. With 1/80 of the discovery in.

Over

73. **TEXT:** Letter from Gary 4-23-02 page 1

(3)

I long to hold you, look in your face
to say good bye. I well never touch, kiss
or hug you. It hurts so much.
  Do you think God will forgive me.
I don't even forgive myself.
  You were the best wife, lover and
mother I ever had. I blow it. I needed
help and couldn't find any. I'm sorry
for what I did, it was wrong. But
I had you and didn't want to loss you.
Maybe I am evil, a mad man, the
devil and a monster. I prayed so
much for the ladies I killed. I prayed
for you, To find someone who could
take care of you. I did a bad job.
of that.
  Why can't I quit cring. I have a
part of my heart missing. I can't seam
to keep it together. Judith why didn't
Sue Petter get you to see me. Just
one last time.
  Is it better to have loved and lost
it. Then to have never love.
  God forgives sinner. Will he ever forgive
me.

                Love You
                Gary L Redgway

74. **TEXT:** Letter from Gary 4-23-02 page 3.

75. Gary Ridgway served in the US Navy in 1969.

76. Tom and Mary Ridgway–Gary's Father and Mother–Early 1990's.

77. Kenworth Union trip to Las Vegas. (left to right) Jim Bailey, Judith, and Gary. 1999.

78. Gary holding Sugar and Oscar, 1993.

79. Judith and Gary–Kenworth Trucking 1998.

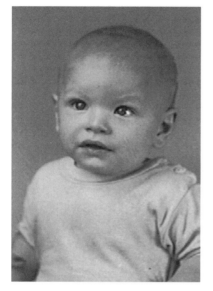 

80. Gary Ridgway, 6 months old, 1949. 81. Judith and Gary on one of many vacations in the 1980's.

82. Judith, 42 years old, 1 year after meeting Gary Ridgway.

(1)

1-1-04

Dear Judith

I am very sorry for hurting you.
I didn't mean to. I'm sorry I lied to you
so many times.
 I was told by Sue Peters (they taped
it) that you weren't going to wright to
me. I was told by Dave Reichert
(they taped that to) you had meet
someone you cared for. I don't want
to stand in your way of starting new.
I don't want you to be sad anymore.
 The day of me pleading Guilty. They
arranged a meeting with Greg + Doreen.
That saturday I sat with them in a room
we hugged I needed you there so much
I cried most of the time. I did some
bad things. I hurt alot of people.
Most of all I hurt you, I'm sorry.
1985? I made a prayer to God, I well stop
killing if I don't get caught. I had to
live with all that in me all those years
I couldn't tell you. I was like a alcaholic
dry for a time. Then fell off the wagon.
I miss you so much.
 Why did God let me do these things.
Why didn't he kill me.

83. **Text:** Letter from Gary 01-01-04 page 1.

On vedeo tape

I asked Sue Petters if I could see you. I had to see you, hug you just one more time. I don't think she ever tried. Ask for your forgivenes. All I got from her was a cold shoulder.

Judith I needed you there to know I was doing the right thing. I feel I let alot of people down.

God had to be there to get me through that. They call me evil, the devil, mad, monster, satin and others.

Right before my sentencing ? They arranged a meeting with Greg + Doreen again. I was so mad I couldn't see you. I cried so much. I would have been able to kiss and hug you, For the last time of our life. Why didn't Sue Petters ask you to come. I think it because of punishing me. They think I'm holding back on something. But I am not. It means so much to me. Judith I'm sorry. Sense the 18th they have me on suicide watch, They come by every fifteen minutes to monetor me. Every day theyhave a head shrink come ask me. if I am going to hurt myself, or others. Why am I here

84. **Text:** Letter from Gary 01-01-04 page 2.

(3)

I long to hold you, look in your face
to say good bye. I well never touch, kiss
or hug you. It hurts so much.
    Do you think God will forgive me.
I don't even forgive myself.
    You were the best wife, Lover and
mother I ever had. I blow it. I needed
help and couldn't find any. Im sorry
for what I did, it was wrong. But
I had you and didnt want to loss you.
Maybe I am evil, a mad man, the
devil and a monster. I prayed so
much for the ladies I killed. I prayed
for you, To find someone who could
take care of you. I did a bad job.
of that.
    Why can't I quit cring. I have a
part of my heart missing. I cant seam
to keep it together. Judith why didn't
Sue Petter get you to see me. Just
one last time.
    Is it better to have loved and lost
it. Then to have never love.
    God forgives sinner. Will he ever forgive
me.
                    Love You
                    Gary L Ridgway

85. **Text:** Letter from Gary 01-01-04 page 3.

⑤ ⑤

Hi Judith   2-14-04

Words just can't express what I feel
to you or for you. What am I suppose to call
you. I can't call you my wife. Because we are
divorced. I can't call you my lover. I broke
your heart. I thought I could call you a
friend. But a friends would never do what
I did to you. Maybe time will come to you
can forgive but will you ever forget.
Every month the dam news brings it
back up again an dagain.
    Are you going to church. In Christ Ministries
helps families to coupe and its free.
    I just received one letter from you 1-27-04
Just think in a couple of days I will be
double nickels. ☺
    My aunt Nancy said she got a letter from
Matthew + Dianne. She in Roswell New Mexico.
I wrote them to thank them for there prayers.
They told me thanks for saying my parents
were good to us kids.
    I did not push you away when I said we
needed a devorce. It was to protect you.
I did not want to disown you for changing your
name. I did it Because I loved you and wanted
you safe. You mean the world to me. People
will go after the families if they can't
get them. me
    Mail has been real screwed up. ☺ One
the letter took 12 days to get here. Its because
of my trip to Monroe. My mail is not
a priority so I alsways get mine late.

86. **Text:** Letter from Gary 02-14-04 page 1.

Friday at 6 or 7 pm Micheles legal mail came. Then at 9 or 10 the other mail came.
Greg and Dorene thanked all the ~~lawer~~ atterneys for the case. He also wanted all phots given back to the familys.
Do you mined if I send ~~a so~~ my copy to you.
I was to controling, selfish when I wanted to see you hold you and kiss you. It was the first and the last time that will happen
Judith, you see how hard it is on you in King County Jail. It is going to be harder here if you decide to see me. Its still betwuu glass for hour or so
Do you get as much rain down south as in Federal way.
They wolk me up friday morning for more blood work. Thir iod and other test it is this ~~thre~~ meant
Please let me know if I am bugging you every week ~~with a letter.~~ I need to no.
I am not a staker or a petis.
Do you use the Amway air cleaner in the home or did you sell it. It would help you maybe.
I have not received any mail from anybody in King County but Gregs and yours. If Linda wants to write me I will write back or ask them if they want me to write them first. I will Its no trouble. I need there address.
I read in some magizine there is a herb that you can take for your skim problem.
                    Love you,
                        Gary I Ridgway

87. **Text:** Letter from Gary 02-14-04 page 2.

Sunday March 21,

Judith
I thought this morning I was going to
(IMU). You went 6 months without a
letter or phone call or any word from
me. Maybe I was wrong to write you.
I probably should not have made any
contact with you I did horible things in
my life. I have to agree with every body
out there I am a monster, the devil and
very evil. I wrote because I love you.
To tell I was sorry for all the I did.
And all I did to hurt you. I never wanted
to get caught because I did not whant
you to find out. Go through all this.
You see by me writing to you it is
still hurting you. Maybe I never should have
writen you. I feel I am just wasting
your time. Like you say you have to
look after your self. Because I am not
there to help you.
Judith this 30 days I can't write to
anybody. Please think pray go deep
down inside whats left of your heart.
Ask your self. What do I get out of
writing to me. Am I going to start living
my own life. Is there a future. What
does Judith want. Where does Judith
want to be. What are Judith needs. Set
back and be honest with you self. Me
sending my mail to Greg and Dorene. Is
this helping me heal. What is Judith
ashamed of. Love your Gary L. Ridgway

88. **Text:** Letter from Gary 03-21-04

I just finished another book. I am on a new one now. I am sure glad you and everyone else, comes to see me. I don't know what the percent of people come to visit is. But it isn't very much.

Sents I been here 3 people went to prison, There has been 3 that went to western State. None have come back yet.

Being in here is an eye opener. People don't no what lonley is till you are in here. It well stay with me for ever, Where ever I am. I have got used to the food here. I take less stomic antacids, with each meal

This is Tuesday I have clean sheets and cloths. I well send you last months calende of events.

Sorry for the bad hand wrighting. It is hard to find anything to talk about. I don't what to have time on my hands to think. Thats not good for anybody in here. Read and do crossword puzzels, Look out the window. I think about you. Nobody showed up tonight.

I well send you my list of what I can order from Comissary. If I don't have money I can order Indigent stuff. I well circle it on back of form.

Love you for ever. Gary

89. **Text:** Letter from Gary 03-21-04 page 2

Judith you do not have to be obligated to write me. I wrote you from the heart. If there is no heart left. Do not force you self. I well understand. No bad. can take your memories.

If I do not hear from you I will no you made the best choise for you.

I will pray for you.

Love you, Gary L Ridgway

90. **Text:** Letter from Gary 03-21-04 page 3

4-14-04

Hi Judith

If you sometime do not know what
to pray for Ask the Holy spirit.
Romans In the same way the Spirit help us in our
8:26 weakness. We do not know what we
ought to pray for. But the spirit
himself intercedes for us with groans
that words cannot express. And he
who searches our hearts knows the
mind of the Spirit because the Spirit
intercedes for the Saints in accordance
with Gods will.
How are you today. I have been sick
with that. acid reflex problem. I did
not have that on the outside. In jail
I took Zantac 3 times aday. Before
meals. Here I take it 2 times a day.
About 9 or 10 Am and 9 pm. At 10
pm I go to bed.
I take 3 Benidral at night for sleep
and sinus drainage. They do not work.
I have to lie down during the day. I feel
all bloated. Yesterday the Dr came and
change the Zantac to Periksac. That
should help. I cent lay down for 5 hours
after I take it. So tonight at 4 pm
I am suppose to take it.
The Psychologist came by about 1 hour
after the Dr left. He is taken me off
Benidral and giving me Diocson? A sleep
aid 50 mg.

91. **TEXT:** Letter from Gary 4-14-04 page 1.

Mail takes a while to get out of the prison. My last letter was dated 4-7-04 I left here monday the 12. Some one stamped my indigent postage slip the 11 of April. That was Easter Sunday. I only wish It did not set around here 5 days before it was mailed.

How have you been. Did you have a nice Easter. We did not have any thing differen for sunday. The Pastor came by Sunday to tell us it was Easter.

How is your brother. I sent a letter to Marcia. I have not heard from here.

I did get a letter from Linda Baily. There doing pretty good, Age is getting them down a little.

There letter was stamped on 4-3-04 I received it 4-12-04.

I do not know if you want me to write letters to you. This mail to you must take 5 to 10 days to get to you. Just let me Know I will stop. If it helps you, To make a new life for yourself.

I had day room yesterday mornning. Thier on the talbe was a Casey Treat book called Living The New Life. It was a new book, but the copy write was 1991. Here in the hospital day room most of the books are religon books I only sent out a few letters last week. I try to get out 10 per week. I only put out one last week.

Love you Gary L Ridgway

92. **TEXT:** Letter from Gary 4-14-04 page 2.

①

May 1 · 04

Hi Judith

How are you doing today. I hope you are well. When you are out looken for a church. Pray before you go in that it is what God wants. 2 John verse 10 "The Father and the son."

2 John → 10
If anyone comes to you and does not bring this teaching do not take him into your home or welcome him. Anyone who welcomes him shares in his wicked work.
Judith if you hate, you will give them your heart and mind. Do not give those two things away. Nelson Mandela spent 27 year in incarceration. The longest political prisoner. Said that

1 John 4:18
Never forget, perfect love drives out fear. Love God must love his neighbor. Because fear has to do with punishment.

Satan Loves to work on your weakness.

Corth 13:5 →
Love Keeps no records of wrongs. Love is slow to anger. Love is patient, love is kind. Love is not rude.

Romans → 8:28
All things work together for good to them that love God.

phesians 4:31-32
"Get rid of all bitterness, rage and anger brawling and slander, along with ever form of malice. Be kind and compassionate to one another, forgiving each other, just as Christ God forgave you."

Not to forgive is to be imprisoned by are past. Happiness is a choice. There is no guilt in you.

93. **TEXT:** Letter from Gary 5-1-04 page 1.

③

What is Prayer

1. Prayer is the key that opens heaven to us on earth.
2. Prayer touches the heart of God through the two way communion love and relationship
3. Prayer is making a request of God. We are expressing our relationship.
4. Prayer lets us worship God, love God hear God, confess to God and submit to God.

He heals and forgives. Healing is in Gods hand in Gods time.
Sick

James 5:14 If anyone of you are sick. He should call the elders of the church to pray over him and anoint him with oil in the name of the Lord And the prayer offered in faith will make the sick person will the Lord will raise him up.

I am 100% accountable for what I've created in my life.
Judith say that 25 times a day it will sit it in your mind. Every day.

Judith did you have that new furniture in storage or is it over at Tom and Tinas house. Just interested.
I heard you had some winds over there. Did you have any trouble.

94. **TEXT:** Letter from Gary 5-1-04 page 3

④

May 3, 04

These are a few of the things I thought you might want to read. It is thrown together for you to pick and chose.

I would have done a better job but I could not think straight. This acid Reflex deases. has flard up. I can only be up for a short lenghth of time. I am getting better slowly I never had that problem at home. If I did it wasn't that bad a couple of anit-acids tablets toke cared of it. I have had it sence friday night. I think it was the tocao meat on friday after noon or the beans. Will next time I wont eat that again. The Dr says stag away from the spice. I am allready staying away of sugar. That feeds the toe fungus. I want my toe fugus under my nails to go away on my left foot.

Judith for a private prayer to God go to Matthew 6:6 to 16 That should help you out alot.

The pastor here is going to look into getting me a New International Version of a study bible for me. I wanted him to look around in the chaplains liberary for a used one Offended Offenders have bibles sent in the might be one there. I think he is going to buy one. The hard leather bond is twice as much as the other one. It has maps and a feferences at the bottom of the pages. That should help. I do not know when that Documentry is going to be. I will let you know.

Love you   Gary L Ridgway

95. **TEXT:** Letter from Gary 5-3-04 page 4

6-17-04

Hi Judith
   Judith when we had it all it was n't
enough. I am very sorry for us. We built
our future on sand. We needed Jesus
Christ in our hearts more. With a strong
Christian life, Church, people, prayer and
fellow ship with God. I know we would
have been better off. Stonger to go through th
   Now we are like strangers. Living day by
day I hear and see the londyness here.
It's hard to really fell love and other
fellings
   I can see your moods in your writing
to me. It bring saddness to my soul. That
I am the cause of all the pain I inflicke
on you.
   I am sorry for all those letters I write
to you asking for Forgiveness. You may
never say it to me. I know life is hard
on you. Forgiveness comes from your heart.
It is between you and God. (Only) Look
back on your life. If you ever had anything
in it to forgive your children. You never
told them, you let them off the hook through
Jesus. When we have trouble with anybody,
Tell Jesus you forgive them. Life is to
short. to harbor anger, hate and any
other bad felling to people.
   It is good you know what your limits are
Judith. Could I make a sugestion. Look in
your nieghborhood or the Yellow pages. For
a Church. Baptist, Assemble of God

96. **TEXT:** Letter from Gary 6-17-04 page 1

2

Nondinominationl, Put the book in the bedroom on the night stand, bed or what ever. Get on you knees before bed time and pray a small pray for guildness. Ask Jesus to help you. Then pray your normal pray. Go to bed look at the churches in the Yellow pages. Do it as long as you hare, 5day - 30days. One Sunday morning. Find out what time a Christan Church starts. Pray then get dress like going to church. Drive to the churches parking lot. Park out far if you want or the handy cap lot. Stop the Engine. Pray that God will help give you the strength to go in. Or some kind of sign. Like some person coming over to envite you into the church. God is sending that person to help you. If you get shacky isk for help pray or leave. If you do leave Celebrate to go in that God gave you the strength to make it that far. See Judith you are winning because God is in you and does not want you to fear. Fear is what the devile want to keep you from going to church. Being closer to God. God desn't want you to be by yourself. If you can do that part. It might help you to stay out side and just listen to the music. If you cry just let it out it will be good. Who Knows you might see some one you know there. By doing that part you beat the devil from taken your soul. The devil will put bad thoughts of fear, depperssion and shame.

97. **TEXT:** Letter from Gary 6-17-04 page 2

Hi Judith   7-31-04

I hear it has been hot over there. Did
any records for heat get broken. How
have you been. Does the home you live
in keep you cool.
How has your body doing with the bone
spurs. There is a program on one of the
radio station that talks about medical
problems. Dr Wong.us is the internet
website site. Bone spurs are caused by to much
calcium in your body. Magnesseum desalve
them. Use Glasomite Magnesseum The other
type sometimes will give you diarea.
Go to the section Achives Articles.
For fibermalsa that problem people need
more oxegen in their body's Need some
more emsims. They had two studies about
that. I do not have a computer but its on
there. 85% to 89% success rate.
Alzimors patients need more fatty acides
They keep the brains nerons soft. So they
transmit the brain nerons. waves
That sites should help you out. Do
you take magnesseum. He says all bone
spurs are soft. It is a high doses of
magnesseum. You could have poor circulation
in yourfeet.
He has articles on Diabetis, One cell.
and two offender are Diebetics. One is
in Stage 1 diabetis.
Each sunday he is on the radio answering
questions. One man had bone spures all
over his body

98. **TEXT:** Letter from Gary 7-31-04 page 1

On the same radio station there is a
site about the Bible. Its called Amazing
Facts.org or Amazing Facts.com. The
Pastors name is Doug Beckler. He answers
all Kinds of questions. They have free
books on the Trinaty, Tongues, plus
one about what Denomanation has the
best teachings of God.
Out there in the real world. There are
a lot of Church's that water down the Bible.
Or only use portens (parts) not the whole
Bible. Both have not meet what God wants
people to learn. A person could lose their
salvation.
Judith words we use in our prayers are
important, but for more valuable is the
attitude of our heart. Talk to him about
anything.
I have a copy of Foot Prints. Let me
Know if you want it.
I will send you a copy of "Attitude".
Quote I am convinced that life is 10%
what happens to me and 90% of how
I react to it.
Judith this year and the next?
I will have to fill out imcome tax.
You might have to send me some forms?
I would ask you to do it for me but.
I do not want to humiliate you by asking.
Mail is not getting to me. If Linda and
Jim or you sent me any letters in July
I did not get any.   Love you Gary.

99. **TEXT:** Letter from Gary 7-31-04 page 2

Emergency Phone Numbers

When in sorrow, call	John 14
When people fail you, call	Psalm 27
When you want to be fruitful, call	John 15
When you have sinned, call	Psalm 51
When you worry, call	Mat 6:19-3
When you are in danger, call	Psalm 91
When God seems far away, call	Psalm 139
When your faith needs stirring, call	Heb 11
When you are lonely and fearful, call	Psalm 23
When you grow bitter and critical, call	Love 1 Cor 13
For the secret to happiness, call	Col 3:12-17
For an idea of Christianity, call	2 Cor 5:15-1
When you feel down and out, call	Rom 8:31-3
When you want peace and rest, call	Mat 11:25-3
When the world seems bigger than God, call	Psalm 90
When you want Christian assurance, call	Rom 8:1-3c
When you leave home for travel, call	Psalm 67
For a great invention/opportunity, call	Isa 55
When you want courage for a task, call	Josh 1
How to get along with people, call	Rom 12
When you think of investment returns, call	Mark 10
When you are depressed, call	Psalm 27
When people seem unkind, call	John 15
When your pocketbook is empty, call	Psalm 37
When you are discouraged about something, call	Psalm 126
When you are losing confidence in people, call	1 Cor 13
When you find the world growing small and you big, call	Ps 19

100. Emergency Phone Numbers

Lonely Psalm 9 - 10 - 13 - 27 - 40

Depressed Psalm 23 - 42 - 43 - 88 Isa 54:1-7 Lam 3:19-24

Discouraged Josh 1:6-9 2 Chron 20:15-17 , 32:6-8

101. Emergency Phone Numbers page 2

12-4-04

Dear Judith

This letter is long over due. I have spent
a lot of time on this. I read books to get
words to say to you. I prayed ask all kind
of questions. The answers are not in books
Its comes from the heart. No book has
it and never will. Mat 5:23;24,
I am sorry for all the hurt I caused you.
I am sorry for killing all those young
women.
I am sorry for ruining so many victims
families and their friends lives.
I am sorry for all the wrong paths I took
in my life. Hurting Matthew so much.
I am sorry I lied so much to you. Causing
so much pain and health problems in your
life. For betraying you and losing your tru
I am sorry for blaming all my problems
on other people in my life. Hurting family.
I am sorry for the tax payers. Paying for
all the bills during all the years. All the
Police, Prosecutors, Attorneys, Psychologis
and everbody else involved.
I hurt and killed a lot of Gods childrer
I have sinned against the Creator. I hop
some day you can forgive me. I am sorry fo
not getting this letter out to you before
this time. I pray I did not leave out anyth
I hope you will know this comes from my
heart.

God Bless you take care.
Gary

102. **TEXT:** Letter from Gary 12-04-04 page 1

103. Birthday Card from Gary
08-15-04

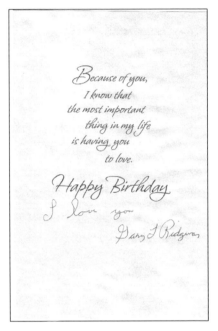

104. Birthday Card from Gary
08-15-04

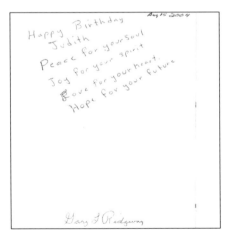

105. **TEXT:** Birthday note handwritten
from Gary 08-15-04

Dear Judith   12-28-01
   The hardest part is the nights. Not
being close to you. You never no how
much I need you. Your soft body
next to me, I love you. I get 2 or 3
hours of sleep. When I do dream its
of you, and the things we did together.
The ocean with oscar + sugar. Running
up the beaches. Walking in the hills with
you. Ridding the bikes to Sea Side.
Isn't it good memories we had.
   In my cell area I think I am the
most active. You have to work out
so you can sleep. I look at books, reed
the newspaper and day dream.
   I wrought a letter to Lorraine + Johnny
thanking them for there card and letter
I called them Thursday night. We
talked for 15 minutes and ranout of
time, They well be over on Sunday.
   Today we have a inspection of our cells.
I don't no what that is yet. My cell
is clean always Some people are not
very clean in there cells. They sure
take long showers. I take my time
in there and get it over with. Gives
me more time on the phone, I take
the full hour out. Sit in the same
place everyday to read, or day dream
in a book or magizene. Just so I
don't go back to my cell.
   The blue cover als are for misdomenon
The red is for more severe crimes.
The white is for people that a dangerus

106. **TEXT:** Letter from Gary 12-28-01 page 1

people, so they say.
I got the three pictures in your last
letter. Make sure you put some of your
perfume on the next one. Day and night
I can smell it and it well bring me back
to the good times. Today after I called
you I called Matthew + Diane they
were working, nobody answered the
phone. I well call them sat if I get
a chance to call them. I well tell them
my hours out that, I can call. I well
have them call you once a week to keep
in touch.
I do have a calendar, Dorine got
for me, It is small and fits on the table.
I cross off every day Im in here on
it. I was to see Savage this week but
he well probly come in on Sat or Sun
morning.
Every inmate in the jail has to stand
in line to get a trail. The system is
to dam slow. I'd loved to change
places with some of these inmates.
By the way I am real embarast I told
you there was a girl in # 7. A little
mexican girl. I was wrong he was
moved up in the upper floor. There
is two she men here. They take hormons
and the what ever. I didn't let the
other inmates no I thought it was a
girl. Im sending you two papers keep
them in a box. Fridays mail well go out
on Monday. They dent have mail on Sat
I Love you. Be strong.

Love you
Gary.

107.**TEXT:** Letter from Gary 12-28-01 page 2

Its about 8:am I work out in my cell. I have about 20 different exercises along with stretching. I do twice a day.

I sit look outside watch the people walking, Just thinking the freedom they have. I have a building under construction to my right. It is going up slowly. I read books and newspaper alot. It takes my mind off whats going on.

At 1115am is lunch. They bring a paper bag with a sandwich, apple or orange chips or pretzels and a cookie or cheeze crackers with peanut butter in them. Today they gave us milk. I trade my sanwich for the apple or orange. Then I brush my teeth. I don't no when someone comes to see me. I don't want to scare them.

My hour out today is 12:30 to 1:30 But I go when I get a chance, today it is 11:45 to 12:45. I phone lout but nd onl is home.

Mail comes between 2 and 6. If is 4:00 PM I have mail. I try to answer it the same day I get it. All books come in later

At 4:15 Commissary came in today. We order on tuesdays and it comes on wednesdays

At 5:15 or so they bring dinner out Unlock the small door. The menu varys every day. They have chicken paddys rice beef patty, beef stew, meat balls, mashed patatos. small green salad (lettuce only) with different dressings, two slices of bread with butter. Mixed vegetables and peaches or some kind of puddings or apple saus. They always Lock the door after the put the tray through.

108. **TEXT:** Letter from Gary

Dear Judith   Sun. Dec 23, 01

I Love you. Do you no, it is hard
to keep white cloths clean. I will
keep my head up. I look out over
Seattles waterfront. This is a beutiful
day. I well call over on Tuesday 25
at Gregs. By the time you get this
Xmass dinner is over.

Try to take a bag, a few boxes
to Christian store. Or Book world.
It was asked how a person would
eat a Eliphent. One peice at a time.
That is the way you remove all
the stuff you don't need, one box
at a time. If they are to heave get help.

I would like you to keep all of the
paper work I send home. Put it in
a box. These are my Attorneys and
Investegators.

AHy
Anthony Savage   Denise Seaffidi
Michelle Shaw   Bettye Witherspoon
Todd Gruenhagen   Elisabeth _____
Mark Prothero
Eric Lundell

Before going to bed, put a little
after shave on my pillow. Hold it
close to you heart. I Love you. It
well help you sleep better.

Take time to find, how much
you get out of the house. I dont
think you can buy a house, Look
at Moble homes in parks. Look
at them with a fine tooth comb.
Find someone to help you get the best.

I haven't had any coffee and only
one cup of tea. I would like a beer,

109. **TEXT:** Letter from Gary 12-23-01.

or a mix drink, even some wine.
Thats not going to happen.
 When you mail me a letter please
put a little perfume on it. It well
remind me of you. I will keep it
close, and smell it before going
to bed at night. When my emotions
are down it well bring back good
memories, of how much you mean to me.
 Im going to buy one pair of
short, some lotion, and a razor.
this weed. I have 2 pair of white
socks. My skin is rough in a few
places. A razor is good. How did
you like my short hair. Taking
a shower everyday dries your skin
out. It doesn't take much time to feel a page.
 Talk to Brenda + Jeremy if its ok
to call them. It wont be everyday
my be once a month. Till them
thank you for all your help. God bless
them. Be safe, take care of yourself.
Keep one of those personal alarms
with you. With new batteries don't be
afraid to use it. There is alot of bad
people out there. Bring me my
bible if you remember. I need it.
 I love you. Where is a true friend.
It is a lonly spot im in. Not one
person ever talks to me from KW.
Some how I need to get word to then
of my visitation times. Maybe then
some one will come see me. I wrote
all of this today it is 5 oclock pm.
Sunday. Good night. I love you, sleep tight.
     I Love you.

          Gary L. Ridgway

110. **TEXT:** Letter from Gary 12-31-01 page 2

48 Victims

In his plea agreement with King County Prosecutor, Norm Maleng, Gary Ridgway admitted to killing the following list of females within the boundaries of King County, Washington. The ages range from 15 – 38.

Wendy Lee Coffield, 16
Gisele Ann Lovvorn, 17
Debra Lynn Bonner, 23
Marcia Faye Chapman, 31
Cynthia Jean Hinds, 17
Opal Charmaine Mills, 16
Terry Rene Milligan, 16
Mary Bridget Meehan, 18
Debra Lorraine Estes, 15
Linda Jane Rule, 16
Denise Darcel Bush, 23
ShawndaLeea Summers, 17
Shirley Marie Sherrill, 18
Colleen Renee Brockman, 15
Alma Anne Smith, 18
Delores LaVerne Williams, 17
Gail Lynn Mathews, 23
Andrea M. Childers, 19
Sandra K. Gabbert, 17
Kimi-Kai Pitsor, 16
Marie M. Malvar, 18
Carol Ann Christensen, 21
Martina Theresa Authorlee, 18
Cheryl Lee Wims, 18

Yvonne Shelly Antosh, 19
Carrie A. Rois, 15
Constance Elizabeth Naon, 20
Kelly Marie Ware, 22
Tina Marie Thompson, 22
April Dawn Buttram, 17
Debbie May Abernathy, 26
Tracy Ann Winston, 19
Maureen Sue Feeney, 19
Mary Sue Bello, 25
Pammy Avent, 16
Delise Louise Plager, 22
Kimberly L. Nelson, 20
Lisa Yates, 19
Mary Exzetta West, 16
Cindy Anne Smith, 17
Patricia Michelle Barczak, 19
Roberta Joseph Hayes, 21
Marta Reeves, 36
Patricia Yellowrobe, 38
Jane Doe B-10
Jane Doe B-16
Jane Doe B-17
Jane Doe B-2

Bibliography

The Green River Killer, King County Journal, Seattle: King County, 2003.

King County Journal (various articles), 2001-2006.

Prothero, Mark, *Defending Gary, Unraveling the Mind of the Green River Killer*, New York: Jossey-Bass, 2006.

Reichert, David, *Chasing the Devil*, New York: Little Brown, 2004.

Rule, Ann, *Green River, Running Red: The Real Story of the Green River Killer—America's Deadliest Serial Murderer*, Free Press.

Seattle Times (various articles), 2001-2006.

Smith, Carlton and Thomas Guillen, *The Search for the Green River Killer*, New York: Signet, 1991.

Index

aftershave, 63, 127
Amway, 90, 154
Aristotle, 161
Auburn, Washington, 4, 84, 97
August 15, 1944, 17
baselines, 167
Bear Creek, 113
Bethlehem Steel, 27, 29, 40, 46, 51
Bible, 130, 131, 147, 156, 158
Boeing, 19, 21, 22, 25, 27, 121, 145
Boeing Field, 121, 145
Chaney, 31
Chehalis, Washington, 17, 18
compartmentalization, 177
connectors, 177
Crystal Mountain, 91
Disneyland, 70, 71, 101
divorce, 56, 59, 80, 81, 86, 89, 115,
    119, 120, 142, 155
DNA, 16, 142, 146, 164
Enumclaw, Washington, 185
Executive Board, 139
FBI, 164
Fluffy, 89, 90
Freud, 162, 170
Friday night Sabbath, 49
Friday the 13th, 145
Gestalt Method, 162
Gonzaga University, 84
Grand Coulee Dam, 70
Grandma M, 118
graphic maturity, 167
Green River Community College,
    4, 84
Green River Killer, 5, 16, 59, 62,
    63, 69, 72, 73, 74, 84, 90, 93,
    96, 97, 110, 112, 113, 115, 116,
    118, 119, 121, 124, 128, 141,
    145, 158, 159, 164, 238

Green River Task Force, 72, 160
Heather, 104, 190
Highway 101, 77
Highway 99, 12, 28, 59, 61, 62, 63,
    64, 65, 69, 88, 89, 91, 96, 98,
    114, 140, 145, 150
holistic, 161, 165, 167
honeymoon, 26, 75, 76, 79, 82, 83,
    140
hypnotherapist, 29, 42
IMU, 147
In the Garden, 95
integration, 177
JC Penney, 68, 87
Judie, 40, 79
Judith, 4, 5, 7, 8, 9, 10, 11, 12, 13,
    14, 15, 16, 17, 18, 20, 21, 22,
    23, 24, 25, 26, 27, 28, 29, 30,
    31, 32, 33, 34, 35, 37, 38, 39,
    40, 41, 42, 43, 44, 45, 46, 47,
    48, 49, 50, 51, 52, 53, 54, 55,
    56, 57, 58, 59, 60, 61, 62, 63,
    64, 65, 66, 67, 68, 69, 70, 71,
    72, 73, 74, 75, 76, 77, 78, 79,
    80, 81, 82, 83, 84, 85, 86, 87,
    88, 89, 90, 91, 92, 93, 94, 95,
    96, 97, 98, 99, 100, 101, 102,
    103, 104, 105, 106, 107, 108,
    109, 110, 111, 112, 113, 114,
    115, 116, 117, 118, 119, 120,
    121, 122, 123, 124, 125, 126,
    127, 128, 129, 130, 131, 132,
    133, 134, 137, 138, 139, 140,
    141, 142, 143, 144, 147, 148,
    149, 150, 151, 152, 153, 154,
    155, 156, 157, 158, 159, 160,
    166, 169, 174, 175, 176, 179,
    180, 181, 182, 183, 184, 185,
    186, 187, 188, 189, 190, 191,

192, 193, 194, 195, 196, 197, 198, 199, 200, 202, 203, 210, 211
Kennewick, Washington, 25
Kennydale, Washington, 21
Kent Valley, 155
Kenworth, 7, 61, 69, 72, 74, 80, 82, 87, 88, 90, 93, 96, 104, 110, 127, 134, 136, 137, 138, 139, 141, 143, 144, 148, 152, 157, 160, 175, 176, 178, 182, 192, 210
Kindercare, 69
King County Fairgrounds, 122
King County Jail, 105, 121, 145
King County Police, 62
KMPS, 122, 185
Korean War, 22, 41, 80
Labor Temple, 139
Lake Geneva, 7, 93
Lake Washington, 7
Leisure Time Resorts, 78, 82
limousine, 43, 45, 71
Lori, 31, 32
Manhunt Live, 84
Maple Valley, Washington, 133
marijuana, 52, 54
Marine Corp Ball, 41
Matt Haney, 13, 98, 102
Medieval, 54, 197
Modesto, California, 70
Mother Ryther, 30
Navy, 80, 150, 209
Old Spice, 63
Oscar, 10, 95, 98, 103, 179, 210
Parents Without Partners, 59, 149
perfume, 63, 127
Petrified Forest, 70
Plymouth Champ, 71
Potatoes, 18, 24
potluck, 74, 76, 77
Pt. Defiance Zoo, 70

Questioned Documt Examiner, 163
Ramsey, Jon-Benet, 163
Red Cross, 20
Red Lion Inn, 98
Renton, Washington, 7, 138, 190
Ridgway, Ed, 93
Ridgway, Greg, 93
Ryther Child Care Center, 30
saliva, 73
Salt Lake City, Utah, 21
Seizure, 26
Siamese cats, 9, 94, 98
Size, 168
slant, 169, 170, 173, 175
Snoqualmie Pass, 122
Soc. for Creative Anachronism, 54
Solitary confinement, 33
speed, 167, 168
St. Helens Hospital, 17, 20
Strip, 174, 175
Sue Peters, 13, 16, 97, 98, 99, 102, 113, 114, 126
Suzuki, 91, 186
Synagogue, 49
Trinity Episcopal Church, 43
Tyee High School, 80
Uncle Si, 17, 18, 19, 20, 21, 22, 23, 24, 25, 28, 78, 184
Union meetings, 48, 139
University of Washington, 48, 51
Vader, Washington, 18, 21, 184
Valley Medical Center, 138
Vietnam, 48, 80, 91
Walla Walla State Penitentiary, 124
Washington State Penitentiary, 146
Western State Hospital, 31, 32, 34, 35, 37
White Shutters, 59, 61, 62, 149
worker-bees, 166
World War II, 17, 19, 20
Wrongway Ridgway, 134
zones, 162, 170, 171